THE NEW AND REVISED

Carlton Fredericks
Cook Book
for Good Nutrition

by Carlton Fredericks, Ph.D.

GROSSET & DUNLAP
Publishers · New York

Dedication

To the housewife, whose dedication to her family's welfare inspired this book, and whose willingness to learn invited its writing; to Dr. I. N. Kugelmass, pediatrician, hematologist, biochemist, and nutritionist, without whose guidance these concepts would have remained academic; to Dr. Richard O. Brennan, founder of the International Academy of Preventive Medicine, who knows that good food is the basis of preventive medicine; to Betty, my dear wife, and April, Dana, Spencer, and Rhonda—my children—whose response to good nutrition was a testing of the theory behind these recipes.

Preface

Ordinarily, the motivation for the writing of a cookbook is the concept that the average woman entering the kitchen can use some expert help in preparing meals which will please her family. You, dear reader, have found for yourself a cookbook which offers that kind of help. Underlying this motivation is another—one which is quite subtle. It has always been my belief that meals and recipes which please the palate and tickle the taste buds but do not meet the needs of the body are a disservice to the cook and her family.

After all, we have long known that there is a very short and undeviating route from the kitchen to the clinic. The great British physician and nutritionist Sir Robert McCarrison showed decades ago that animals eating the "national" diet of a country developed the sicknesses which crowded the hospitals and medical offices of that country. He showed, too, that the diet of a healthy people was reflected by good health in the animals.

The advancing knowledge of modern nutrition has begun to pick out details in these broad generalizations. This refining of our nutritional knowledge has allowed us to treat many of man's ills with diet, vitamins, and other nutritional factors. This newer knowledge brings with it a collateral benefit, for what nutrition improves or cures, it ordinarily helps to prevent. The mathematics of nutrition is therefore simple arithmetic. The body requires from the daily diet some fifty-odd nutrients which it cannot manufacture for itself. If these factors are provided in the proper balances and amounts—and "proper" is a term with different meanings for every person, for we are all highly individual—the reward will be the achievement of the potential with which we were born. If the dietary does not supply proper quantities and balances of these nutrients, there will be a penalty. It may show itself in deviations from normal health, either physical or mental, and the consequences may take years to appear. The lapse is often so prolonged that the effects of long-continued poor diet are frequently confused with and identified as the toll of "normal" aging. Thus, poor nutrition becomes a time bomb, ticking inexorably.

Generalizing about the American diet is risky what with individual differences in food selection, nutrient needs and food tolerances. However, it can be said about Americans that:

—they eat too much of the wrong foods—especially sugars and overprocessed starches.

—they sometimes eat too little—making good nutrition difficult, if not impossible, to achieve (this seems to apply most frequently to women).

—their diets are often deficient in protein, unsaturated fats, roughage, Vitamin B Complex and Vitamin E.

The recipes in this cook book are aimed at helping the cook please her family as well as overcoming the deficiencies in our national diet.

Carlton Fredericks, Ph.D.

Contents

CONTENTS

The Basic Idea

1

The Basic Idea

Whether a veteran cook or a beginner, your responsibility is to prepare food for the best possible nutrition and palatability. After all, most people eat what they *like,* good for them or not. Contrary to the Puritan legend that what is good for you must be endured, good nutrition and palatability are not mutually exclusive. Properly cooked meat is more tender and succulent; it is also more digestible, and its amino acids become more available to the body. A white bread with higher protein, vitamin, and mineral values tastes better than the "bubblegum" commercial variety. Homemade cake with elevated nutritional value can make the product of a cake mix taste like what it is: a triumph of the chemist over common sense, of the processor over the laws of nature. Properly cooked vegetables are more nutritious, and taste better for it.

The "best possible nutrition" is a phrase with built-in, hidden traps. Best possible for whom? Man's heredity varies, and his nutritional needs with it. On a uniform diet, chickens of the same heredity don't turn out the same. Some grow slowly, some faster; some are sickly, others function; some are superbly healthy; most live, some die. The chicken eats what is available; man, what pleases him. Unfortunately, man seems no better able to detect

15

the relationship between his diet and his health than does the chicken (it has been said that the last discovery made by a deep-sea fish would be salt water).

The broiler of today reaches marketing weight in a fraction of the time it took thirty years ago. Yet the poultry scientists of that day were sure they knew practically everything about feeding fowl, exactly as our nutritionists today write about human nutrition, with the assurance that all knowledge is at hand, and all members of a species have the same nutritional requirements.

Before World War II, the Japanese accepted their shortness as an hereditary trait. Now with their children growing taller than their parents, the Japanese realize that their prewar short stature was an adaptation of their bodies to limitations in the national diet. Yet Japanese nutritionists of the 1930s were quite sure they knew all the major answers to questions about human dietary needs. Which brings into sharp focus the attempt of our Food and Drug Administration to *legislate* a uniform requirement for vitamins and all other nutrients needed by two hundred million Americans.

A half-ounce cake of compressed yeast, given good nutrition continuously, would grow to a billion tons in *one* week. Do our yeast growers provide such a balanced diet for these cells (assuming that all varieties have the same requirements, which they don't)? Don't be silly: we'd be up to our ears in yeast, instead of having intermittent shortages. Yet our knowledge of the nutritional needs of yeast is more detailed and complete than our understanding of the much more complicated requirements of man. Moreover, yeast doesn't scramble its genes as does man with haphazard mating; nor complicate matters by requiring a restricted diet for allergies; nor insist, as we do, on consuming foods with additives known to interfere with efficient reproduction. (Your very vitamin pills are probably colored with some kind of additive. It is also found in most lipsticks.)

Question: how do you know your nutrition is not—in some subtle or even in some explicit ways—forcing your body, your nervous system, or your brain into a compromise, an adaptation

16

to an unfavorable internal environment such as the Japanese unknowingly made? How do you know what kind of chicken you are? What makes you sure, if you *are* sure, that your sicknesses are not related to your choices and methods of preparation of foods? The U. S. Department of Agriculture has made up its mind: "Up to 90 percent of our common diseases," their literature flatly states, "could be mitigated or wiped out, if we ate properly."

How do you know that your child's hyperactivity is not a direct price for the artificial colors and flavors in the convenience foods you have innocently served? A recent report blamed a drug action of these chemicals for the hyperactivity which in some states impairs the functioning and the educability of up to 40 percent of our school children. It disappeared, the American Medical Association was informed, when the chemicals were eliminated from their diets, and reappeared when they were re-introduced. Questions: do you read the fine print on the labels of your favorite brands of foods? With understanding?

Finally, how do you *know* that you don't fall short of meeting your nutritional requirements and those of your family, exactly as the yeast growers and the chicken breeders fall short of providing the ideal nutritional environment for the living cells they feed? Before you answer: one of my professional friends, a fine medical nutritionist, made a small improvement in the diets of eight hundred professional men and their families. It resulted in a measurable improvement in their mental and emotional functioning—yet they all considered themselves to be at least reasonably well fed before the research began—and theirs were typical American diets of affluent families. The removal of one single food from the diet of a "neurotic hypochondriac" woman restored her normal cheerful personality, her psychiatrist—an orthomolecular practitioner, using nutrition instead of the couch —reported. Removal of much of the sugar from the diets of school children not only dramatically lowered tooth decay but their rate of illness also declined, and their school grades rose; yet their parents had thought them "well fed." So the question: are your

17

food choices intelligent? is not an idle one. And in your preparation of your meals, which can make a tremendous difference in their nutritional values, are you retaining vital nutrients, or throwing the baby out with the bath water?

All this distinctly doesn't mean munching on raw foods, though there is a place in your menus for some which are delightful and healthful. It doesn't commit you to drinking alfalfa juice laced with blackstrap molasses. There's nothing wrong with health foods, but something very wrong with the concept that foods good for you must be exotic, unpalatable, and the choice only of little old ladies in tennis shoes. All foods are supposed to be healthful to the degree that they supply the body's requirements. All additives should be harmless, and all processing innocent of negative effects on food values, and both should fulfill a function benefiting the consumer. Unhealthful additives and harmful processing should be stopped, and will be, if you exercise your ballot in the market place.

It is an affront to common sense that supermarkets should stock health foods on a special counter. Should not all the foods they sell deserve that title? It just isn't sensible, either, that we should have health food stores, for the reason that foods good for you should be universally available. But it is just as illogical that you should feel chary about patronizing a health food store. For certain items, it is a necessity; yet not every product so named is worth buying.

It is obvious that I am a nutritionist with very definite ideas about what you should eat to improve your diet. It is equally true that you are a peace-loving homemaker with a family with very definite ideas about what it *will* eat. Put your mind at rest: I am a nutritionist who will settle for less than the millennium— for the good reason that experience has taught me its unattainability. I have learned that it is wiser (and more effective) to outflank the family's resistance, rather than attack it head-on. That leads to Rule #1 (and 2 and 3): never place a dish or a meal before your husband and the children, and announce that it's (a) a new one, and (b) good for them. Eating things that are good for one is taking care of one's self. That is essentially a feminine philosophy, which is why this book is addressed to you. American men, doubtful about their masculinity, suffer great anxiety when asked to participate in something they consider feminine. They therefore are charter-bound to reject anything that is good for them. So you are, from this point on, a happy participant in a conspiracy between good nutrition and you.

To prove to you that these are not the idle dreams of a theorist, let me tell you about my experience as nutrition director of two summer camps. I violated all the traditions of mass feeding by using the foods, recipes, and menus recommended in this cook book. There were some three hundred and twenty-five children (and two hundred adult staff members) who couldn't have cared less about good nutrition, addicted as they were to summer camp menus built around bologna sandwiches, nitrated hot dogs, imitation pancake syrup, cereals that whistle from the plate, etc. A little boy coming out of the mess hall, munching on one of Betty's Cookies (for my wife's supernutritious and delightful recipe see page 266) said, "Uncle Doc," (my camp name) "are dese th' McCoy, or somefin else?" He couldn't tell by taste; he was merely suspicious that he was eating a nutritional Mickey Finn—and he was right. We baked our cookies for high-protein, high-vitamin values, and yet you couldn't tell; they were delicious. But it obviated the need to stand over the child at dinner, and exercise coercion—which is always a boomerang with children—by saying, as so many mothers have said: "You can't have your dessert unless you finish your meat" (fish, fowl, or whatever). We served the cookies at all meals and as snacks because they supplied the protein needed, but bypassed by many of the children.

If space permitted, I'd devote pages to the story of the camps, where our children had salad twice a day, fruit with all meals, real maple syrup on pancakes made from our own mix, high in protein, vitamins, minerals, and unsaturated fats. They drank fruit juice instead of what the industry calls "bug juice"—powdered soft drink mixes. The bread, muffins, cakes, cookies, rolls, frankfurter rolls and hamburger buns—all topnotch nutrition, carefully disguised—assured that the children were being well fed, but like the little boy, they couldn't prove it. *We* could. Sitting at the same tables, our overweight children lost weight— some of them successful for the first time—and our underweights gained. A brain-injured child went back to school to be promoted to a class for normal children. Asthmatics had fewer attacks, and children gaited for many "summer colds" were suddenly resistant to them. Complexions improved; hair took on new sheen and improved texture. But this is not a book about camp menus, though camps would do well to apply this thinking and this experience, and use these recipes. Nor is it a nutrition textbook, though I have parted the curtain, now and again, to give you a glimpse of the scientific research which backs my philosophy. This is a cook book for good nutrition, and it is my hope that you now realize it is needed, that you should read it, and that its teachings should be applied.

If you are a modern homemaker with a sincere desire to provide your family with good nutrition, you should read carefully the following discussions about vegetable and meat cookery before proceeding to the recipe sections. This is especially recommended if you are a beginner, or if you learned to cook peering from behind your mother's apron or into cookbooks made obsolete by contemporary needs, the quality of contemporary foods, and revised or new concepts about preserving food nutrients.

Mother may have been the best cook in the world, but her cooking methods and her ideas about food were not geared to modern nutritional knowledge or requirements. Think back to the dinners of your childhood, or reread some of her cherished recipes (inherited, probably, from the best cook in the world of her generation—your grandmother). Do you find instructions to sear the meat invariably—to roast it in a very hot oven—to drown it in flour gravy—to boil vegetables for a long time, adding baking soda to "retain color"?

Among the facts to emerge from modern scientific nutrition test kitchens is one which reveals that ordinary, old-fashioned

20

cooking methods may mean the loss of up to 95 per cent of the vitamins and minerals in certain foods. Even under ideal conditions, cooking often subtracts sizable percentages of nutrients from foods' assayed raw values—one reason why you will find, in this cookbook, the use of special-purpose foods as recipe ingredients. They are introduced to help offset losses which may have occurred in the raising or processing of food, or in cooking.

For many women, the following instructions may mean discarding long-held habits and acquiring new ones. If you have been accustomed to cooking methods which contradict mine, there is a very good chance that you have been innocently depriving your family of vitamins, minerals, and proteins—as well as flavor —in the meals you serve.

VEGETABLE COOKERY

On the subject of vegetable cookery I am stubborn. There is no separate chapter in this book with lots of lovely recipes reading from *artichokes* to *zucchini*, although there are plenty of recipes using vegetables as ingredients. Vegetables taste fine just the way they are—some of them raw, others briefly cooked to permit the retention of their color and flavor and a decent amount of whatever vitamins and minerals they were born with. Anything elaborate you do to them is likely to demand more exposure to light, air, and heat (all nutrient robbers) than I care to think about.

Cook the freshest vegetables you can find in the following ways: Steaming, pressure-cooking, sautéing, broiling, or baking; creaming them when half-cooked in a sauce to which you add extra nutrients (milk, milk solids, cheese, wheat germ, yeast flakes); simmering them in milk and using the milk; or cooking them very quickly in an absolute minimum of water and using the water. They should be cooked only until they are tender, not soft, and not a second longer.

Frozen vegetables are preferred to "fresh" varieties which may have suffered nutrient losses owing to premature harvesting, transportation, and storage or display without refrigeration. Because frozen vegetables are partially precooked at the source to arrest enzymic action and "lock in" nutritive value, flavor, and texture, follow carefully the producers' instructions, printed on the packages, to cook them briefly.

If family palates or prejudices insist that vegetables be embellished as an alternative to being uneaten, then for goodness' sake do it in such a way as to add nutrition, not subtract it.

A fine embellishment is lemon juice, for it replaces some of the easily destroyed vitamin C which starts vanishing as soon as a vegetable is wrenched from earth, stalk, or vine.

Excellent would be a judicious addition of wheat germ or yeast flakes for the sake of B vitamins and vitamin E, lacking in many of the foods you eat.

Simmering in milk is good, because milk adds its protein and calcium and is in less danger of being thrown away than water.

Creamy sauces made with unbleached or whole-wheat flour, with or without cheese, have nutritional value—but perhaps they are best avoided unless someone at your house is on a weight-gaining diet or won't drink milk straight in the recommended quantity. Aside from adding more calories than you probably need, heavy sauces take up too much appetite room to be considered wholly desirable.

Whenever possible, dice, slice, or shred vegetables. They'll cook faster, keeping nutrient losses to a minimum. Also, whenever possible, prepare and cook vegetables just before serving and try to cook only as much as will be eaten during the meal for which they are intended. If any are left over, refrigerate or freeze them without delay and refer to the recipes in the section on leftovers.

MEAT COOKERY

If you still cook meat without using a meat thermometer, I shall pause long enough for you to run out and buy one. From now on, any meat you cook "plain" by braising, broiling, pan-broiling, roasting, or sautéing (the preferred methods) will be certain of success, both gastronomic and nutritional, if you serve it when the proper thermometer reading is reached and provided you *take the time to cook meat slowly, at low temperatures.*

Braise meat over low range heat or in a low oven.

Broil meat at a low temperature if your broiler has a heat control; if not, place meat to be broiled from 4 to 6 inches from the source of heat.

Pan-broil meat over low range heat.

Roast at low (300°) temperature, unless the recipe specifies otherwise. If your oven is not equipped with an accurate oven thermometer, buy one and use it as directed by the manufacturer, using also your meat thermometer.

Sauté over low range heat.

AN EXPLANATION OF RECOMMENDED MEAT COOKERY TERMS

Braise: To Cook by Steam

Less tender cuts of meat retain flavor and nutrients if carefully braised. Brown the meat on all sides in a heavy utensil— slowly, over low heat, without adding fat. To intensify browning and add flavor in some recipes, the meat may first be dredged with whole-wheat flour; in this case, it is necessary to add a small amount of oil or fat to the pan. When the meat is browned, place it on a rack in a heavy utensil which can be covered tightly. Add a small amount of liquid (stock or vegetable water), cover closely, and cook over low heat until tender or for time specified in recipe. A little lemon juice or vinegar added to the liquid shortens cooking time and acts as a tenderizer. Braising may also be done in a very low (200°) oven. Brown as directed, place on rack, add liquid and lemon juice or vinegar, cover closely, and set in a slow oven until meat is tender and proper thermometer reading is reached.

23

Broil: To Cook by Exposing Meat Directly to Heat

To broil successfully, do not preheat broiling compartment. Keep heat low, if your broiler has a temperature control, and place meat on the top rack. If your broiler has no temperature control, place meat from 4 to 6 inches from the source of heat. Leave broiler door open. Broil one side for half the total cooking time; turn meat, insert meat thermometer, and finish cooking to state of desired doneness (rare, medium, or well done) according to proper thermometer reading.

Pan-broil: To Cook in a Pan over Direct Heat

Place meat in a heavy skillet without adding fat or water. Do not cover. Turn occasionally, and pour off or remove fat as it accumulates. Cook over low heat for amount of time specified in recipe.

Roast: To Cook by Surrounding Meat with Dry Heat

Place meat, fat side up, on a rack in an open shallow roasting pan. Insert a meat thermometer so that its bulb is in the center of the largest muscle. The bulb should not touch bone or rest in fat. Add no water, and do not cover. Roast at oven temperature specified for the amount of time given in the recipe, or until thermometer reading indicates the state of doneness at which you wish to serve the meat (rare, medium, well done).

Sauté: To Cook in a Minimum of Fat

Add to pan only enough oil or fat to prevent food from sticking. Meat may be dredged with whole-wheat flour or whole-wheat bread crumbs, or it may be sautéed without dredging. Start cooking meat over moderate heat, sear for only 1 or 2 minutes on each side, reduce heat to low (or remove pan to a low unit, if you use an electric range), and continue cooking over low heat for amount of time specified in recipe.

RECOMMENDED COOKING METHODS, TIMES, AND TEMPERATURES FOR MEAT AND POULTRY *

Note: The cooking times given in the following table apply only to meat and poultry at room temperature. Allow more time if chilled. Frozen meats or poultry should be defrosted before cooking.

Cut	Cooking Method	Time to Allow	Oven Temperature or Surface Heat
		MEAT	
Beef:			
Standing or rolled rib roast	Roast	Rare: 18–20 min. per lb. Medium: 22–25 min. per lb. Well done: 27–32 min. per lb.	300°
Round, rump, or chuck roast	Roast	Rare: 45–50 min. per lb. Medium: 55–60 min. per lb. Well done: 60–70 min. per lb.	250°
	Braise	60 min. per lb.	Very low (simmer)
Steaks, tender cuts (sirloin, porterhouse, T-bone, club)	Broil	*2-in. steaks* Rare: 30–40 min. Medium: 45–50 min. *1-in. steaks* Rare: 25–30 min. Medium: 35–40 min. *½-in. steaks* Rare: 12–15 min. Medium: 17–20 min.	Low, 4 in. from source of heat

* Unless otherwise specified in individual recipes.

Cut	Cooking Method	Time to Allow	Oven Temperature or Surface Heat
Steaks, less tender cuts (chuck, round)	Broil	*1-in. steaks* Rare: 35–45 min. Medium: 45–50 min. *½-in. steaks* Rare: 18–20 min. Medium: 22–25 min.	Very low, 5–6 in. from source of heat
Ham:			
Whole or half	Roast	25–30 min. per lb.	300°
Tenderized	Roast	20–25 min. per lb.	300°
Steaks: Not tenderized	Broil or pan-broil	*1-in. steaks* 40–45 min. *½-in. steaks* 20–25 min.	Low, 4 in. from source of broiler heat, or over low heat on range
Tenderized	Broil or pan-broil	*1-in. steaks* 20–30 min. *½-in. steaks* 15–20 min.	
Lamb:			
Leg	Roast	25–30 min. per lb.	300°
Shoulder	Roast	40–45 min. per lb.	275°
Breast	Roast	30–35 min. per lb.	300°
Chops or steaks	Broil	*2-in. chops* 40–45 min. *1-in. chops or steaks* 20–30 min.	Low, 4 in. from source of broiler heat
Pork:			
Loin cuts	Roast	35–40 min. per lb.	300°
Shoulder	Roast	40–45 min. per lb.	300°
Fresh ham	Roast	35–40 min. per lb.	300°

Cut	Cooking Method	Time to Allow	Oven Temperature or Surface Heat
Chops	Broil (be sure to use meat thermometer)	1½-in. chops 40–45 min.	Low, 4 in. from source of broiler heat
	Pan-broil	1-in. chops 30–35 min.	Low heat on range
Veal:			
Leg	Roast	25–30 min. per lb.	300°
Loin	Roast	30–35 min. per lb.	300°
Shoulder	Roast	40–45 min. per lb.	300°
Chops (¾–1 in.)	Braise	45–50 min.	Low heat on range
Cutlets (½ in.)	Braise	30–35 min.	Low heat on range

POULTRY

Cut	Cooking Method	Time to Allow	Oven Temperature or Surface Heat
Chicken:			
Parts	Broil, pan-broil, sauté	45–50 min.	Low, 4 in. from source of broiler heat, or over low heat on range
Whole	Roast	35–45 min. per lb.	300°
Turkey:			
Small (8–13 lb.)	Roast	20–25 min. per lb.	300°
Large (14 lb. or over)	Roast	15–18 min. per lb.	300°
Duck	Roast	25–30 min. per lb.	300°
Goose	Roast	25–30 min. per lb.	300°

Throughout this cookbook, whenever other cooking methods are used—as for stews, meat loaves and patties, casseroles, etc.—

specific cooking times and temperatures are given. All organ meat recipes also include specific instructions.

WHY SPECIAL-PURPOSE FOODS?

In many recipes in this cookbook, you will note several special ingredients with which you may or may not be familiar, for example: wheat germ, wheat-germ oil, brewers' yeast, yeast flakes, skim-milk solids, monosodium glutamate, sugarless sweeteners, soybeans or soybean flour, whole-wheat pastry flour, etc. My students and listeners to the "Living Should Be Fun" broadcasts are aware of the nutritional values of these special-purpose foods. For those to whom emphasis on good nutrition is a new idea in home cookery, let me say briefly here that these are foods whose contributions to diet cannot be overstated. They provide protective amounts of proteins, vitamins, and minerals much needed in modern diets. The index will refer you to further discussions.

WHERE TO FIND SPECIAL-PURPOSE FOODS

Happily, as emphasis on good nutrition for good health continues to grow in schools, medical research laboratories, government agencies, and the public awareness, the special-purpose foods mentioned throughout this book are becoming more and more available from more and more sources. There was a time, not too many years ago, when you would have had to go to a farmers' feed and grain store to find blackstrap molasses, to a brewery for brewers' yeast, to flour mills for wheat-germ and whole-grain flours and cereals, to the military quartermaster or a dairy farm for skim-milk solids.

While some of the special flours and other items must still be sought out, most of the special-purpose foods can be found on the shelves of your favorite supermarket. If your store does not have them, ask the manager to stock them and persuade your friends and neighbors to request them also. These foods are—or soon will be—commercially available and nationally distributed.

The housewives of America may not realize it fully, but they are the ones who determine to a large extent what foods, of what quality, are offered by the retailers. If there is sufficient demand for special-purpose foods, your local merchants will be happy to stock them.

For your general guidance, suggested sources for special-purpose foods are given below. When more than one source is given, the listing (reading from left to right) is in an order indicating the most reliable and usually the most realistically priced sources.

Banana flakes: Food chain and independent grocery stores; drugstores.

Brewers' yeast: Leading mail-order vitamin firms; drug stores; breweries;* health-food stores.

Cereals, whole grain, no sugar added: Many varieties to be found in food chain and independent grocery stores. Otherwise— at independent local mills;* local and state farmers' exchanges;* organic gardening clubs;* health-food stores.

Flour, unbleached: Food chain and independent grocery stores.

Flour, 100 per cent whole wheat: Occasionally to be found at food chain and independent grocery stores. Otherwise—see next listing.

Flour, whole rye, buckwheat, soybean, potato, whole-wheat pastry: Independent local mills;* large milling companies;* local or state farmers' exchanges;* organic gardening clubs;* health-food stores.

Gelatin, whole or natural, unsweetened: Food chain and independent grocery stores, health-food stores.

Macaroni products, made with wheat germ and containing 20 per cent protein: Food chain and independent grocery stores, health-food stores.

Monosodium glutamate: Under various brand names, in food chain and independent grocery stores. Otherwise—leading mail-order vitamin firms; drugstores; health-food stores.

Rice, brown or converted: Food chain and independent grocery stores; independent local mills;* health-food stores.

Skim-milk solids (nonfat dry milk, nonfat milk powder): Food chain and independent grocery stores.

Sugarless sweeteners: Under various brand names, at food chain or independent grocery stores, usually on shelves where dietetic foods are displayed; drugstores; health-food stores.

Undegerminated corn meal: See "Cereals, whole grain, no sugar added."

Wheat germ: Food chain and independent grocery stores; independent local mills;* milling companies;* organic gardening clubs;* health-food stores. (Defatted wheat germ has lost its saturated fat and Vitamin E. It is a good food, but inferior to natural wheat germ. Buy natural wheat germ in vacuum packing, if possible; like all good foods it is perishable.)

Wheat-germ oil: Leading mail-order vitamin firms; drugstores; health-food stores.

Yeast flakes: See "Brewers' yeast."

Special note about salt: Although the recipes in this book do not specify it, the author sincerely hopes that all table and cooking salt used in your home is *iodized* unless contraindicated by a physician. Iodized salt is available in all food stores.

Special note about labels on food packages: Learn to read labels carefully. Food packagers are required to list ingredients. No product is 100 per cent whole grain unless the label states that it is. No product contains wheat germ or any other special nutrient unless it is specified on the label. Salt and/or sugar additions are stated. Artificial flavorings and colorings are similarly identified, as are preservatives.

Special note about brewers' yeast: Yeasts vary tremendously in nutritional values—particularly protein and the B Complex vitamins. They also vary in taste, from awful to quite palatable. As a starter, try Delecta yeast for incorporation in most recipes. Where a bacon flavor is acceptable, try Bakon Yeast. Both are available in health food stores.

---

* Consult the yellow pages of your telephone book, or write to the sales department of a firm producing the end commercial product—beer, flour, macaroni, etc. Your country or state farm bureau or the agricultural department of a nearby college or university can usually supply you with a list of your area's organic farms, distributors of organically grown produce, and mills offering whole-grain cereals and flours for sale.

Good Nutrition
Starts the Day Right

2

Good Nutrition
Starts the Day Right

THE IMPORTANCE OF BREAKFAST

Holding this book in your hands makes you one of two kinds of people. You're either a seeker after good nutrition, or you're a cookbook fan. If the former, and especially if you are familiar with my broadcasts, you won't be surprised by nonconformity. If the latter, you will find that in this cookbook not only are the ideas and recipes unorthodox, but also their sequence.

This chapter concerns breakfast, the most valuable but unfortunately the most neglected meal of a typical American day. The next chapter, on the other hand, concerns something which realistically appraises the typical American enthusiasm for those little snacks, goodies, and diet dodges you find so irresistible.

By raising the curtain on breakfast, the author hopes to hold your attention long enough to convert you and your family into a group of virtuous breakfasters, eating good, nutritious, body-sustaining breakfasts instead of the little glass of fruit juice, piece of buttered toast, and cup of sweetened coffee, which masquerade as a morning meal in most households.

The starch-and-sugar breakfast of the average man, woman, or child is pitifully inadequate to sustain any human being at an efficient level of working or thinking capacity until lunchtime. Starches and sugars enter the blood stream rapidly, causing blood-sugar levels to rise like geysers and creating a deceptive feeling of satisfaction. These carbohydrates are so quickly burned up that the spurting blood-sugar levels drop with a thud, resulting in the all-too-familiar "midmorning slump." By contrast, a protein breakfast—one emphasizing eggs, meat, cheese or extra milk along with the fruit juice, toast, and beverage—maintains blood-sugar levels in better equilibrium until the next meal.*

Understanding and even agreeing with the idea that the body requires a substantial breakfast is one thing. Putting a substantial breakfast into family routine is another matter.

The hurried, harried housewife and mother is usually blessed with a husband and children who have obstinate ideas about breakfast, when they eat it at all. Unnerved by their complaints, disdain, or outrageous demands, she finds it far too much trouble to boil or poach eggs for Papa, fry them for Sonny, and scramble them for Sis; therefore she deems it wise not even to offer a choice of more substantial dishes. She has found it expedient to put a loaf of bread near the pop-up toaster, plug in the percolator, and go back to bed.

Even when she is willing, if not eager, to prepare and serve a decent meal in the morning, there are other obstacles. One of the most common complaints brought to my attention by women sincerely interested in correct nutritional habits for their families is: "My child simply won't eat breakfast. What can I do?" Very often this problem is complicated by another one. Thousands of worried mothers have told me that when they coax, threaten, or force their children to eat breakfast, physical distress follows. These mothers have a depressing choice—an improperly nourished child or a nauseated one.

There are many reasons why a child may get sick after eating a breakfast he knew beforehand he did not want. Sometimes it is

* There is recent evidence that protein at breakfast raises blood amino acids; protein at dinner does *not*. A good high-protein breakfast is obviously the most important meal of the day.

34

nervousness in the rush of getting off to school. (The solution here would be to get the child up earlier.) Sometimes the nausea is a physical manifestation of an emotional conflict. The child wishes to reject school, cannot, and so rejects his breakfast instead. On an adult level the same emotional factors may be involved if you substitute *job* for *school,* but much breakfast-skipping is a simple matter of an acquired bad habit compounded by neglect or laziness until the body sets up a stubborn block against change.

Adolescent girls frequently scorn breakfast when they become interested in boys. They sacrifice the morning meal, which they suspect of harboring hateful calories, to retain their willowy slimness. The goal is commendable, but the method for achieving it is not. There is overwhelming evidence that breakfast-skipping, which lowers functional efficiency, may ultimately lead to health problems. While a teen-age girl may not be impressed by your concern with her health, she is likely to pay some attention if you point out that good nutrition has a positive bearing on good looks. The well-nourished adolescent female has physical as well as physiological advantages over her poorly nourished sister—a fresh, smooth complexion, shiny hair, good teeth, clear eyes, and the energy to keep up with the dates forthcoming from admiring adolescent males. Skipping breakfast does not lower calory intake, anyhow. The teen-ager unconsciously compensates—with calories from the wrong foods at lunch and dinner.

There are at least two ways of tackling the problem of the reluctant breakfaster. One is to make breakfast so concentrated that you can get a whole meal into a glassful of liquid. The other is to make it so enticing it is irresistible.

The child who absolutely refuses to eat anything solid in the morning can usually be cajoled into accepting a glass of something liquid, if it tastes nice. And few children of any age, which includes husbands, can resist the holiday spirit of a stack of pancakes or waffles.

Serving breakfast in the do-it-yourself style of the hunting set is an excellent idea. In gracious English homes, the breakfast room sideboard is aglitter with silver chafing dishes keeping a variety of tempting foods warm for self-service. Translated into American, the kitchen counter or dinette table can bear electric skillets and saucepans, automatic bean-pots and candle warmers. Your family probably won't clap hands in delight over bloaters, kippers, or kidney pie at 7 A.M., but many of the recipes in the pages to follow lend themselves readily to buffet breakfasts.

There is nothing in nutrition which insists on ritual. The point is to get good, enjoyable food into your family at regular intervals, especially in the morning. One little girl of the author's acquaintance eats soup for breakfast. She likes it.

EYE-OPENERS

BANANA-ORANGE MILK SHAKE

1 fully ripe banana (or 1 scant tablespoon concentrated banana flakes)
½ cup unsweetened orange juice
1 tablespoon honey
pinch of salt

¼ teaspoon almond or vanilla extract
1 eight-ounce glass of cold milk
2 tablespoons skim-milk solids
(2 egg yolks)

Mash banana and beat with fork until creamy. (If you use banana flakes, stir them into the orange juice until well blended.) Beat in orange juice, honey, salt, and extract, using either a rotary beater or electric blender. Add milk and milk solids and beat until all ingredients are well blended. Serve at once. For greater nutritive value, especially when dealing with breakfast rebels, add 2 egg yolks as you beat in the milk. *Serves 2.*

MORNING MAPLE

2 whole eggs
2 teaspoons brewers' yeast
1¾ cups cold milk
2 tablespoons skim-milk solids

4 tablespoons freshly made coffee
2 teaspoons honey
1 teaspoon maple syrup

Beat eggs thoroughly with rotary or electric beater, gradually adding brewers' yeast and continuing to beat until lumps disappear. Add milk, milk solids, coffee, honey, and maple syrup, and beat until mixture resembles thick malted milk. *Serves 2.*

36

SPOON PRUNE

1 cup pitted, cooked prunes *   2 tablespoons skim-milk solids
1 cup cold whole milk   1 cup crushed or shaved ice

Chop prunes. Combine all ingredients with electric beater or blender for half a minute, until smooth. Serve at once in sherbet glasses, to be eaten with spoons. (Save syrup remaining after all prunes have been used. Refrigerate, and substitute for sugar or honey in milk shakes and eggnogs.) *Serves 2 to 3.*

BABY FRUIT NOG

1 egg yolk   3 tablespoons any strained baby-
1 cup cold milk   pack fruit (peaches, apricots,
1 tablespoon skim-milk solids   etc.)
                                       1½ teaspoons honey

Combine all ingredients and beat well with rotary or electric beater. *Serves 1.*

PURPLE COW

½ cup sugarless grape juice   1 egg yolk
½ cup cold milk   1 teaspoon honey
2 tablespoons skim-milk solids   1 teaspoon brown sugar
1 teaspoon lemon or lime juice

Combine all ingredients and blend very thoroughly with rotary or electric beater. Serve at once. *Serves 1.*

For the delight (and equal nourishment) of little breakfast balkers, this recipe can be transformed into a Pink Piglet by using cranberry, raspberry, or strawberry juice instead of grape.

HOT FRUIT RAINBOW

Choose any combination of fruits and berries according to the supply of the season, your family's preferences, the cans on your

---

* *To cook prunes.* Drop 1 pound of dried, unsweetened prunes into 2 cups of boiling water. When water returns to boil, cover saucepan and reduce heat to simmer. Cook for only about 15 minutes, until prunes are tender. Remove from heat; sweeten with 2 tablespoons of honey. Refrigerate until used.

pantry shelf, or the packages in your freezer. The suggestions given here are a guide to quantities.

2 or 3 small, sweet, seedless oranges divided into sections
1 cup seedless grapes or pitted cherries
1 cup peach halves or whole pitted apricots or plums
1 cup canned figs

1½ cups juices from canned fruits, or 1 cup orange juice
1 teaspoon grated orange peel
1 teaspoon lemon juice
½ teaspoon almond or vanilla extract
⅛ teaspoon cinnamon or nutmeg —or both

Put fruit, juice, and grated peel into large skillet over medium heat and simmer gently for 10 minutes. Remove from heat and flavor with lemon juice and extract. Sprinkle with cinnamon and/or nutmeg, and serve while hot. If you have used tart fruits, sweeten to taste with honey. *Serves 4 to 6.*

BREAKFAST BROTH

1 cup any condensed cream soup (canned)
¾ cup whole milk
⅓ cup skim-milk solids

2 teaspoons brewers' yeast or yeast flakes
yolk of hard-cooked egg

Stir condensed soup until smooth, in pan placed over low heat. Add milk and milk solids, stirring to blend thoroughly. Bring to just below boiling point. Remove from heat and stir in yeast until there are no lumps. Sprinkle with crumbled egg yolk and serve with buttered whole-wheat toast for a simple, somewhat unusual but nutritious hot morning drink. *Serves 2.*

GOOD-NUTRITION CEREALS

If you are in the habit of feeding your family the average packaged cold breakfast cereal, you should be interested in the following account of a visit to one of this country's celebrated breakfast-food factories. Although the cereal described here is cornflakes, the procedure is essentially the same for all cold cereals not specifically labeled "whole grain."

First I saw machinery removing the outer coat, then the germ (in other words, the life) from corn. This, my guide explained, was to prevent their cornflakes from "rancidity and spoilage." He said they sent the discarded husks to "fox farms and other places where they feed animals." What was left of the corn at this point was of an unlifelike pallor as befits any corpse. Masses of this corpselike substance (I refuse to call it corn) were put in large pressure cookers, heated to a temperature of 250 degrees and held at that temperature for two and a half hours when it was ready to be mixed with artificial flavoring and coloring to make it look and taste less like the corpse it really was. The entire mass was then cooled until it reached a stage at which it was ready to be run through machines to flake it. At this point it began a journey on endless belts that passed it through heaters where it reached a temperature of 450 degrees, thus assuring loss or deterioration of nutritional elements that might have survived up to this point. The process set the flakes to prevent them from sticking together. Now it was ready for packaging in wax-paper lined cartons. This, said the guide, would keep their product "as fresh as a daisy." The factory was sending out sixty-five carloads of this foodless pap and other breakfast foods every day to be eaten by human beings. A tank car full of corn germ oil left . . . every month for the pharmaceutical houses. The little foxes got the rest of it.[*]

With the foregoing in mind, you may want with all your heart to revise your cold-cereal purchasing but anticipate objections from your habit-inured family. Until you can persuade your housemates to accept a morning bowlful of entirely whole-grain cereal I suggest you do the following—in easy stages, if necessary:

1. Read labels. Avoid cereals to which sugar has been added.
2. To each serving of cereal add 1 or 2 teaspoons of wheat germ.
3. Mix customary cereal with equal portions of whole-grain types.
4. Add 2 tablespoons skim-milk solids to each cup of milk served with cereal.
5. Sweeten cereal with honey, dark molasses, or banana flakes. If you cannot turn a deaf ear to pleas for sugar, fill the sugar bowl with brown sugar. The family will use less.

---

[*] From *Open Door to Health*, by Fred D. Miller, The Devin-Adair Company, New York, 1959.

Cooked Cereals

GRANULAR WHOLE WHEAT, UNDEGERMINATED CORN MEAL, QUICK-COOKING OATS

In water:

2 cups water
1 cup cereal
1 teaspoon salt

honey, dark molasses, brown
    sugar, or banana flakes

In heavy saucepan with tight-fitting lid, bring water to a rolling boil over high heat. Add cereal slowly as water continues to boil, and stir briskly, adding salt. Reduce heat to gentle boil, cover tightly, and cook for 5 to 7 minutes. Add honey, dark molasses, brown sugar, or banana flakes to taste when served. *Serves 2.*

In milk:

2 cups milk
2 tablespoons skim-milk solids
1 cup cereal

½ teaspoon salt
honey, dark molasses, or brown
    sugar

Combine milk and milk solids and heat to simmer stage. Add cereal very slowly to prevent cooling of milk. Add salt, cover, and simmer for 5 minutes. Add honey, dark molasses, or brown sugar to taste when served. *Serves 2.*

WHOLE WHEAT, WHOLE BUCKWHEAT, WHOLE GRITS, ROLLED OATS

In water:

3 cups water
1 cup cereal
1 teaspoon salt

honey, dark molasses, or brown
    sugar

Bring water to rolling boil, add cereal slowly as water continues to boil, and stir briskly. Add salt, reduce heat to gentle boil, cover tightly, and cook for 10 to 15 minutes. Add honey, dark molasses, or brown sugar to taste when served. *Serves 2.*

40

In milk:

2 cups milk
2 tablespoons skim-milk solids
1 cup cereal

½ teaspoon salt
honey, dark molasses, or brown
  sugar

Combine milk and milk solids and heat to simmer stage. Add cereal very slowly to prevent cooling of milk. Add salt, cover, and simmer for 10 to 15 minutes. Add honey, dark molasses, or brown sugar to taste when served. *Serves 2.*

Note: For even better nutrition and very slight variation in taste, add to each cup of dry cereal before cooking 1 teaspoon brewers' yeast or yeast flakes.

SPECIAL CORN-MEAL RECIPES

SCRAPPLE

If you're going to take the trouble to prepare this excellent source of protein and vitamins, you might as well make a lot. It can be stored in a refrigerator freezing compartment for three months, in a full freezer for six months. Before freezing, however, be sure to slice chilled scrapple into individual serving pieces and separate them with double thicknesses of cellophane or Saran. Wrap and seal securely.

To make 4 pounds of scrapple:

2½ pounds lean raw pork, cut
  into small pieces—or 2
  pounds lean raw pork and ½
  pound raw pork liver
2 quarts cold water (use water

saved from cooking vegetables, if possible)
1 teaspoon salt
½ teaspoon black pepper

Cover meat with water and add seasonings. Bring to a boil, reduce heat, and simmer for 2 hours. Remove and grind or shred meat. Strain cooking water and remove 2 cups of it, allowing it to cool. Continue to simmer remaining broth—very slowly, and well covered.

41

Blend together

2 cups undegerminated yellow
　corn meal
¾ cup wheat germ
1 teaspoon salt

½ teaspoon black pepper
1 teaspoon sage or savory
dash of cayenne

To this blend add the 2 cups of cooled broth, gradually. Keep it from lumping. When smooth, add slowly to the simmering broth, stirring constantly. Still stirring, add the ground or shredded meat. If you use an electric stove, reduce heat to lowest temperature. If you use a gas range, place pan on a low flame covered with an asbestos mat. Continue to cook slowly for 2 hours, stirring occasionally. Pour into long, narrow pans which have been rinsed in cold water. Let stand in a cool place until firm. To serve: Heat slices over moderate heat in skillet with only enough oil or shortening to prevent sticking.

FLUFFY BUTTERMILK SPOON BREAD

1 quart buttermilk
4 tablespoons skim-milk solids
⅔ cup undegerminated yellow
　corn meal

⅓ cup wheat germ
1½ teaspoons salt
2 tablespoons butter or margarine
4 eggs

Combine buttermilk and skim-milk solids and heat in top of double boiler. Do not boil. Mix corn meal, salt, and wheat germ and add to milk, stirring until thickened and smooth. Cover, reduce heat, and let cook while you preheat oven to 425°. Remove from heat and add butter. In large bowl beat eggs until light and frothy. Stir eggs into corn-meal mixture, blending well. Pour into well-greased baking dish and bake 50 minutes to 1 hour. Serve hot, topped with sliced fruit, honey, or maple syrup.

BANANA SPOON BREAD

2½ cups water
½ cup undegerminated yellow
　corn meal
½ cup wheat germ
2 tablespoons butter, melted
¾ teaspoon salt
2 egg yolks, lightly beaten

1½ cups milk
3 tablespoons skim-milk solids
2 egg whites, beaten stiff
1 cup mashed banana, or 1 jar of
　puréed baby-food banana, or
　¼–½ cup banana flakes

42

Using top of double boiler, bring water to boil over direct heat. Combine corn meal and wheat germ and stir into boiling water. Set boiler top in its bottom part filled to proper level with boiling water. Cook 15 minutes over boiling water, remove from heat while you preheat oven to 425°. When mixture is slightly cooled, add butter, salt, egg yolks, and milk (combined with milk solids) and beat for 2 minutes with rotary or electric beater at low speed. Fold in stiffly beaten egg whites and banana pulp or flakes and pour into greased 2-quart baking dish. Bake 40 minutes.

BREAKFAST DUMPLINGS

BAKED FRUIT DUMPLINGS

1¼ cups unbleached flour
⅛ teaspoon salt
1½ teaspoons baking powder
1 tablespoon skim-milk solids
1½ tablespoons butter or margarine

½ cup milk
¼ cup wheat germ
2 teaspoons brown sugar
1 cup sliced apples, peaches, apricots, plums, or bananas

Sift flour with salt, baking powder, and milk solids. With fork, work in butter. Add milk and blend into a doughlike ball. Pat or roll out on a floured board to a thickness of about ½ inch. Cut dough into 4-inch squares. Combine wheat germ and brown sugar and stir into sliced fruit until it is evenly coated. Place several slices of fruit in center of each dough square. Moisten edges of dough and fold, pinching edges together firmly to seal. Put dumplings, not touching each other, in a well-greased shallow baking pan. Carefully pour boiling water in pan to a depth of ¼ inch. Without covering, bake dumplings at 350° for 30 to 35 minutes, until browned. Serve hot with warm fruit juice, honey-sweetened or unsweetened cream, or light sour cream. *Serves 4.*

43

BOILED YEAST DUMPLINGS WITH FRUIT

Good for late Sunday or holiday breakfasts.

½ yeast cake or ½ package dry
    yeast
1 cup lukewarm milk
2 cups unbleached or whole-wheat
    flour

1 teaspoon sugar
1 teaspoon salt
2 tablespoons skim-milk solids
2 eggs, well beaten
stewed, fresh, or frozen fruit

Crumble or sprinkle yeast over ¼ cup of the warm milk and let stand while you sift together the flour, sugar, salt, and milk solids. Add dry ingredients and beaten eggs to yeast mixture along with remaining milk and knead well in bowl until smooth. Cover with towel and set aside in a warm place (80°) to rise until double in bulk, about 1 hour. Pat down, shape into balls about the size of large walnuts, and place them on a floured board. Cover and let rise again. When double in bulk (1 hour or less), drop one by one into lightly salted boiling water. (Use pan large enough to hold at least 2 quarts of water, with room to spare.) Boil gently for 10 to 20 minutes, covered. Test by removing one dumpling (recovering pan immediately) and pulling it apart with two forks. Dumplings are properly done when inside is dry and spongy, not doughy. Remove dumplings with slotted spoon and serve at once with any stewed, fresh, or defrosted frozen fruit. You may warm the fruit, but the contrast between hot dumplings and cool fruit is pleasant. *Serves 4.*

GOOD-NUTRITION PANCAKES AND WAFFLES

Pancakes and waffles can be as nutritious as they are seductive to early-morning appetite laggards.

It is a temptation, in this day of food processors who do everything for the busy housewife except set the table and wash the dishes, to buy a prepared pancake or waffle mix which requires only that you add liquid and introduce the stove. There are, happily, some mixes available which make an honest effort to charge their ingredients with good nutrition, and the thoughtful homemaker can serve these with a clear conscience.

For nutritional security and creative satisfaction, you should prefer to make your own batters.* Inasmuch as a genuine breakfast may almost constitute a new habit for you and your family, perhaps I can get you to put into those batters a strong dose of important B vitamins, a certain amount of vitamin E, and a nice margin of proteins. (I am assuming that fruit and fruit juices will provide a morning portion of the vitamin C you must have daily, and hoping that—in time—you will be using the bread section in this book to give meaning to carbohydrate intake.)

You will note in the recipes to follow that whenever baking powder or (rarely) baking soda is included as a concession to the morning rush, there is also mention of a generous amount of skim-milk solids, wheat germ, and brewers' yeast or yeast flakes. Let me tell you why, lest you dismiss the subject too lightly in the belief that eggs and milk are enough, or that these products are fad foods and therefore expendable.

For one thing, there are natural B vitamins in yeast you literally get from no other source in quite the same balance. Wheat germ and wheat-germ oil supply valuable unsaturated fatty acids and vitamin E, inadequately present in most modern foods. For another thing, there is an alkali in baking soda and to a lesser degree in baking powder which destroys a high percentage of the B vitamins in the recipe ingredients milk, flour, and shortening. Extra milk solids, a yeast product, and wheat germ in your breakfast menus offset the loss—the milk solids by providing complete proteins which neutralize the alkali, and the yeast and wheat germ by providing more B vitamins than the baking powder can destroy.

Those of you who will take the time to make all-yeast pancakes (page 48) or waffles (page 54) can do away with baking powder or soda entirely while treating the family to a new taste thrill.

---

* There are a few pancake mixes available that are nutritious, and which are not seasoned with chemicals of dubious safety. Most of these are in the health food stores. Occasionally, there is a brand in the supermarkets. Read labels carefully.

Pancakes

Use a very heavy griddle or skillet and make it ready by heating it slowly. When it is properly hot, a few drops of water will sputter and bounce on the griddle surface. For the most part, a heavy enough griddle requires no greasing—or, at most, a very light coating of oil. Some cooks like to rub the griddle with a salt-filled cheesecloth bag or an oiled cloth, cleaning it also this way between uses.

To be sure of good results, batter should be medium, not thick, and not too thin except where specified for paper-thin pancakes to be filled. Milk can be added to batters that seem too thick, and extra wheat germ to those that are too thin.

Pour batter from a pitcher, or drop it by the spoonful onto the hot griddle, baking no more than 3 or 4 pancakes at a time. Turn pancakes only once—when bubbles break on the uncooked surface and the edges appear slightly dry, usually in 2 or 3 minutes. After you have flipped them with a wide spatula or pancake turner, the second side will brown nicely in about 1 minute.

If possible, serve pancakes at once on heated plates rather than stacking them and keeping them warm.

APPLE CINNAMON PANCAKES

1¼ cups unbleached or whole-wheat flour
1 teaspoon baking powder
(1–2 tablespoons brewers' yeast or yeast flakes)
2 tablespoons skim-milk solids
¼ cup wheat germ
½ teaspoon ground cinnamon
1 tablespoon brown sugar

1½ tablespoons butter or margarine, melted (1 teaspoon of this amount may be wheat-germ oil)
2 eggs, beaten
1 cup finely chopped raw apples (or applesauce)
1 cup milk

Combine dry ingredients, mixing well. Add melted butter, beaten eggs, and apples and blend thoroughly. Stir in milk gradually to make a smooth batter. *Makes about 16 pancakes.*

BACON AND EGG CORNCAKES

1 cup boiling water (use water in
    which vegetables were
    cooked, if possible)
1 cup undegerminated yellow
    corn meal
2 tablespoons bacon fat
½ cup chopped bacon
¼ cup unbleached or whole-wheat

    flour
¼ cup wheat germ
1 teaspoon baking powder
(1–2 tablespoons brewers' yeast
    or yeast flakes)
(2 tablespoons skim-milk solids)
1 egg, beaten
1 cup milk or buttermilk

Pour boiling water over corn meal in a bowl and let stand while you fry chopped bacon slowly until crisp. Pour off bacon fat, reserving 2 tablespoons. Combine dry ingredients and mix with softened corn meal. Stir in 2 tablespoons bacon fat, beaten egg, and milk. Add crisp bacon and mix thoroughly. *Makes about 16 corncakes.*

BERRY SOUFFLE PANCAKES

4 eggs, separated
1 tablespoon brown sugar
¼ teaspoon salt
¼ cup unbleached or whole-wheat
    flour

½ cup heavy sour cream
½ cup drained, naturally sweet
    berries—whole blueberries,
    crushed raspberries, or sliced
    strawberries

Beat egg yolks until light. Add sugar, salt, flour, sour cream, and berries, stirring to mix well. Beat egg whites until stiff and fold in. *Makes about 8 pancakes.*

BREAD PANCAKES

1 cup coarse whole-wheat bread
    crumbs
1 cup milk
1 egg, well beaten
¼ cup unbleached or whole-
    wheat flour
¼ cup wheat germ

2 teaspoons baking powder
½ teaspoon salt
(1–2 tablespoons brewers' yeast
    or yeast flakes)
(2 tablespoons skim-milk solids)
2 tablespoons butter or marga-
    rine, melted

Soften bread crumbs in milk—for an hour, if you have the time. Add beaten egg. Combine and add dry ingredients and melted butter. Mix well. *Makes about 8 pancakes.*

47

OATMEAL PANCAKES

1½ cups milk
2 cups quick-cooking oats
⅓ cup oil or melted ham or bacon
     fat
2 eggs, beaten

⅓ cup unbleached flour
2 tablespoons wheat germ
(1–2 tablespoons brewers' yeast)
(2–3 tablespoons skim-milk sol-
     ids)

Heat but do not boil milk, and pour over oats and shortening. Cool slightly. Add and beat in eggs. Add and blend in remaining ingredients, mixing thoroughly. *Makes about 12 pancakes.*

WHOLE-GRAIN YEAST PANCAKES

1 cake fresh yeast, or 1 package
     dry yeast
1½ cups warm milk
1 tablespoon dark molasses, hon-
     ey, or brown sugar
2 eggs, beaten
2 tablespoons shortening, melted

(butter, margarine, oil, or
     ham or bacon fat)
1 cup whole-wheat or whole-buck-
     wheat flour
½ cup wheat germ
(¼ cup skim-milk solids)
1 teaspoon salt

Stir yeast into warm milk and let stand 10 minutes. Stir in sweetener, beaten eggs, and shortening. Combine dry ingredients and stir into liquid. Mix thoroughly. Batter may be used immediately, may be allowed to rise in a warm place for 30 minutes to an hour, or may be prepared before bedtime and stored overnight in the refrigerator. *Makes 12 to 16 pancakes.*

SOUR-DOUGH PANCAKES

These deserve special mention. I have taken some nutritional liberties with the traditional sour dough as it was thrown together by gold prospectors in Alaska and the old West. They, of course, knew nothing about wheat germ as a separate ingredient—their flour sometimes contained it.

To make the sour-dough starter: Peel, dice, and boil four or five potatoes until they are soft. Reserve the potatoes for some other use—it's the water you need.

2 cups warm potato water
2 cups unbleached flour
1 tablespoon sugar

1 teaspoon salt
1 yeastcake, crumbled, or 1 package dry yeast

Mix these ingredients and put them in a crock. Cover loosely and let stand in a warm place overnight or for 2 days, until the starter is "working" and giving off a yeasty, somewhat sourish smell. It is then ready for use.

Mix together in a bowl and let stand overnight in a warm place:

2 cups sour-dough starter
1 cup unbleached flour

1 cup water

Add to bowl:

¼ cup wheat germ
¼ cup skim-milk solids
1 egg, lightly beaten

2 tablespoons butter or margarine, melted

Combine all ingredients by stirring well, and let stand for 5 minutes. Ladle about ¼ cup of batter for each pancake onto hot griddle. *Makes 12 to 16 pancakes.*

PAPER-THIN PANCAKES, TO BE FILLED AND ROLLED

2 eggs
1¼ cups milk
½ teaspoon salt

1 cup sifted unbleached flour
1 tablespoon sugar
oil for griddle

Beat eggs until light. Stir in milk and salt. Sift flour and sugar together and stir into liquid. Beat very rapidly, but not too long, until smooth. Use a small, heavy skillet for these, make them one at a time, and coat the skillet thinly with oil before each pancake. Pour about 2 tablespoons of batter into hot skillet, tilting it in all directions to spread batter evenly. Turn when bubbles break. *Makes 12 to 16 pancakes.*

FILLING SUGGESTIONS FOR PAPER-THIN PANCAKES

Each recipe will yield approximately 1 cup of filling. Blend ingredients well and place 1 tablespoon of mixture slightly off center of pancake. Roll and top with fruit, fruit pulp, honey, dark molasses, or sweet or sour cream.

1 cup chopped fresh, canned, or defrosted frozen peaches or cherries
1 tablespoon crystallized ginger, chopped fine
2 teaspoons grated lemon or orange rind

1 cup cottage cheese
1 tablespoon grated orange rind (or banana flakes)
yolk of egg which has been coddled 1 minute in water just under boiling point

1 cup cottage cheese
1 tablespoon honey or brown sugar
¾ teaspoon ground cinnamon
¼ teaspoon grated nutmeg
¼ teaspoon grated lemon or orange rind

½ cup fine-curd cottage cheese or cream cheese
½ cup cranberry sauce or applesauce; crushed pineapple; whole blueberries; or crushed raspberries, blackberries, or strawberries

HIGH-PROTEIN FILLINGS

When these fillings are used, omit sugar from pancakes.

Sautéed Chicken Livers

½ pound chicken livers—or any kind of liver cut into very small pieces
basil or nutmeg

1½ tablespoons butter or chicken fat
⅔ cup warm sour cream

Sprinkle liver with few grains of basil or nutmeg. Sauté liver in butter or chicken fat until cooked through and just tender. Add sour cream and mix thoroughly.

Creamed Chipped Beef

2 tablespoons butter or margarine
2 tablespoons unbleached or whole-wheat flour

1 tablespoon skim-milk solids
¾ cup warm milk
¼ pound chipped beef

Melt butter in top of double boiler. Add and blend in flour and milk solids, making a smooth paste. Slowly add warm milk, stirring to avoid lumps. Let cook over boiling water, stirring occasionally, for 10 minutes. Separate layers of chip beef, cut into 1-inch pieces, and stir into sauce.

50

Waffles

Like pancakes, waffles can be good food as well as good fun. The recipes given here pay tribute to the complete proteins which belong in breakfast but are usually sparse or lacking. Once your family has tasted these waffles topped with fruit or, if they insist, with sauces (made with honey or molasses, as on page 54), it is improbable that they will ever again cheer the empty calories of ordinary white-flour, white-sugar waffles.

Waffle batter should not fill the baking iron completely—about half an inch from the outer edge is a good general rule. The iron should be hot enough to make a drop of water boil, but not sizzle. After you have poured the batter and closed the iron, resist the temptation to peek until the steaming has stopped.

Some cooks insist that eggs to be used in waffles must be separated and the yolks beaten and added before the stiffly beaten whites are folded in. This may make the waffles somewhat airier, but it is no crime to take a short cut and beat the whole eggs. Nutritionally speaking, the less air beaten into food the better.

BACON OR HAM WAFFLES

½–1 pound sliced bacon—or 1 cup diced or minced cooked ham
2 cups unbleached or whole-wheat flour
3 teaspoons baking powder

3 tablespoons skim-milk solids
1 teaspoon salt
2 teaspoons brown sugar
2 tablespoons wheat germ
2 cups milk
2 eggs

Fry bacon slowly until crisp. Remove from pan, drain, and crumble. Reserve ⅓ cup of the bacon fat. Combine dry ingredients and mix thoroughly to distribute well. Add milk and mix thoroughly. Beat in eggs, one at a time. Add and stir in bacon fat (⅓ cup). Pour small amount of batter on waffle iron and sprinkle with crisped bacon pieces—or diced or minced ham. (In place of bacon fat, you may use 6 tablespoons melted butter or margarine, or 3 tablespoons each of melted butter and liquid shortening.) *Makes 6 waffles.*

CHEESE WAFFLES

2 cups unbleached or whole-wheat
  flour
1 teaspoon salt
3 teaspoons baking powder
3 tablespoons skim-milk solids
2 tablespoons wheat germ
3 eggs, beaten

2 cups milk
6 tablespoons butter or margarine, melted—or 3 tablespoons each melted butter and liquid shortening
1 cup grated unprocessed yellow or Swiss cheese

Combine dry ingredients (except cheese) and mix thoroughly to distribute well. Combine and stir or beat well-beaten eggs, milk, shortening, cheese. Add to flour mixture and stir thoroughly. *Makes 6 waffles.*

CORN-MEAL WAFFLES

1½ cups boiling water
¾ cup undegerminated yellow corn meal
¼ cup wheat germ
1 teaspoon salt
4 tablespoons liquid or melted shortening (rendered bacon or ham fat preferred)

2 eggs, beaten
1 cup unbleached or whole-wheat flour
2 teaspoons baking powder
½ teaspoon baking soda
3 tablespoons skim-milk solids
(1–2 tablespoons brewers' yeast)
1⅛ cups milk

Combine corn meal and wheat germ in top of double boiler. Pour boiling water over this mixture. Add and stir in salt and shortening. Cook for 10 minutes over boiling water, remove from heat, pour into batter bowl, and cool. When cool, add and stir in beaten eggs. Sift flour with baking powder, soda, milk solids (and brewers' yeast). Add flour mixture to bowl alternately with milk and mix thoroughly. *Makes 6 waffles.*

OATMEAL WAFFLES

1 cup unbleached or whole-wheat flour
½ cup quick-cooking oatmeal
½ cup wheat germ
1 tablespoon brown sugar
3 teaspoons baking powder

(1–2 teaspoons brewers' yeast)
½ teaspoon salt
2 eggs, beaten
1¼ cups milk
6 tablespoons liquid shortening

Combine all dry ingredients, mixing thoroughly. Add beaten eggs, milk, and shortening. Blend thoroughly. *Makes 6 waffles.*

PEANUT BUTTER WAFFLES

¼ cup peanut butter
¼ cup wheat germ
3 tablespoons butter or margarine
2 eggs, beaten
1½ cups milk
1½ cups unbleached or whole-
    wheat flour

2 teaspoons baking powder
3 tablespoons skim-milk solids
    (1-2 tablespoons brewers' yeast)
¼ teaspoon salt

Blend peanut butter, wheat germ, and butter until creamy. Add and stir beaten eggs and milk, mixing well. Sift flour with baking powder, milk solids (and brewers' yeast), and salt and add to liquid mixture. Blend thoroughly, with rotary or electric beater, until smooth. *Makes 6 waffles.*

SPICE WAFFLES

1¼ cups unbleached or whole-
    wheat flour
3 teaspoons baking powder
3 tablespoons skim-milk solids
1 teaspoon salt
1-2 teaspoons ground ginger, nut-
    meg, or cinnamon—or combi-
    nation

1 cup wheat germ
(1 tablespoon brewers' yeast)
4 tablespoons butter or marga-
    rine, melted
2 eggs, beaten
4 tablespoons dark molasses
2 cups milk

Sift together flour, baking powder, milk solids, salt, and spices. Add and stir wheat germ (and brewers' yeast), distributing well. Combine and blend remaining ingredients and add liquid mixture to flour mixture. Beat until smooth. *Makes 6 waffles.*

SWEET POTATO-ORANGE WAFFLES

1 cup unbleached or whole-wheat
    flour
2 teaspoons baking powder
(1-2 tablespoons brewers' yeast)
2 tablespoons skim-milk solids
⅛ teaspoon nutmeg
2-3 tablespoons wheat germ

4 tablespoons butter or marga-
    rine, melted
1 egg, beaten
1 cup milk
½ cup orange juice
1 cup mashed sweet potatoes

Sift together flour, baking powder (and brewers' yeast), milk solids, and nutmeg. Stir in wheat germ. Combine liquids with mashed sweet potatoes and blend well. Add to dry ingredients and beat until smooth. *Makes 6 waffles.*

WHOLE-GRAIN YEAST WAFFLES

1 cake fresh yeast—or 1 package dry yeast
2 cups warm milk
2 tablespoons dark molasses or honey
3 eggs, beaten
6 tablespoons butter or margarine, melted (1 teaspoon of this may be wheat-germ oil)
1½ cups whole-wheat or whole-buckwheat flour
½ cup wheat germ
1 teaspoon salt

Stir yeast into warm milk and let stand 10 minutes. Stir in sweetener, beaten eggs, and shortening. Combine dry ingredients and stir into liquid. Mix thoroughly. Batter may be used immediately, may be allowed to rise in a warm place for 30 minutes to an hour, or may be prepared before bedtime and stored overnight in the refrigerator. *Makes 6 to 8 waffles.*

Good-nutrition Hot Sauces for Pancakes or Waffles

HONEY SAUCE

1 egg yolk
½ cup milk
½ cup honey
1 tablespoon butter or margarine, melted
(⅛ teaspoon ground cinnamon or nutmeg)

Beat egg yolk. Stir in milk, then honey. Add butter (and spice). Cook over boiling water for about 10 minutes, stirring until thickened. *Makes about 1 cup.*

MOLASSES SAUCE

½ cup dark molasses
2 tablespoons butter or margarine
½ cup warm milk
1 tablespoon skim-milk solids
(⅛ teaspoon ground ginger)

Heat but do not boil molasses. Stir in butter. Remove pan from heat. Combine warm milk with milk solids and slowly stir into molasses. (Add ginger.) Blend well. *Makes about 1 cup.*

BREAKFAST EGGS . . . PLUS

Eggs are fine for breakfast, supplying as they do high-quality complete proteins, an impressive list of important vitamins, and a good measure of the food minerals phosphorus, iron, and calcium. However, many people with the best of nutritional resolutions innocently believe that a breakfast egg—or, virtuously, two breakfast eggs—will provide optimum protein nutrition throughout the early part of the day. Don't misunderstand me: One or two eggs for breakfast will assuredly help stave off nutritional hypoglycemia, the low blood sugar condition so prevalent today among people of all ages, in all walks of life. But when we speak of "optimum" protein nutrition we must take into account the fact that we are aiming at an ideal—not just "adequate" or "sufficient" protein nutrition.

One egg provides the protein value of 1 ounce of meat. Even the most opportunistic of roadside stands would not insult customers by offering 1-ounce hamburgers. In order to receive the nutritive benefit of an average serving of meat, therefore, you would have to eat *three* eggs. Even this dedicated nutritionist cannot delude himself that anyone except possibly an athlete, farmer, manual laborer, or another dedicated nutritionist would willingly sit down to a three-egg breakfast as daily routine. It is a pleasant thought, but an unrealistic one; the professional nutritionist is in a position of appraising realistically the nation's eating habits by studying public health surveys and observing the traffic in physicians' offices, dental clinics, and hospitals.

Medicine and nutrition are fields of much weighty opinion, varying judgments, and sometimes arbitrary pronouncements. Many of these center about the (theoretical) roles of animal fat and cholesterol in hardening of the arteries. Despite evidence from the American Cancer Society that egg-eaters probably outlive egg-avoiders, these theories have terrified millions of people into avoiding eggs, butter, cheese, whole milk, liver and other meats, and, unbelievably, have induced pediatricians to feed babies on what is essentially an experimental diet, for which lifetime effects cannot be predicted: skimmed milk, and low fat. Actually, the majority of our cholesterol is manufactured in the body, and dietary cholesterol is a threat only to a group whose biochemical management of it is inefficient; and sugar is more of a threat (and to more people) than either fat or cholesterol. If your blood chemistry has induced your physician to taboo or limit eggs for you, remember that high quality protein is important to everyone, and can be obtained from fish, fowl, and permitted meats. With all the disagreements, though, most nutritionists who are free of commercial pressures agree that we'd be better off if we reduced our intake of carbohydrates, particularly sugar and overprocessed starches, in favor of the whole grains; took up to 20 percent of our total fat intake from vegetable oils, with corresponding reduction of animal fats, and brought our intake of efficient (animal) proteins up to a satisfactory level. It is not easy to achieve optimal nutrition with three meals daily, and some do better with six small ones; doing it with two meals is really making life difficult.

For breakfast, meat has nutritional advantages which cannot be overemphasized. That's why so many of the recipes in preceding and succeeding pages incorporate it in pancakes, waffles, omelets, and soufflés.

As for the recipes to follow, I assume that you know how to boil, fry, poach, and scramble eggs. Apart from urging you to prefer poaching or short boiling to frying, to fry slowly over low heat in a minimum of fat, and to add grated yellow cheese or extra skim-milk solids to milk when scrambling eggs in little or no grease in top of a double boiler, I shall concentrate here on only the more elaborate egg dishes representing good to excellent start-of-the-day protein nutrition.

EGGS BENEDICT WITH CHEESE OR HOLLANDAISE SAUCE

Traditionally served with hollandaise, which is very nice but a little tricky to make early in the morning if the original European recipe is followed, eggs benedict are also enjoyable topped with a smooth cheese dressing. In order not to horrify the purists entirely, a nonconforming recipe for hollandaise is also given.

2 English muffins *	4 eggs, poached
4 slices boiled or baked ham	1 cup cheese or hollandaise sauce

* A recipe for making these with whole-wheat flour is on page 215.

Break or cut muffins in half and toast them. Place a slice of ham on half a muffin, top with a poached egg, and spoon the sauce over it. *Serves 4.*

Cheese Sauce

2 tablespoons butter or margarine
2 tablespoons unbleached flour
2 tablespoons skim-milk solids
1½ cups warm milk

1 cup grated unprocessed yellow cheese
½ teaspoon salt
pepper or paprika to taste

Melt butter in top of double boiler, add flour and milk solids, and blend to a smooth paste. Slowly add warm milk, stirring to avoid lumps. Add cheese and seasonings and stir until cheese melts. Cook, stirring occasionally, until sauce is smooth—about 10 minutes.

Nonconforming Hollandaise Sauce

¼ pound butter
1–2 teaspoons lemon juice
3 egg yolks, lightly beaten with a fork

1 tablespoon cream
pinch of salt

Melt butter, remove pan from heat. Stir in remaining ingredients in order. Mix well, return pan to very low heat, and stir constantly until sauce thickens.

EGGS RANCHO

1 4-ounce package chipped beef
1 large onion, chopped
¼ cup chopped green pepper
3 tablespoons butter, margarine, or vegetable oil
6–8 eggs
½ teaspoon Worcestershire sauce

(¼ teaspoon Tabasco sauce)
dash of fresh-ground black pepper, or cayenne
½ cup chopped watercress or parsley
¾ cup cottage cheese

Fry chipped beef, onions, and green pepper in melted shortening, using large skillet. Stir eggs with fork until blended, season, and add to beef. Stir with fork in skillet until eggs begin to congeal; then add watercress (or parsley) and cottage cheese, stirring continuously until eggs are firm. *Serves 4.*

57

EGGS CORRAL

2 medium potatoes	1 tablespoon chopped parsley or
8 slices bacon	watercress
1 tablespoon butter or margarine	6–8 eggs
¼ cup chopped green or sweet red pepper	1½ cups milk
	½ teaspoon salt
¼ cup chopped onion	pepper to taste

Boil potatoes in their jackets, peel, and chop. Fry bacon slowly until crisp, remove from skillet, drain, and crumble. Pour off all but 2 tablespoons of the bacon fat. Add to skillet butter, pepper, onion, and parsley (or watercress), and cook until onions brown slightly. Add chopped potatoes and mix well. Turn heat low and stir mixture occasionally to prevent burning. Stir eggs with milk in a bowl and add seasonings. Pour over potato mixture in skillet; stir to distribute all ingredients evenly and continue cooking over low heat until eggs are firm. *Serves 4.*

EGGS IN HAM-POTATO NESTS

1½ cups mashed potatoes (white or sweet)	1 egg, beaten
¼ cup wheat germ	4 eggs
½ cup finely diced or minced cooked ham	

Mix mashed potatoes with wheat germ, ham, and beaten egg. Shape this mixture into 4 balls and put them on a lightly greased baking sheet or in a shallow baking dish. Press centers of balls to form cups. Break an egg into each cup. Bake at 350° for 15 to 25 minutes, depending on how firm you want the eggs. *Serves 4.*

OMELETS

From a nutritional standpoint, omelets are superior breakfast fare. Their special quality makes them appealing to drowsy morning appetites, and they are, besides, excellent vehicles for high-quality proteins—and not only those in the eggs themselves, but also the proteins in their fillings.

There are probably as many ways of making omelets as there

58

are cookbooks. Some home cooks hold fast to the theory of separately beaten egg yolks and whites, some insist that perfect omelets can be made only in special omelet pans, while others try first one and then another method—fail—and give up forever in discouragement. Omelets, like soufflés, require a little self-confidence, but they are neither difficult nor fussy to make.

INDIVIDUAL OMELET

1 or 2 eggs
1 or 2 tablespoons cream
¼ teaspoon salt

dash of pepper
1 tablespoon butter, margarine, or oil

This omelet is the easiest of all and requires no tilting. Use a 6- or 7-inch heavy skillet. Preheat slowly until very hot; then turn heat very low. Lightly beat eggs with a fork. Stir in cream, salt, and pepper. Melt butter in pan, making sure sides are coated. Pour in egg mixture and cover immediately. Let cook over lowest possible heat for 2 to 3 minutes. To remove omelet, loosen edges with spatula and turn it out on a warm plate. Fold in half.

With cheese filling: After pouring egg mixture into pan, sprinkle about ½ cup of coarsely grated unprocessed yellow cheese over it, then cover immediately. Cook 3 to 4 minutes. Cheese will be melted, egg will be done, omelet will be ready for removing, folding, and serving.

With other high-protein fillings:

Bacon: Fry 3 or 4 slices slowly until crisp. Crumble and sprinkle over omelet before folding and serving.

Ham and cottage cheese: Combine ¼ cup each of minced or deviled ham and cottage cheese and spread over omelet just before folding and serving.

Liver: ¼ pound of chicken, calf, beef, lamb, or pork liver. Chop or cut coarsely and sauté in butter or chicken fat until cooked through and just tender (a little longer for pork liver). Mix with 1 or 2 tablespoons of sour cream and spread over omelet just before folding and serving.

Kidney: ¼ pound beef, calf, lamb, or pork kidney. With scissors, remove membranes and fat. Cut into small pieces, sprinkle with 1 teaspoon of lemon juice or mild vinegar, and let stand for 20 minutes. Drain; then sauté in any shortening for 5 minutes, stirring to brown evenly. Mix with 1 or 2 tablespoons sour cream (or use leftover gravy) and spread over omelet just before folding and serving.

LARGER OMELETS

6–8 eggs
¼ cup milk
2 tablespoons skim-milk solids
1 teaspoon salt

dash of pepper
2 tablespoons butter, margarine, or oil

Use a large (12-inch), heavy skillet. Preheat slowly until very hot; then turn heat very low. Lightly beat eggs with a fork, stir in milk, milk solids, and seasonings. Melt butter in skillet, making sure sides are coated. Pour in egg mixture, cover, and cook over lowest heat for about 5 minutes. If top looks runny, lift edges with spatula, tilt pan, and let uncooked egg flow beneath cooked portion. Cover again, cook 5 minutes more. Slide onto warm plate, fold, and serve. *Serves 3 or 4.*

For filled larger omelets: Double or triple the amounts given for individual omelets.

ORANGE OMELET

eggs, lightly beaten
cup milk
teaspoon salt
cup orange juice

1 teaspoon grated orange rind
2 tablespoons butter, margarine, or vegetable oil

Combine all ingredients except shortening and mix thoroughly. Cook as directed for larger omelets. *Serves 2.*

FIRM BANANA OMELET

1 large ripe banana (or 1½ tablespoons banana flakes)
6 eggs, lightly beaten
2 tablespoons cream
2 teaspoons brown sugar or molasses

½ teaspoon salt
2 tablespoons butter, margarine, or vegetable oil

60

Mash banana with fork until pulpy. Combine this (or banana flakes) with all other ingredients except shortening. Cook as directed for larger omelets. *Serves 4.*

HALF-BAKED BREAD-CRUMB OMELET

¾ cup hot (not boiled) milk
3 tablespoons skim-milk solids
¾ cup soft whole-wheat bread crumbs
¼ cup wheat germ

6 eggs
¾ teaspoon salt
dash of pepper
2 tablespoons butter, margarine, or oil

Combine milk and milk solids and pour over bread crumbs and wheat germ in large bowl. Mix thoroughly and let stand until cool. Beat eggs with salt and pepper, combine with crumb mixture, and beat until thoroughly mixed. Cook in hot shortening over medium heat until bottom is light brown; remove skillet to 300° oven and bake until top is dry. *Serves 4.*

SOUFFLES

It is likely that only the most enthusiastic cooks attempt a soufflé for breakfast, and then probably only on a Sunday or holiday morning. The creation of a classic soufflé is time-consuming and reputedly fraught with anxiety. It must be composed with tenderness, self-confidence, and a light hand and served immediately or it will deflate. This means getting the whole family at the table, forks in hand, before the soufflé comes out of the oven in all its lofty splendor.

However, there are short cuts and reassurances in all good-nutrition cooking without sacrificing art or savor, although tradition may have to go. Three approaches to the soufflé are given here—one neoclassic, one ingenious, and one downright practical. The choice of method is yours, for any one of them provides the good nutrition which is the principal concern of this book.

BASIC SOUFFLE NO. 1

Preheat oven to 350°.

4 tablespoons butter or margarine
4 tablespoons unbleached flour
4 tablespoons skim-milk solids
1½ cups milk

1 teaspoon salt
dash of pepper
6 eggs, separated—room temperature

Melt butter or margarine in top of double boiler. Add flour and milk solids, and blend to a smooth paste. Add milk slowly, a little at a time, stirring to avoid lumps. Stir in salt and pepper. Cook, stirring, for about 5 minutes. Remove from heat and allow to cool slightly. Beat egg yolks until light and stir into cream sauce. Have ready a large round or oval ungreased casserole (about 2-quart size). Beat egg whites until stiff but not dry and fold into sauce. Pour immediately into casserole and with back of teaspoon make a circular groove in the top of the soufflé, about 1 inch from rim of casserole. Bake 40 minutes. *Serves 4 to 6.*

Note: If you have time, preheat oven to 300° instead of 350°, set casserole in pan of hot water, and bake for 1 to 1½ hours.

BASIC SOUFFLE NO. 2

Preheat oven to 350°. Requires no flour—thickened with tapioca.

4 tablespoons quick-cooking tapioca
1½ cups milk
4 tablespoons skim-milk solids
(1 tablespoon brewers' yeast or yeast flakes)

1 teaspoon salt
dash of pepper
6 eggs, separated—room temperature

Combine tapioca, milk, milk solids (yeast), and seasonings. Cook in saucepan over moderate heat until boiling point is reached. Remove from heat and allow to cool slightly. Beat egg yolks until light and stir into mixture. Beat egg whites until stiff but not dry and fold into mixture. Pour into ungreased casserole, set in pan of hot water, and bake for 50 minutes to 1 hour. *Serves 4 to 6.*

62

BASIC SOUFFLE NO. 3

Preheat oven to 300°. No flour added—made with condensed cream soup.

1 can condensed cream soup (celery, mushroom, chicken, etc.)	(1 tablespoon brewers' yeast or yeast flakes)
4 tablespoons skim-milk solids	6 eggs, separated—room temperature

Combine soup with milk solids (and yeast) without adding liquid and stir over low heat until smooth. Remove from heat and allow to cool slightly. Beat egg yolks until light and stir into soup. Beat egg whites until stiff but not dry and fold into mixture. Pour into ungreased casserole, set in pan of hot water, and bake for 1 hour. *Serves 4 to 6.*

Soufflés Plus

Each of the preceding recipes can be enhanced with other ingredients for taste, variety, and added food value.

CHEESE SOUFFLE

Choose any of the three basic recipes. Add 1 to 1½ cups grated unprocessed yellow or Swiss cheese to double boiler or saucepan in first step. Cook and stir over low heat until cheese is melted and blended. Proceed as directed.

FRUIT SOUFFLE

Choose either No. 1 or No. 2 of the basic recipes. Add to cooled sauce 1 cup diced naturally sweet peaches or apricots; prune pulp or mashed banana; or 1 8-ounce jar of puréed baby fruit. Proceed as directed.

HIGH-PROTEIN SOUFFLE

Choose any one of the three basic recipes. Add to sauce, just before adding beaten eggs, one of the following:

1 cup minced or finely diced cooked ham, bacon, or tongue
1 cup sautéed drained sausage meat
1 cup ground cooked liver, kidney, or heart
1 cup diced cooked sweetbreads or brains
1 cup flaked cooked fish
1 cup drained canned salmon or tuna fish

PEANUT BUTTER WHEAT-GERM SOUFFLE

Preheat oven to 375°.

6 tablespoons butter or margarine
½ cup peanut butter
½ cup wheat germ
1½ cups scalded milk

½–1 teaspoon salt, depending on
  saltiness of peanut butter
4 eggs, separated—room temperature

Melt butter or margarine in top of double boiler. Add peanut butter and wheat germ, and blend until smooth. Add scalded milk a little at a time, stirring to avoid lumps. Add salt and continue stirring and cooking until sauce thickens. Remove from heat and cool slightly. Add beaten egg yolks and fold in stiffly beaten egg whites. Pour into lightly greased casserole, set in pan of hot water, and bake for 30 to 40 minutes. *Serves 4 to 6.*

Good Nutrition
Can Be Fun

3

Good Nutrition Can Be Fun

APPETIZERS AND MEAL-STARTERS

Before-meal appetizers and snacks, which also brighten cocktails, dinner, or late parties, are not only gracious and friendly; they can also contribute rather a lot to the cause of good nutrition. Avoid those which depend on carbohydrates for their appeal, take the trouble to prepare fresh fruits or fruit juices instead of opening cans, and add one or more of the food fortifiers to a tasty tidbit.

Appetizers of all kinds are usually consumed enthusiastically because, besides being attractive, they are offered at the time of keenest appetite. The best meal-starter of all, perhaps, is a large but not too substantial salad made with mixed salad greens and a nutritionally meaningful dressing. The California custom of serving the salad course at the beginning of a meal is a fine one, for it catches people when they're hungry enough to eat it if only to kill time. The most hardened salad-haters surprise themselves when visiting California by actually enjoying this course. Back home, they tend to revert to their contempt of "rabbit food," excusing their Western lapse on the grounds of vacation abandon.

Whether the meal-starter is a salad, a beverage, or a fancy canapé, it should combine eye appeal and taste appeal and provoke anticipation of what's to come. There is no law (not even in nutrition) which forbids you to serve caviar or oysters preceding meat loaf, or antipasto preceding sukiyaki, but it seems to make better sense if you try for a little togetherness.

Fruit or fruit juice can introduce any main course, and so can tomato, cranberry, or sauerkraut juice or a cup of hot, chilled, or jellied consommé.

Soup? From a nutritionist's point of view, while correctly made soup (pages 107-131) can be a readily assimilated amalgam of delicious proteins, vitamins, and minerals, its proper place is not at the beginning of the day's heaviest meal. If you admit to being an average American, by the time you sit down to dinner you have consumed less than half of the nutrients required daily for optimum health. Bulk and fillers, yes—you've satisfied your appetite but not, usually, your body's true hunger for blood-building, tissue-repairing, resistance-bolstering food elements. If dinner is to supply anything like the other half of your nutritional requirements, better skip soup. No matter how full of nutrients it may be, it is too filling (and, usually, too caloric) to be serviceable as a provider of proteins more generously supplied by the meat course. By all means enjoy and benefit from soup at lunch or for supper when you had dinner at noon —but it is preferable to begin the main meal of the day less ambitiously.

Getting extra nutrition into leaner, lighter meal-starters is not difficult. A few suggestions follow:

Save the water in which you have cooked vegetables, mixing it in a large refrigerator bottle. Any vegetable water will do— even cabbage or cauliflower in discreet amounts. To make a pleasant and nutritious predinner cocktail, mix equal parts of the vegetable water and tomato juice. To each cupful add ½ teaspoon lemon juice, salt, pepper, and a dash of onion juice.

If you start the meal with straight sauerkraut or tomato juice:
1. Try mixing them, half and half.
2. To either, add 1 tablespoon yeast flakes per cup.

3. Serve the juice with whole-wheat or wheat-germ crackers or with a tray of finger vegetables: carrot curls, green celery sticks, green or red pepper rings, sliced unpeeled cucumbers, radishes, raw cauliflower or cabbage wedges.

If you start with fruit juice: Wait until diners are seated at the table before pouring it.

If you start with melon: Serve with slices of boiled ham, salami, or bologna filled with cottage cheese and rolled.

If you start with a sea-food cocktail: Serve on a bed of crisp lettuce and surround with watercress or fresh parsley in the hope that the garnishes will be eaten.

GOOD-NUTRITION SAUCE FOR SEA-FOOD COCKTAIL

½ cup catsup
½ cup chili sauce
2 tablespoons lemon juice or mild vinegar
1 tablespoon horse-radish (or more)
½ teaspoon Worcestershire sauce
1 tablespoon chopped parsley
1 hard-cooked egg or 2 yolks, chopped fine or mashed with fork
1 tablespoon brewers' yeast or yeast flakes
¼ teaspoon wheat-germ oil
salt if needed
few drops of Tabasco sauce if desired

Makes 1½ cups. Leftover sauce may be stored in the refrigerator and stirred up before next use.

CANAPES AND DIPS

The mixtures suggested may be spread on melba toast, assorted dark-bread rounds, or whole-wheat crackers, but many modern hostesses deplore the way moist appetizer spreads make even the crispest crackers or toast limp and soggy. They prefer to offer their concoctions in attractive bowls with a tray of breadstuffs or potato or corn chips. Hostesses even more modern discreetly forbear to tempt weight-watching weaklings with carbohydrates and surround the appetizers instead with a variety of nutritious lower-calory dippers, spreadables, or toothpick dunkers. These are limited only by your larder and your ingenuity. They include cooked shrimp or chunks of chicken or lobster; cubes, oblongs, or wedges of unprocessed cheese or delicatessen meats; and a gardenful of crisp vegetables—raw.

Unless otherwise specified, the following recipes will serve from 4 to 6.

AVOCADO AND CHEESE

pulp of 1 large or 2 small ripe avocados
1 cup cottage cheese
1 tablespoon wheat germ or yeast flakes

1 tablespoon lemon juice
1 teaspoon minced onion
¼ teaspoon salt
2 tablespoons sour cream or milk

Mix thoroughly.

ENRICHED GUACAMOLE

pulp of 1 large or 2 small ripe avocados
1 soft-ripe tomato
1 tablespoon brewers' yeast or yeast flakes

1 tablespoon minced onion, or 1 teaspoon onion juice
1 tablespoon lemon juice
¼ teaspoon wheat-germ oil
salt to taste

Mash avocado pulp; mix with tomato cut into small pieces; add and blend thoroughly remaining ingredients. Taste before adding salt.

EGG PASTE

1 cup cottage cheese (or 1 large package cream cheese)
2 hard-cooked eggs or 3 egg yolks, mashed with fork
2 tablespoons mayonnaise
½ teaspoon wheat-germ oil

1 teaspoon prepared mustard
3 tablespoons sour cream or milk
1 tablespoon skim-milk solids
½ teaspoon Worcestershire sauce
½ teaspoon salt
dash of pepper or paprika

Mix thoroughly.

GARLIC CHEESE

½ cup cottage cheese
1 small package cream cheese
2 tablespoons milk, cream, or sour cream
1 tablespoon skim-milk solids
1 clove garlic (or more, depending on your guests' sophistication)

¼ teaspoon salt
½ teaspoon Worcestershire sauce
dash of paprika
(½ cup chopped ripe black olives)

Combine cheese and milk, blending to a smooth paste. Put garlic through garlic press or mince and stir into cheese mixture. Add seasonings and blend thoroughly. (The olives are optional, but nice.)

LIVER PATE

1 cup diced chicken, beef, calf, or lamb liver (half of this amount may be chicken hearts)
2 tablespoons chicken fat or oil
1 hard-cooked egg, mashed with fork

2 teaspoons minced onion
½ teaspoon salt
dash of pepper
1 tablespoon butter or margarine

Sauté liver in chicken fat or oil until tender. (Parboil chicken hearts for 5 minutes, dice, and sauté until tender.) Combine with all remaining ingredients and blend to a smooth paste.

CHOPPED CHICKEN LIVER ISRAELI *

¼ cup minced onions
6 tablespoons chicken fat
1 pound chicken livers
2 hard-cooked eggs

1¼ teaspoons salt
⅛ teaspoon black pepper
(⅛ teaspoon garlic powder, optional)

Sauté onions in 3 tablespoons of the chicken fat until lightly brown. Remove from heat. Cut chicken livers in half and broil one side for 5 minutes; then turn and broil 1 minute longer. Grind livers and hard-cooked eggs, or chop in wooden bowl until very fine. Combine with sautéed onion, remaining chicken fat, and seasonings. Blend thoroughly.

SALMON OR TUNA SPREAD

1 7½-ounce can salmon or tuna
1 cup cottage cheese
3–4 tablespoons sour cream

1 tablespoon skim-milk solids
(1 tablespoon wheat germ)

Mix thoroughly.

---

* Much commercial chicken production is accelerated by the use of arsenic compounds. The use of such feeds is supposed to be stopped well before the fowl are slaughtered, but FDA inspections indicate the rule is frequently ignored, with the result that commercial chicken liver may contain undesirable amounts of arsenic. If you can find organically raised fowl—which some health food stores stock—the extra cost may be well justified.

SARDINE SPREAD

1 can boneless sardines (3½ ounces)
2 hard-cooked eggs
2 tablespoons lemon juice
2 tablespoons mayonnaise
1 tablespoon chopped parsley
1 teaspoon onion juice

½ teaspoon salt
dash of cayenne
(1 tablespoon yeast flakes)
(½ tablespoon monosodium glutamate)
2 tablespoons skim-milk solids

Mash sardines with a fork. Mince egg whites, reserving yolks. Combine all ingredients except yolks and mix well. Heap in small bowl and garnish with crumbled egg yolk.

BACON–HORSE-RADISH SPREAD

3 slices bacon
1 cup cottage cheese—or 1 large package cream cheese
2–3 tablespoons white horse-radish

(1 tablespoon wheat germ or yeast flakes)
salt if needed

Fry bacon slowly until very crisp. Drain and crumble. Combine with other ingredients and mix thoroughly.

SEA-FOOD SPREAD

½ cup minced clams, shrimp, herring fillets, crab, or lobster meat
3 hard-cooked eggs, mashed with fork
1 teaspoon minced onion
1 teaspoon lemon juice
1 tablespoon finely chopped green

celery, green pepper, or parsley
1 tablespoon mayonnaise or sour cream
(1 tablespoon wheat germ, brewers' yeast, or yeast flakes)
½ teaspoon salt—or ¼ teaspoon garlic salt

Mix thoroughly.

SOUP DIP

1 can condensed black bean, pea, asparagus, or cream of mushroom soup
1 cup cottage cheese—or 1 large package cream cheese
1 medium onion, minced or finely chopped

2 tablespoons chopped parsley or watercress
2 tablespoons low-calory salad dressing (pages 101-102)
(½ teaspoon wheat-germ oil)
salt and pepper to taste

Combine all ingredients and blend thoroughly. An electric blender is helpful.

CARAWAY DIP

1 cup cottage cheese—or 1 large package cream cheese
4 tablespoons sweet or lightly salted butter or margarine
1 teaspoon salt

2 tablespoons sweet paprika
1 teaspoon powdered dry mustard
4 teaspoons whole caraway seed
(1 tablespoon wheat germ)

Cream the cheese and butter together until soft and well blended. Add remaining ingredients and mix thoroughly. Chill, removing from refrigerator about 1 hour before serving.

VEGETARIAN SPREAD

1 cup cottage cheese
¼ cup chopped onion or scallions
1 tablespoon grated raw carrot
¼ cup chopped unpeeled cucumber

¼ cup chopped green pepper
1 tablespoon chopped pimiento
¼ cup sour cream
(1 tablespoon wheat germ)
salt and pepper to taste

Mix thoroughly.

LEFTOVER SPREAD

2 slices bacon
1 cup cold leftover cooked meat—ham, tongue, beef, liver, poultry (not lamb or pork)
1 hard-cooked egg
1 small onion
1 tablespoon chopped green pepper or pimiento
1 tablespoon chopped sweet pickle
2 tablespoons finely chopped green celery

1 tablespoon brewers' yeast or yeast flakes
¼ teaspoon curry powder
(¼ teaspoon chili powder)
½ teaspoon olive oil—or ¼ teaspoon each cooking oil and wheat-germ oil
salad dressing or mayonnaise
salt and pepper to taste

Fry bacon slowly until crisp. Drain and crumble. Chop or grind meat together with egg and vegetables and combine with yeast. Blend curry (chili) powder with oil and stir into mixture. Add crumbled bacon and enough salad dressing or mayonnaise to make a spreadable paste and season with salt and pepper.

73

HOT HORS D'OEUVRES

FRENCH FRIED FISH FRITTERS

1 cup unbleached or whole-wheat flour
1½ teaspoons baking powder
1 tablespoon skim-milk solids
1 tablespoon brewers' yeast
½ teaspoon salt
2 tablespoons wheat germ
1 cup tuna, salmon, or flaked cooked fish

½ cup milk
1 egg
2 tablespoons butter or margarine, melted
deep fat for frying
grated yellow, Romano, or Parmesan cheese

Sift flour with baking powder, milk solids, brewers' yeast, and salt. Stir in wheat germ. Add fish, milk, beaten egg, and butter, and mix well. Drop by the spoonful in deep fat heated until it browns a cube of bread in 1 minute. Fry until golden brown—about 2 or 3 minutes. Drain on paper towel. While still hot, roll in grated cheese.

STUFFED MUSHROOMS

12 large mushrooms
3 tablespoons butter, melted
½ cup finely chopped cooked liver, chicken, turkey, shrimp, lobster, or crab meat
¼ cup wheat germ
1 egg, lightly beaten
1 tablespoon chopped parsley
1 tablespoon flavoring: for liver

or poultry, minced onion or onion juice; for any seafood, sherry with a dash of lemon juice
½ teaspoon salt
2 tablespoons grated yellow, Romano, or Parmesan cheese
2 tablespoons fine whole-wheat bread crumbs

Remove stems from mushroom caps. Chop stems and sauté in 1 tablespoon of the melted butter—no longer than 2 minutes. Remove from skillet and mix thoroughly with all other ingredients except remaining butter, grated cheese, and bread crumbs. Brush mushroom caps with remaining butter and broil, cap side up, for 2 minutes. Remove from broiler; fill hollows of caps with stuffing mixture. Combine grated cheese and bread crumbs, sprinkle over mushrooms, return them to broiler for 2 minutes more, cap sides down.

CHEESE PUFF TURNOVERS

1 pound mild unprocessed yellow
    cheese
6 cups unbleached flour
1 cup wheat germ
2 teaspoons salt

½ cup solid shortening
1 egg, well beaten
1½ cups (vegetable) water
deep fat for frying

Grate cheese into thin slivers, using half-moon side of grater, and set aside. Combine flour, wheat germ, and salt in a large bowl and cut in shortening. Add beaten egg and, gradually, the water. Mix into a dough, turn it out on a lightly floured board, and knead until soft and light. Use small quantities of additional flour if needed to prevent the dough from sticking. The kneading is important to this recipe, for the lighter and softer the dough, the bigger and airier the puffs.

Shape dough into a roll about 1½ inches in diameter. Cut off a slice about ½ inch long. With a lightly floured rolling pin, roll the slice to ⅛ inch thickness and cut into 2½-inch circles with cookie cutter. Place 1 tablespoon of the slivered cheese on half of the circle, folding the other half over it and pressing the edges together firmly with the tips of your fingers and a lightly floured fork. Cut, roll, and finish one slice at a time until all dough is used.

In hot (375°) deep fat fry two or three of the crescents at a time, basting with the hot fat until they swell and turn golden brown. Drain on paper towels. *Makes about 40.*

COCKTAIL MEATBALLS

2 pounds ground beef
2 cloves garlic, minced or pressed
½ cup minced onion
½ cup fine whole-wheat bread
    crumbs
¼ cup wheat germ
1 tablespoon brewers' yeast or
    yeast flakes
1 tablespoon skim-milk solids

½ cup milk
2 eggs, lightly beaten
1 teaspoon salt
¼ teaspoon ground black pepper
(pinch each of cayenne, ground
    cloves, and basil if spicier
    meatballs are desired)
1 teaspoon brown sugar
¼ cup cooking oil

Mix together thoroughly all ingredients except oil. Shape into balls—30, more or less, depending on size. Let stand in refrigerator for 1 hour or more. Brown on all sides in oil in large skillet. They may be served on toothpicks or, for a nutritious variation, rolled in wheat germ to be eaten with the fingers.

LIVER KNISHES

½ pound beef liver
3 tablespoons cooking oil or chicken fat
4 medium potatoes
2 eggs, beaten
¼ cup wheat germ

1 teaspoon salt
½ teaspoon monosodium glutamate
¼ teaspoon black pepper
4 tablespoons minced onion

Brown liver on both sides in 2 tablespoons of the oil or fat. Chop or put through fine blade of grinder and reserve. Boil potatoes in their jackets, peel, and mash. Add beaten eggs, wheat germ, and seasonings. With moistened hands, shape potato mixture into balls about the size of large walnuts and make a dent in the center of each. Place on a well-greased baking sheet and bake at 350° until browned—about 30 minutes. While potato shells are baking, sauté onion in same skillet as you browned the liver, adding the remaining tablespoon of oil. Add and reheat ground liver. Mix liver with onions and put a teaspoonful of the mixture in the dented center of each potato shell. *Makes 25 to 30.*

LIVER CUPS

12 thin slices whole-wheat bread without crusts
1 tablespoon chopped or minced onion
2 tablespoons cooking oil, butter, or chicken fat
½ pound mushrooms, sliced thin

¾ pound chicken, calf, or beef liver
pinch of basil
½ cup warm sour cream
salt and pepper to taste
dash of nutmeg

Press bread slices into lightly greased muffin cups and toast in 350° oven until set and lightly browned. Sauté onion in oil, butter, or fat until glazed but not brown. Remove from pan and reserve. Sauté sliced mushrooms for 2 minutes. Remove from pan and reserve. Cut liver into very small pieces and sauté until tender—about 3 minutes for chicken liver, 4 for calf, 5 for beef.

Return sautéed onion and mushrooms to pan, and stir. Add basil and warm sour cream. Season with salt and pepper. Heat (but do not boil) for 2 or 3 minutes and spoon mixture into bread cups. Sprinkle with nutmeg.

COCKTAIL ROLL-UPS

12 thin slices whole-grain bread without crusts
one or more of the following: chopped or minced ham, chicken, corned beef, tongue, liverwurst, salmon, tuna fish, crab or lobster meat, slivered yellow cheese, cream cheese with chopped olives, chopped Swiss cheese with green pepper, peanut butter with crumbled crisp bacon and wheat germ

Put bread slices on sheet of waxed paper and dampen slightly with water or milk. Cover with waxed paper and flatten bread with palm of hand or rolling pin. Uncover and let dry until bread can be handled without tearing. Spread the slices with any of the above suggestions. Roll carefully into fingers and secure with toothpicks. Broil until toasted.

FRENCH TOAST CHEESE AND BACON SANDWICHES

4 slices bacon
4 eggs
1 cup milk
¼ cup skim-milk solids
½ teaspoon salt
⅛ teaspoon pepper

8 slices whole-wheat bread or white bread containing wheat germ
½ pound unprocessed yellow cheese
(2–3 tablespoons shortening)

Fry or broil bacon until crisp. Drain, crumble, and reserve. Beat eggs lightly with fork and stir in milk, milk solids, and seasonings. Coarsely grate or sliver cheese. Make sandwiches of bread, cheese, and crumbled bacon. Press together and soak, one at a time, in egg mixture. Remove carefully with pancake turner onto plate, and cut each sandwich into 4 equal squares or triangles. Heat shortening until it browns a cube of bread in 30 seconds—or use grease from bacon. Brown sandwiches on both sides, until cheese melts. Drain on paper towels. *Makes 16.*

CHEESE-PASTRY FILLED TURNOVERS
Pastry

3 small (3-ounce) packages cream
   cheese
½ cup butter or margarine,
   softened

1½ cups unbleached flour
¼ cup wheat germ

Combine cream cheese and butter or margarine and blend thoroughly. Add and blend in flour and wheat germ, kneading lightly with fingers until smooth. Shape into ball and refrigerate for 1 hour or more.

Filling

1½ cups any cooked fowl, meat,
   or fish—chopped fine or
   ground
1 tablespoon minced onion or
   chives
1 tablespoon chopped green celery
1 teaspoon chopped parsley

1 egg, lightly beaten
1 tablespoon yeast flakes
¼ teaspoon sage, thyme, or
   poultry seasoning
½ teaspoon salt
⅛ teaspoon ground black pepper

Preheat oven to 400°. Mix filling by blending all ingredients thoroughly. Taste, add other seasonings if desired (pinch of basil or oregano—dash of cayenne, curry, or ginger). Punch chilled pastry ball down with hand and roll on lightly floured board until thin. Cut into rounds with cookie cutter. Place a tablespoonful of filling on half of each round and fold dough over. Press edges together firmly with fingers and floured fork. Bake on ungreased baking sheet until brown—about 15 to 20 minutes. *Makes 24.*

DIET DODGES

Not all of the day's food intake—of whatever nutritional contribution—can be measured in terms of breakfast, lunch, and dinner. The term "three square meals" is an old-fashioned figure of speech, for the average modern American eats more than three meals of some kind during a 24-hour period. The school child has a fourth meal at homecoming and perhaps a fifth one before bedtime. The adult female usually manages a teatime snack between lunch and dinner and joins her husband (who had a coffee break between breakfast and lunch) for some icebox raiding during television commercials.

Actually, most people do better when they eat four or five comparatively light meals during the day than if they stuff themselves at any one meal to the point of inertia—and indigestion. There is nothing nutritionally wicked in the pleasures of between-meal nibbles, either, provided they do not rob the individual of appetite needed for more substantial meals or add too many useless, empty, obesity-causing calories to a diet which may be oversubscribed already.

Food is not only the fuel and building material of life itself; it is also one of life's major pleasures. No one realizes this more keenly than the individual who makes a deliberate attempt to lose or control weight without foregoing entirely the between-meal snack. To brighten diet doldrums, here are a few suggestions which are comparatively low in calories but high in essential nutrients:

BREADLESS "SANDWICHES"

Cucumber and Cheese

Slice peeled or unpeeled cucumber into ¼-inch rounds. Put thin slices of unprocessed yellow cheese between rounds.

Lettuce and Meat

Roll slices of cooked ham, beef, or chicken in large green lettuce leaves.

Meat and Cheese

Spread thin slices of ham, tongue, chicken or turkey roll with hoop, farmer, or skim-milk cottage cheese.

STUFFED CELERY HEARTS

Stuff green celery hearts with hoop, farmer, or skim-milk cottage cheese softened with skim milk. (About a third of the cheese may be Roquefort or bleu.) Sprinkle with paprika.

DEVILED EGGS

4 hard-cooked eggs
1 teaspoon lemon juice
1 tablespoon tomato juice
1 teaspoon minced onion

½ teaspoon dry mustard
½ teaspon salt
⅛ teaspoon pepper
dash of ginger or chili powder

Cut peeled eggs in half lengthwise and remove yolks. Mash yolks and blend throughly with all other ingredients. Fill hollows of egg whites with mixture. *Makes 4 servings.*

LIVER LOAF

½ pound beef liver
1 medium onion
½ cup coarsely cut raw carrots
½ teaspoon salt

⅛ teaspoon pepper
2 tablespoons Basic Dressing No. 1 (page 101)

Broil liver close to source of heat for 3 minutes on each side. When cool enough to handle, cut into pieces and put through the grinder with onion and carrots. Add and mix seasonings and dressing until smooth. Press into small loaf pan and chill in refrigerator.

CHICKEN LOAF

1 cup finely chopped or minced cooked chicken
¼ cup each grated carrot and finely chopped green celery

2 tablespoons finely chopped apple
¼ cup Basic Dressing No. 2 (page 101)

Blend all ingredients thoroughly. Press into small loaf pan and chill in refrigerator.

CHEESE BALLS

1 cup farmer or skim-milk cottage cheese
½ cup wheat germ
2–3 tablespoons Basic Dressing No. 3 (page 102)

(about) ¼ cup fine whole-wheat bread crumbs or yeast flakes

Blend cheese, wheat germ, and dressing and shape into balls. Roll in crumbs or yeast flakes.

SPICED MEATBALLS

1 pound lean ground beef
⅛ teaspoon each of ginger, ore-
    gano, pepper, and cloves

pinch of cardamom and curry
1 small onion, minced
1 egg, lightly beaten

Combine beef with herbs and seasonings and mix with onion and beaten egg. Blend well. Shape into balls and broil close to source of heat, turning once, to desired doneness—from 1 to 3 minutes on each side for rare or medium, 4 to 6 minutes for well done. *Makes 12 to 16.*

TOOTHPICK SHRIMP

2 quarts water
1 bay leaf
1 teaspoon peppercorns
1 teaspoon salt
3 stalks celery with leaves—or 1
    tablespoon celery flakes

¼ teaspoon cayenne
¼ teaspoon curry powder
1 onion, sliced
1 tablespoon lemon juice
1 pound shrimp in shells

Bring water to boil and add all ingredients except lemon juice and shrimp. Allow this to boil for 15 minutes. Add lemon juice and shrimp and simmer for 15 minutes. Remove from heat and allow to cool in cooking water. Peel and devein shrimp. Impale on toothpicks and serve with a sauce made by combining equal parts of soy sauce and mustard (hot or mild). Or—marinate shrimp for 1 hour or more in refrigerator in one of the basic dressings.

BROILED SCALLOPS

1 pound scallops
1–2 tablespoons lemon juice or
    any basic dressing (pages 93–
    94)

¼ cup wheat germ
2 teaspoons parsley flakes

Place scallops on shallow baking sheet and broil quickly until brown on one side. Turn and brown other side. Toss scallops in lemon juice or any basic dressing. Roll in wheat germ mixed with parsley flakes.

FISH KABOBS

Use any fillet of fish you can cut into 1-inch chunks—or use shrimp, scallops, or langostinos. Marinate in Basic Dressing No. 2 (page 101) for 1 hour or more in refrigerator. Thread on skewers, separating pieces with chunks of raw green pepper, tomato, mushrooms, and—if you like—small white onions. Broil, turning a few times, for 5 minutes.

SNACKS THAT MAKE SENSE

PIZZA

Nutritionists think of our adolescents as the pizza-pop-hamburger-pie generation. This *Cook Book for Good Nutrition* has uttered trenchant advice on soda pop, and given you pie recipes elevated to better nutrition. Now let's do something about pizza. Principal faults of the commercial variety: too much of the wrong kind of dough; and correspondingly too little protein (cheese). This enjoyable dish can be started with a thin layer of dough made from the Cornell Mix (page 229). It will take several hours for the dough to rise, after you have patted an even layer of it into oiled pie plates. Stewed tomatoes—homemade or canned—are now drained, and arranged on the dough, with the traditional spicing: basil and oregano. Add any grated hard cheese, and bake in an oven that has been preheated to about 350°. When the crust is thoroughly baked—in 20 or 30 minutes—you can put on a finishing touch by putting the pizza under a broiler to brown the cheese. Add sardines, olives, anchovies, mushrooms, if you wish, a few minutes before the baking is terminated.

LOW-CARBOHYDRATE SNACKS

There are many reasons for building better nutrition into snack foods. The primary one is that the commercial snacks are usually un-nutritious food, and more often than not laden with preservatives and additives better avoided. A secondary motive for creating snacks that are low in carbohydrates is the demand for those

82

on a low-carbohydrate diet who are often required to eat six meals daily; diabetics; and hypoglycemics (sufferers with low blood sugar, who must also eat frequently and limit carbohydrates).

The best way to pave the road to rejection of high-starch, high-sugar snacks is to begin in childhood. The remarkable, if impossible, Fredericks children did have our own cookies (Betty's Cookies, page 266), but in place of the potato chips, confections, and cakes, we always had platters of cheese, ham, tongue, and other high-protein foods, as well as fresh fruit available, which the children would snatch on their endless missions around the house, like the brass ring seized by the young riders on the merry-go-round.

For those on a low-carbohydrate diet here are some suggestions for between-meal, low-starch, low-sugar snacks:

Ground Meat Pizza

½ pound ground meat, kneaded with added pepper to taste
2 fresh tomatoes
1 large onion
¼ small can tomato paste
pinch of oregano
paprika
sweet basil

Line 6-inch Pyrex dish with the meat. Chop the tomatoes, and mix with the diced onion, spices, and tomato paste. Fill the meat-lined pan with the mixture, top with the pinch of oregano, and bake at 350° to preferred finish. This will make from 2 to 4 portions of snacks, depending on the specifications of the low-carbohydrate diet.

Quick Tuna Fish Snack

½ cucumber, hollowed out and stuffed with 1 ounce of tuna fish, mixed with 1 teaspoon mayonnaise.

Blanketed Cheese

A thin piece of ham, tongue, chicken roll, or turkey roll is wrapped around ½ ounce of Gouda or other preferred cheese.

83

Celery-Cheese Snack

Press pot cheese through strainer. Add buttermilk, skim milk, or a little yogurt to moisten. Add small pinch sea salt to taste. Chop pimiento, watercress, and green pepper, mix with cheese, and fill celery stick.

Yogurt Fizz

½ cup plain yogurt (the varieties with jam and preserves may have more calories from sugar than from yogurt) in tall glass, and fill with club soda. Refreshing in warm weather.

Café au Lait

Dilute nonfat milk with half the specified amount of water, and blend thoroughly. Heat ⅓ of cup just short of boiling, and add coffee (decaffeinated for hypoglycemics and diabetics) to taste.

Stuffed Egg Snack

To make six stuffed egg halves:

3 eggs
1 ounce margarine, melted
⅛ teaspoon sea salt,
very small pinch pepper
⅛ teaspoon prepared mustard

½ teaspoon minced onion
about ⅙ cup of flaked tuna, chopped shrimp, or crab meat

Hard-cook eggs, peel, cut lengthwise, remove yolks, and set whites aside. Mash yolks thoroughly, till crumbly, add margarine and all other ingredients, and mix well until smooth. Refill hollows in whites, garnish with olives.

Peanut Butter Snacks

Commercial peanut butter is laden with sugars and additives. Yet peanuts are a fine, relatively low-carbohydrate and high-protein food, rich in unsaturated fat and vitamin-mineral values. Many health food stores will grind fresh peanut butter for you without chemicals. This has two disadvantages: it is somewhat tacky in the mouth, and when stored its oil tends to rise to the top. The tackiness can be partially offset by adding orange juice to taste—and it *is* an agreeable combination. The problem of the oil rising can be overcome by storing the peanut butter upside down, and stirring before use. Brewers' yeast is a good addition to peanut butter, particularly the smoked variety that tastes like bacon. Start with 1 tablespoonful to the 8-ounce jar; you will discover the level below which you must stay. Such peanut butter on your Cornell mix rolls is a fine snack for the children. In a celery stick, it is an excellent snack for those on low-carbohydrate diets. (Seed grinders for home use, low-priced, are available.)

Quick Low-Carbohydrate "Bavarian Cream"

Pour a little low-calorie ginger ale over 2 tablespoonfuls of non-fat milk powder and stir.

Sautéed Tomato Snack

Cut tomatoes in ½-inch slices, and dip in fresh milk and wheat germ, seasoned with ½ teaspoonful sea salt, and cumin or caraway seeds to taste. Sauté in 2 tablespoons butter or margarine, till golden brown, about 10 minutes.

Low-Carbohydrate Macaroons

Use 1 egg white, 6 small walnuts, liquid artificial sweetner to taste. Add sweetener to egg white, and beat until stiff. Chop nuts very fine, fold into egg white. Put wax paper on cookie sheet, and drop mixture by spoonfuls onto wax paper. Brown in moderate (350°) oven. Two are average allowance on low-carbohydrate diet.

Mushroom Snack

Mushrooms are better food than most people realize, and fit nicely into low-carbohydrate diets. Wipe small button mushrooms with a damp cloth. Do not peel, but break off stems. On caps heap paste made from pot cheese, curry powder, and pinch of sea salt. Do not eat great quantities of mushrooms. They are *very* heavily sprayed with pesticides during commercial production; FDA regulations allow higher residues of insecticides on mushrooms, on the grounds that they are not likely to be consumed in large amounts.

Pear Snack

½ small pear, partially scooped out, and filled with soft Camembert cheese.

The School Lunchbox

4

The School Lunchbox

GOOD NUTRITION GOES TO SCHOOL

Conscientious mothers who deplore the frequently pallid fare offered by many school cafeterias send their children off in the morning with judiciously packed lunchboxes. This growing habit is heartily approved by the nutritionist who sympathizes with the school dieticians' plight but would prefer to see on students' trays fewer of the ubiquitous "white specials"—creamed fish, chicken, or shreds of overdone meat; gravied mashed potatoes; macaroni or spaghetti; recipes based on white rice.

A child's lunch should supply up to a third of the day's total nutrition, depending on the size and number of his other meals, and that means up to a third of the animal proteins, minerals, and natural vitamins in food along with the carbohydrates represented by starches that are washed down, too often, with soda pop.

Youth is the ideal time to instill good nutrition habits, and it is worth the inevitable struggle with children who seem to be rebels but are actually almost total conformists.

Usually it is a fear of being different which brings about protest when the contents of the school lunchbox resemble real food instead of blackmail payments in the form of white-bread sandwiches, sugary cookies, and candy bars. As one youngster com-

89

plained to his newly nutrition-conscious mother, "I'm the only one in my whole class who brings crazy-looking bread to school. Besides, all the other fellows get candy for dessert, and you expect me to eat this darned old banana or apple every day. They think I'm a square."

The child's mother patiently pointed out that he was also the only one in his class to go without a cold lately, and that most of the other fellows spent their Saturday mornings in a dentist's chair. Needless to say, the hero of this story was not impressed, preferring the anonymities of tribal resemblance (sniffles and cavities) to the dubious distinction of being uniquely healthy.

The school lunchbox need not contain crazy-looking food to be healthful, but neither need it be patterned after nutritional nonentities. Even that good old stand-by symbolizing youth's solidarity—the peanut butter sandwich—can be made eminently (and undetectably) nutritious (page 93).

It does seem a shame, however, that mothers must connive in order to provide their young with proper nutrition. Actually, changing youthful eating habits is less of a losing game than one would suspect, although of course starting from scratch is easier—and preferable. Children brought up from infancy on superior foods prefer whole-grain cereals and breads to sugary sawdust crackles and too-soft, too-white, too-tasteless breads. They even prefer fruits to candies, and milk or fruit juices to soda pop.

When good nutrition enters the child's home late in his life, it is still possible to guide him away from sweets based on sugar by offering similar toothsome fare in sugarless or sugar-minimum forms. It is only in the most adamantly nutrition-insistent homes that ordinary breakfast cereals, wax-wrapped white breads, cakes, cookies, pies, and other "normal" staples of American diet are absent. As wisdom in the ways of good health through nutrition filters through to homemakers, the unfortunate tendency is to go all-out faddish in an extreme of zealous concern. This cannot help but make nutrition a nasty nine-letter word, especially to husbands and children. They must eat the new

order of meals in this matriarchal society, but they seldom do it
in gracious silence.

A living proof that good nutrition does not necessarily mean
cold or unfamiliar foods—or stark deprivation—are the author's
own offspring. No children could be more normal, cantankerous,
or conformist with their peers than April, Dana, Spencer, and
Rhonda. At one time or another, one of them has announced an
intention of eating ''out,'' but this problem usually comes up
after they have attended parties where parents serve the sort of
junk ordinarily served at such affairs. Even so, all four have later
confessed they really didn't find such goo appetizing, preferring
the ''real food'' they get at home and in their lunchboxes. The
author will admit that Rhonda expressed dismay that her mother
didn't marry Dean Martin, who ''at least gives candy to his children.'' She is now reconciled to accepting her present father,
despite his obvious failings.

The recipes and suggestions which follow will, I think, give a
harried mother some wealth of choice about those lunchboxes.

"SOMETHING HOT"

It is always nice for each meal to contain a hot dish. Remember, however, that a cold dish or meal with superior nutrients in
it is far preferable to one whose chief claim to virtue lies in the
fact that it's hot.

Rather than rely on school cafeteria steam tables, it may be a
good idea to equip the child's lunchbox with a wide-mouthed
thermos in which a variety of hot foods can be carried to school.
There's always soup, and most children like it—especially if they
can enjoy the home-forbidden delight of ''drinking'' it instead
of spooning it up like little ladies or gentlemen, neither of which
most of them care to be.

If you cook soup by the can-opener method, you can fortify
it in a number of ways. Heat cream-style soups as directed with
a can of whole milk, but add two or three tablespoons of skim-
milk solids for extra protein and calcium. Canned tomato soup,
diluted with milk and milk solids, is delicious with an added
tablespoonful of yeast flakes per cup. Good canned vegetable,

beef, or chicken soup becomes better if you add chunks of left-over cooked meat or chicken. All soups can be accompanied by whole-wheat, whole-rye, or wheat-germ crackers to be dunked.

The wide-mouthed thermos can also contain nutritious versions of fish chowders, macaroni * and cheese, spaghetti * and meat-balls, Spanish rice,* stews, and casseroles.

Indignant school cafeteria dieticians may point out that their steam tables destroy no more nutrients than are lost because of the length of time home-prepared foods remain in the thermos before being consumed. There is a certain justice in this, except that you can pack much more nutrition in a hot dish than is usually found at school. Be generous with the use of skim-milk solids, wheat germ, brewers' yeast, and yeast flakes—sources of vitamins and proteins greatly needed by growing bodies.

KEEP LUNCHBOXES GREEN!

Children who ordinarily scorn the dinner salad course may take more kindly to salad ingredients packed in lunchboxes. They can be eaten with the fingers without parental admonishment. Taken crisp from the refrigerator and tucked in a plastic bag, a few leaves of lettuce, celery stalks (filled with soft cheese, perhaps), radishes, carrot curls, green or red pepper rings, and whole small tomatoes may find their way into young stomachs at lunchtime after serving a useful purpose as targets, guns, darts, or Indian headdresses.

THE INEVITABLE SANDWICH

Sandwiches can and should provide excellent nutrition. If the children object to whole-wheat bread exclusively, take a hint from fancy tearooms which offer sandwich plates of bite-size sandwiches made with a variety of breads. If little sandwiches are too dainty for your youngsters or take too much trouble to

---

* Macaroni and spaghetti made with wheat germ and supplying 20 per cent protein are commercially available. Rice should be brown or converted.

prepare, at least vary the lunchbox sandwich bread by using more than one kind, or making triple-deckers with at least one slice of whole-wheat. Bake your own white bread (see page 222) or look for a commercial white bread made from unbleached flour, wheat germ, soy, nonfat milk, and other nutritious ingredients. For reducers: double the protein content of the sandwich, omit the top piece of bread, and wrap tightly in foil.

One sure way to get a child to accept whole-grain bread is to make it yourself. Even after it has been wrapped in waxed paper or sandwich bags, there's something about the smell of home-baked bread that is irresistible. Its taste is so much more delicious that once they've been exposed to it children grow dissatisfied with pasty and gummy white breads and accept more readily the commercial whole-wheat varieties which have a firmer texture and a breadier smell.

SANDWICH FILLINGS

PEANUT BUTTER

If you own an electric blender, you can make your own peanut butter and be absolutely certain of its chemical purity as well as its content of unhydrogenated (unsaturated) fat. Put shelled peanuts in the blender a handful at a time and let them agitate at low speed until they are powdery. Either start with salted peanuts or add salt before the next step. (The little red-skin Spanish peanuts contain more nutrients than the big naked kind. Use skins and all.) Pour the pulverized peanuts in a jar or bowl and mix with peanut oil or any other vegetable oil until the desired consistency is reached. (Up to one-fourth of the oil can be wheat-germ oil if a jar of peanut butter disappears in your house within two weeks.)

This homemade peanut butter may separate, unlike the homogenized kind bought in stores. A good trick is to stand the jar upside down on the shelf, where the oil will rise to the *bottom*. The other alternative is to stir it up before each use. A bit more trouble—but a bit more nutrious, too.

Whether you use store-bought or homemade peanut butter, you can make it doubly nutritious if you mix it with equal parts of wheat germ. The kids don't have to know you've monkeyed with it. Simply save your last empty jar of a favorite chunk-style brand. Fill it and an empty new jar with the double amount of peanut butter yielded when you extend it with an equal quantity of wheat germ. When your young critic mentions that this batch tastes swell (he might) tell him your secret. I suggest this not only because I believe in being as truthful with a child as you hope him to be, but also because he may subsequently, with your encouragement, decide to add wheat germ to breakfast cereals and other foods.

For the school lunchbox or the after-school snack, a peanut butter sandwich can furnish additional food value if it contains bits of crumbled crisp bacon and even more if it also includes a slice of unprocessed yellow cheese.

OTHER SANDWICH FILLING SUGGESTIONS

chopped hot dogs with pickle relish and mustard or chili sauce
chopped chicken or turkey with minced celery, parsley, and mayonnaise
ground or minced ham with grated yellow cheese, chopped hard-cooked egg, and mayonnaise
tuna fish or salmon with chopped green peppers and celery
boneless sardines mashed with hard-cooked egg and lemon juice
chopped yellow cheese with crisp bacon
sliced meat loaf with chopped pimientos
minced shrimp, lobster, or crab meat with cream cheese
cottage cheese with chopped raw vegetables
chopped cooked liver with hard-cooked egg yolk and mayonnaise
sliced roast beef, lamb, pork, or veal with sliced tomato
sliced tongue with mustard pickle and slivered yellow cheese
liverwurst, salami, or bologna with cole slaw

SWEET SANDWICHES

cottage cheese and honey or dark molasses
cream cheese, minced ham, and crushed pineapple
any soft cheese mixed with chopped nuts and dark molasses
cream cheese with chopped cashew nuts and chopped crystallized ginger
cottage cheese with grated orange rind
grated carrots and raisins moistened with honey
cottage cheese mixed with skim-milk solids and wheat germ, moistened
     with cream, and sweetened with honey or dark molasses

LUNCHBOX DESSERTS

With a hot dish and/or a sandwich or two, the school lunchbox is only indifferently filled, according to the children who are going to eat its contents. What they are looking for is a special treat. Fruit, they may admit grudgingly, is all right once in a while—especially bananas. But for Pete's sake, can't they have cookies and cake like the other kids? On the playground stock market, fruit is sold short in active trading. If you want to make financiers out of your youngsters, you'll give them something that commands a high price in a bullish market. The result will most likely be that they'll reserve their attractive holdings for themselves.

Good nutrition, let it be repeated, need not—should not—be dull. Perfectly nutritious cakes and cookies are possible, but you'll probably have to make them yourself. If you're really serious about this business of giving your children a better start in life by feeding them nothing but the best in nutrition, please look in the index for cake and cookie recipes.

LUNCHBOX BEVERAGES

Don't fill the narrow-mouthed thermos bottle with milk. The children can usually buy a container at lunchtime for a dime or so, and they drink plenty of it at home. Fill the thermos with fruit juice instead—fresh or frozen—and vary the juices from day to day.

The strategy here is not only to get extra vitamin C into growing bodies which need it, but also to cut down on the consumption of bottled sodas. The hard work of study or play causes thirst, as any youngster with a bottle in his hand will remind you. (To this observer, it would appear that the soda pop bottle has become a modern biological mutation, permanently attached to a small hand.) Don't make the mistake of telling your child that sweet sodas only make them thirstier, whereas fruit juices

95

truly quench thirst. It happens to be true, but juvenile reasoning and logic are strange to each other. Tell them, instead, that fruit juices will make them stronger and better outfielders or skaters, if boys, or prettier and better outfielders or skaters, if girls. In any case—if you are driven to an extremity, become a Stern Parent. Cola beverages are so acid that skilled laboratory workers can identify, by tooth erosion, a rat given one single drink of these concoctions. Their caffeine content is high enough to make the parent who allows these and forbids coffee at very least, inconsistent. The others contain artificial colors and flavors of dubious safety, and they supply five teaspoonfuls of sugar per bottle, which at best is a contribution to weight problems, and at worst a pathway to diabetes, hypoglycemia, hardening of the arteries, and heart disease. If you get the familiar argument that Johnny's mother lets him drink them, respond with: "Some mothers let their children ride bicycles in heavy traffic, but that doesn't mean we must, or that it's a safe thing to do."

Last thought on beverages: the "natural" sugars of fruit juices are also mischief-makers, but at least are accompanied by body-building substances missing from the sodas, and don't contain food additives. Even these should not be overdone: the Greeks did have a word for it, and it makes nutritional sense—*moderation*.

Salads and
Salad Dressings

5

Salads and
Salad Dressings

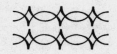

WHAT IS A SALAD?

From a good-nutrition standpoint, every meal except breakfast
should either include a salad or begin with one. The author does
not, however, believe that all of the dressing-drenched, fancied-up
concoctions of meat, fish, fowl, cooked vegetables, or macaroni
products deserve to be called "salads." In my nutrition lexicon,
a salad is composed of raw green leaves—any number, variety,
or combination of green leaves (and there are a couple of dozen
of them)—with or without other raw vegetables.

These ingredients should be as fresh as possible, kept under
refrigeration until prepared, washed briefly under running cold
water, dried quickly, and refrigerated again until served. Just
before serving they should be tossed lightly with a small amount
of dressing.

To list the greens and raw vegetables suitable for salads would
be a waste of space, because such a list would include practically
every vegetable that grows above or below the ground. Almost

any vegetable that can be eaten cooked can be eaten raw. There are a few exceptions, of course. Your common sense will tell you that mushrooms, for example, should be cooked a little before eating, but only because that's how their flavor is best. Even such vegetables as eggplant, beets, turnips, squash, asparagus, and white or sweet potatoes can be added profitably to salads if they are grated, diced, shoestringed, or sliced thinly. Garden-fresh corn kernels are delicious raw if picked while still young, before the cobs toughen.

No formal recipes for salads as such are given in this book. Any other cookbook in print will give you from 20 to 50 pages or more of vegetable names and how to combine them. As far as I'm concerned, they are all good. In any mixture, any raw vegetable salad represents the good nutrition advocated in these pages. I'd like to think you'll eat more of them, more often than you do now.

As for salad dressings, the supermarket shelves are loaded with good ones of all flavors and varying caloric content. Unless you prefer to make your own (pages 101-103) they are perfectly all right to use—always in moderation. Dressings are supposed to enhance the flavor of salad ingredients, not drown it.

Special Note: The nutritive contribution of both commercial and homemade salad dressings can be raised tremendously by the addition of small amounts of wheat-germ oil, which is a concentrated powerhouse of B-complex vitamins, vitamin E, unsaturated fatty acids, phosphatides, and other important nutrients.

HOW TO USE WHEAT-GERM OIL IN SALAD DRESSINGS

In commercial dressings: Begin by adding 1 teaspoonful to an 8-ounce bottle. When you have used some of the dressing in the bottle, add another teaspoonful. When you discover that this remarkable nutrient has not changed the taste of your salad dressing, which is consumed without comment by your family, use it in increasingly greater amounts—up to 2 tablespoons per 8-ounce bottle.

In homemade dressings: Begin by using 1 teaspoonful to replace 1 teaspoonful of oil, gradually increasing the amount until, in subsequent usages, you are replacing one-fourth of the oil with wheat-germ oil.

Fruit salads? They're fine—when made of fresh fruit in any combination and served as a dessert course, at lunch, or between meals. Generally speaking, you would do better to eat fruits in the hand rather than fussing as much as you must when making a salad of them. The less air, heat, light, and time they are exposed to when their skins are broken, the better.

Other popular "salads"—chicken, sea food, cold cuts, etc.— are fine also when served as the main course of a light meal. They do not represent the superb nutritional equilibrium provided by a raw leaf and vegetable salad eaten in conjunction with a dinner's content of meat, cooked vegetables, and carbohydrates.

BASIC LOW-CALORY SALAD DRESSINGS

NO. 1. VINEGAR DRESSING

½ cup mild vinegar
¼ cup water
1 clove garlic, sliced or minced
½ teaspoon salt
¼ teaspoon paprika

½ teaspoon liquid sugar substitute
1 tablespoon chopped fresh parsley or chives

Combine all ingredients in a bottle. Shake and chill. *Makes ⅔ cup.*

NO. 2. CITRUS-HERB DRESSING

½ teaspoon unflavored (whole) gelatin
1 tablespoon cool water
½ cup boiling water
½ teaspoon liquid sugar substitute—or 1 tablespoon brown sugar

½ teaspoon salt
⅔ cup lemon juice
¼ teaspoon onion juice or onion powder
⅛ teaspoon garlic powder
⅛ teaspoon curry powder
⅛ teaspoon paprika

Moisten gelatin with cold water; then dissolve in boiling water. Add sweetener and salt. When thoroughly dissolved, remove from heat and cool. Combine in a bottle with all other ingredients, shake well, and chill. *Makes 1 cup.*

NO. 3. CREAM-STYLE DRESSING

½ cup plain yogurt or buttermilk
½ cup liquid skim milk
1 tablespoon white vinegar
¼ teaspoon salt

⅛ teaspoon white pepper
¼ teaspoon dry mustard
dash each of garlic and onion salt

Combine all ingredients in a bottle, shake, and chill. *Makes 1 cup.*

OTHER GOOD-NUTRITION SALAD DRESSINGS

FRENCH DRESSING

1 tablespoon wheat-germ oil
5 tablespoons olive, peanut, or salad oil
2 tablespoons lemon juice—or 1 each of lemon juice and vinegar

1 teaspoon brown sugar
¼ teaspoon salt
¼ teaspon paprika
1 clove garlic

Combine all ingredients except garlic in a bowl or electric blender. Mix vigorously with rotary or electric beater until thoroughly blended. Pour into jar or bottle and add garlic. Refrigerate, and shake before each using. If this amount has not been consumed within a week, remove the garlic. *Makes ½ cup.*

To vary this dressing, as you enjoy more and more salads, add one of the following from time to time to ½ cup, just before serving. Shake well:

¼ teaspoon basil, oregano, tarragon, dry mustard, chili powder, or mixed herbs
2–4 tablespoons Roquefort or bleu cheese
¼ cup chopped onion
2 tablespoons catsup or chili sauce
1 tablespoon horse-radish
1 tablespoon each of chopped anchovies and capers
2 tablespoons chopped fresh parsley, mint, or watercress
¼ cup sweet or sour cream (beat this in slowly)

MAYONNAISE

2 egg yolks
½ teaspoon salt
¼ teaspoon paprika
⅛ teaspoon dry mustard

3 tablespoons lemon juice
1 tablespoon vinegar
2 tablespoons wheat-germ oil
¾ cup olive, peanut, or salad oil

Chill bowl and all ingredients except seasonings in refrigerator before starting. Using either a wire whisk or your electric mixer or blender, beat egg yolks thoroughly. Add and beat in dry ingredients until well blended; then add alternately—and slowly—the lemon juice, vinegar, and oils. If mayonnaise shows a tendency to separate or curdle, beat another chilled egg yolk in a cold bowl and slowly stir into this the mayonnaise. This will solve the problem—and provide still better nutrition. If the dressing seems too thick, stir in enough sweet or sour cream to thin it to the desired consistency. *Makes 1 large cup.*

RUSSIAN DRESSING

To ½ cup mayonnaise, add

¼ cup chili sauce
1 teaspoon Worcestershire sauce
1–2 tablespoons chopped pimiento, green pepper, or pepper relish

THOUSAND ISLAND DRESSING

To ½ cup mayonnaise, add

2 tablespoons chili sauce
1 tablespoon catsup
1 tablespoon chopped pickles or olives
1 teaspoon minced onion
1 teaspoon each of chopped green pepper and pimiento
yolk of hard-cooked egg, grated

SOUR CREAM DRESSING

¾ cup heavy sour cream
¼ cup skim-milk solids
½ teaspoon minced onion or onion juice
(pressed juice of ¼ clove garlic if desired)
1 tablespoon chopped parsley, watercress, or chives
¼ teaspoon celery salt
¼ teaspoon salt
dash of pepper, paprika, or cayenne
2–3 tablespoons lemon juice or vinegar

Beat sour cream until smooth and add all other ingredients in order—lemon juice or vinegar last—beating until creamy. *Makes 1 large cup.*

Beautiful Soup

6

Beautiful Soup

Soup is art and philosophy combined, reflecting the ingenuity, creativity, and thought processes of the one who prepares it.

Anyone with a minimum of manual dexterity is able to open a can, and what's inside is frequently satisfying and tasty. Canned soups are also, as their advertisers proclaim, "nourishing." They contain calories and varying amounts of proteins, minerals, vitamins, fats, and carbohydrates. No one can deny it. No one can deny either that soup unadorned out of a can tastes like canned soup, or that soup made by the vatful lacks the aroma, grace, and reassurance of love which emanate from a steaming pot on the back of Mother's range.

Gourmet and psychological considerations aside, there is much to be said nutritionally in favor of homemade soup—even if the "home" part of this consists only in fortifying and glorifying the 10 ounces of densely concentrated base that slurps out of a can. The chances are your vegetables won't be any fresher than those used by the cannery—but they'll be cooked more briefly and they'll be consumed sooner. The meat, fowl, or fish you use will be present in more generous quantities. And if you are conscientious, the water you use for homemade soup will not be plain H_2O, but the repository of nutrients from vegetables you have cooked for other purposes. If you have the time and the will, you'll extract the best part of bones—their calcium and proteins—by cracking them before adding them to the soup pot. You'll also save vegetable parings, outer leaves, meat scraps, and cooked leftovers of all kinds to contribute their otherwise wasted food value. Like America itself, the soup vessel is a melting pot—and one that can contribute greatly to good nutrition.

Granted, you must be soup-minded in order to see beauty in the ragged end of a roast, the leaves and peelings of vegetables, the uneaten bowl of oatmeal, the skin and bones of broiled or roasted chicken, the clean, meaty bone a kind neighbor or butcher donates to your dog (through you as intermediary). But here's a little secret: If you privately yearn to achieve the reputation of being a fabulous cook, you can sail toward your goal on every plateful of homemade soup you put before your family or guests. All the bits and scraps you toss into the soup pot along with water saved from last night's—or last week's—vegetables have a way of blending together like a fine orchestration. It requires only for you to taste, sip, criticize, and correct.

SOUP STOCKS

ECONOMY STOCK FROM BONES, RAW MEAT SCRAPS, ETC.

Crack bones, if they are large. Brown them and the meat scraps in a small amount of their own fat or oil, or other shortening. Remove from pan and pour off melted fat. Put bones and browned scraps in bottom of heavy pot and pour over them enough water to cover to twice their depth. Bring to a brisk boil, cover pot, lower heat, and simmer for 3 or 4 hours. Decant liquid and allow it to cool. Fat will rise to the top and can be removed easily. Return stock to clean pot and enrich further by adding whatever vegetable parings or top leaves you have, along with cooked table scraps. Bring to a boil again and simmer for 30 minutes. Strain, cool, and again remove fat if any has accumulated.

You now have an economical, perfectly good stock suitable as a base for all kinds of soups or gravies or as a more nutritious liquid than plain water for stews and pot roasts. Seasonings are not added to this basic stock, for the use to which you put it later will determine the seasonings. Store in freezer or refrigerator.

ECONOMY POULTRY STOCK

An excellent chicken-flavored stock can be made with the raw feet, necks, hearts, and gizzards, plus discarded cooked skin and bones without sacrificing the bird itself, which you may prefer fried, broiled, or roasted.

Cover poultry feet with boiling water and boil for 5 minutes. Discard water and remove skin, being careful not to throw away the jellylike substance between the small bones. Cut or break the bones into smaller pieces and add them to a pot containing the hearts, gizzards, and cooked skin and bones. Cover these with (vegetable) water to twice their depth and bring to a brisk boil. Lower heat and simmer, covered, for 2 hours.

Without interrupting boil, at end of 2 hours add tops and outer stalks of celery, along with a few outer leaves of lettuce, and, if you have them, carrots, peas, white turnips, parsnips, squash—alone or in combination—a total of ½ cup. Boil for 30 minutes more. Strain. Discard bones, but if you have pets by all means give them the skin, gizzards, hearts, and vegetables. When broth is cool, remove fat and store in freezer or refrigerator.

ECONOMY VEGETABLE STOCK

Good cooks with an eye on nutritional values can have constantly on hand a fine supply of vitamin-rich vegetable stock for use in gravies, pot roasts, stews, and casseroles, as well as soup— and, odd as this may seem to you, for use in baking also.

All you have to do is save (under refrigeration, please) a week's supply of the vegetable parts ordinarily and profligately thrown away—peelings, tops, unused stalks, roots, and shoots. Keep a large polyethylene bag in the refrigerator to receive these valuable discards. Also, keep a 2-quart jar on the top shelf and pour into this the *small* amount of water you use when you cook vegetables for the table. When the jar is full, you should have collected enough solid material to make a batch of stock:

Wash the vegetable discards and pick them over for obvious defects. Chop them, or put them through the coarse blade of your meat grinder. To each 2 cups or more of chopped vegetables, add 2 quarts of vegetable water. Bring to a boil, lower the heat, and simmer for ½ hour or longer. If you must have fairly clear stock, remove the vegetables. Nutrition is best served by putting everything through a food mill or forcing it through a sieve. This yields a purée. For thinner liquids, simply add more vegetable water.

Needless to say, it's up to you to use some discretion in the choice of vegetable discards and/or water which go into the stock. If you use overlarge quantities of "strong" vegetables like onions, cabbage, broccoli, and turnips, the stock will be strong. Carrots, parsnips, and the pods of green peas tend to sweeten the stock. A judicious combination of many different-flavored vegetables will blend deliciously, no one predominating —unless you want it to.

ECONOMY MUSHROOM STOCK

Save the stems, peelings, and broken pieces when you prepare mushrooms as a side vegetable or to use in recipes. Wash quickly in a sieve or colander under running water.

Sauté these mushroom remnants in a little butter—just enough to prevent sticking—and stir them just long enough to coat them (about 2 minutes). To each cupful of mushroom pieces add 2 cups of vegetable water. Bring to a boil, lower heat, and simmer for 5 to 10 minutes. This may be used as is, or you may strain it and use only the liquid if you have any qualms about eating the peelings—which you shouldn't have.

RICH BEEF STOCK

2 pounds lean beef plus bones	1½ cups chopped mixed raw vegetables
2 teaspoons salt	
2 quarts cold (vegetable) water	½ cup raw or canned tomatoes

110

Cut about a third of the beef into small pieces and crack as many of the bones as you can. Brown these quickly in a little beef fat. Put the browned beef and bones and the rest of the raw beef and bones in a large kettle, salt them, cover, and let stand for 1 hour. Add the (vegetable) water, bring to a boil, lower heat, and simmer for 3 hours.

Do not, unless you absolutely insist on clear stock, remove the scum which bubbles to the top. It is rich in nutrients.

At the end of 3 hours add the vegetables and simmer for another ½ hour. Pick out the pieces of lean meat; then strain the stock and let it cool. When cold, remove all but a little of the fat which has risen to the top. The stock is a ready-made soup after you have tasted it and corrected the seasoning. It can be stored as a rich beef stock for use as the base of other soups or for adding proteins to meatless casseroles.

As for the meat and vegetables, they have lost most of their prime nutritive value after such long cooking, but they still have some virtue. Meat can be shredded and added to heavy soups like minestrone, gumbo, bean, or split pea. It can be minced and mixed with the yolk of a raw egg and wheat germ as a sandwich filling. It can be used with raw chopped meat for stuffed peppers and similar recipes, or in spaghetti sauce. As a last resort, mix it in with your pet's food along with the vegetables.

CHICKEN STOCK NO. 1

stewing fowl, about 5 pounds
3 quarts (vegetable) water
1 cup chopped celery stalks
1 cup celery leaves—or 1 tablespoon celery flakes

¼ cup chopped carrots
½ medium onion—or 1 small onion cut in half
1 teaspoon salt

Cut fowl into pieces, add water, cover, bring to a boil, lower heat, and simmer for 2 hours. Add vegetables and salt and simmer for ½ hour longer. Cool and remove fat. If soup has jellied, heat it until it is liquid again and strain. (Use the cooked chicken, of course, for fricassee, salad, à la king, or sandwiches.)

CHICKEN STOCK NO. 2

2–3 pounds of chicken backs, wings, and necks
2 quarts (vegetable) water
1½ cups chopped mixed vege-

tables, including some leaves of celery or lettuce, and onion
1 teaspoon salt

Proceed as for Chicken Stock No. 1. The meat can be carefully separated from the bones and used in croquettes, soufflés, sandwiches, or pancake fillings.

GOOD-NUTRITION SOUPS

ARTHUR'S POTATO AND SWISS CHEESE SOUP

4 medium potatoes
1 large onion
4 tablespoons butter or margarine
1 tablespoon unbleached or whole-wheat flour
½ cup warm milk
1 quart boiling stock, mild vegetable water, or (in a pinch)

plain water, to which add 2 or 3 bouillon cubes
salt and pepper to taste
dash of nutmeg
4–8 tablespoons grated Swiss cheese
4 teaspoons finely chopped parsley

Peel and dice potatoes and onion, and brown lightly in 2 tablespoons of butter or margarine. Melt remaining 2 tablespoons of butter or margarine in a heavy soup kettle and add flour, stirring to a smooth paste. Stir in ½ cup of warm milk slowly to avoid lumps. Add boiling stock (or water) and browned potato-onion mixture and stir thoroughly. Season to taste. Simmer gently until potatoes are tender. Add dash of nutmeg, stir again, and pour over grated cheese in soup plates (1 or 2 tablespoons per plate, depending on how much you like cheese). Sprinkle with parsley. *Serves 4.*

VEGETABLE-CHEESE SOUP

3 tablespoons butter, margarine, or peanut oil
½ cup thinly sliced or diced carrots
½ cup thinly sliced green celery
1 cup cut green beans
2 cups boiling stock or (vegetable) water

3 tablespoons whole-wheat or unbleached flour
3 tablespoons cold water
1 quart milk
½ cup skim-milk solids
1–2 cups grated unprocessed yellow cheese

112

Heat butter, margarine or peanut oil in heavy soup kettle. Cook vegetables until they are well coated—about 5 minutes. Add boiling stock (or water), cover kettle, and simmer over low heat until vegetables are tender but not soft—about 10 minutes. Make a smooth paste of the flour and water and add slowly to the kettle. Simmer, stirring, until soup thickens slightly—about 3 minutes. Combine milk and milk solids and add to kettle. Add cheese and stir over low heat until cheese melts and blends. Do not boil. *Serves 8.*

BORSCH

4 or 5 medium beets
2 or 3 large carrots
1 small head green cabbage
2 medium onions, chopped
1 stalk green celery with leaves, chopped
2 tablespoons butter or margarine
1 quart stock or (vegetable) water

1 cup tomato purée or stewed tomatoes
1 tablespoon lemon juice
salt and pepper to taste
(1 tablespoon brewers' yeast)
sour cream
(optional: 4–6 tablespoons dry red wine)

Scrub well but do not peel beets and carrots. Shred them and the cabbage fairly fine. Melt butter or margarine in heavy soup kettle and sauté onions and celery until well coated but not brown —3 to 4 minutes. Add stock or vegetable water, tomatoes, and lemon juice and bring to a boil. Add shredded vegetables and simmer 10 to 15 minutes. Season to taste (and add brewers' yeast) and stir. Ladle into bowls or soup plates. (Stir in 1 tablespoon dry red wine per adult serving.) Serve with side dishes or bowl of sour cream for topping. *Serves 4 to 6.*

FRESH PEA POD SOUP

2 pounds fresh young peas in pods
1 bay leaf
2 quarts (vegetable) water
(1 ham bone or lean end of tongue, if you have it)

2 tablespoons skim-milk solids
¼ cup milk or light cream
salt and pepper to taste
3–4 tablespoons yeast flakes

Wash peas in their pods, shuck them, and, reserving the peas, put pods only in soup kettle with bay leaf and water (and ham bone or tongue). Bring to a boil, lower heat, and simmer for 1

113

hour. Drain, saving the broth and discarding the pods, bay leaf, ham, or tongue. Cover reserved peas with pod broth and boil very gently for 1 to 12 minutes until peas are soft. Force through food mill or sieve, or purée in electric blender. Return purée to kettle. Combine milk solids with milk or cream and stir into purée. Add seasonings and yeast flakes and heat, but do not allow to boil. *Serves 6 to 8.*

ONION SOUP

Of course you can tear open an envelope of dehydrated soup mix, add water, bring to a boil, and serve a creditable onion soup. But fine French onion soup is not difficult to prepare, so why not treat the family or guests occasionally and bask in their admiration? Besides, you'll be serving more excellent onion nutrients at one sitting than you probably do in any average week.

1 pound onions (at least), sliced into very thin crescents
2 tablespoons butter
2 tablespoons whole-wheat or unbleached flour
6–8 cups stock—or vegetable water, adding ½ bouillon cube per cup
salt and pepper to taste
(2–4 tablespoons yeast flakes)
6–8 slices crusty French bread
grated Parmesan cheese
(6–8 tablespoons sherry)

Sauté thinly sliced onions in butter, using heavy saucepan and stirring to coat well. Avoid excessive browning. When onions are glazed and golden in color, sprinkle flour over them, stir, and cook for 1 minute. Add stock slowly, stirring constantly. When smooth and well blended, add seasonings. If you have time, remove the pan from heat and allow it to stand for an hour or more. Bring slowly to serving temperature (add yeast flakes at this time) while you sprinkle slices of French bread with Parmesan cheese and toast them in the oven until the cheese melts and browns. Ladle soup into bowls or plates. (A tablespoonful of sherry per serving is delicious—for adults.) Float a piece of toast in each; pass more Parmesan cheese for the gourmets. *Serve 6 to 8.*

114

VEGETABLE SOUP

The vegetables called for in this recipe are not fixed by law. You can vary them in any way you see fit, provided you maintain approximately the same proportion of vegetables to liquid. Green beans, yellow beans, lima beans, turnips, parsnips, chopped spinach or cabbage, shredded outer leaves of lettuce, etc.—are all excellent soup material. Use what you have on hand or choose vegetables in good seasonal supply.

2 tablespoons butter
½ cup thinly sliced celery, along with some leaves
¼ cup chopped or sliced onion
1 cup diced carrots
2 cups diced potatoes
1 cup fresh, frozen, or canned peas
4 whole tomatoes, coarsely cut, or 1 can whole or stewed tomatoes
1 or 2 green peppers, seeded and cut into small pieces
1 tablespoon chopped parsley
1 bay leaf
salt and pepper to taste
(2 tablespoons brewers' yeast or yeast flakes)
2 quarts stock or vegetable water

Melt butter and sauté celery and onions for 2 or 3 minutes. Add these along with all other vegetables and seasonings (and yeast) to stock in soup kettle. Bring to boil, lower heat, and cook for about 30 minutes. Remove bay leaf before serving. *Serves 6 to 8.*

BEET-TOP SOUP

You can use spinach instead, but beet tops are higher in nutritive value and are often discarded when fresh beets are served —a phenomenon absolutely incomprehensible to a nutritionist.

3 tablespoons butter
1 medium onion, minced or finely chopped
2 pounds beet tops, washed,
drained, and coarsely chopped
4 cups stock or vegetable water
salt and pepper to taste

Melt butter and cook onion over low heat until golden but not brown. Add beet tops and stir them around with a fork to coat them. Add stock and seasonings, stir, and simmer until greens are tender. *Serves 4 to 6.*

ITALIAN SPINACH SOUP

If you have beet tops, combine them with the spinach to yield the amount of greens called for.

2 quarts boiling stock or vegetable water	½ cup diced carrots
½ cup chopped onion	2 cups cooked chopped spinach
1 tablespoon chopped parsley	2 tablespoons olive oil
½ cup thinly sliced celery	2 cups cooked brown rice
4 coarsely cut tomatoes—or 1 can whole Italian tomatoes	salt and pepper to taste
	grated Parmesan cheese

Add to boiling stock the onion, parsley, celery, tomatoes, and carrots and simmer until celery is just tender—about 12 to 18 minutes. Sauté spinach in olive oil, stirring to coat well—about 2 minutes. Stir into simmering stock, add rice and seasonings, and cook for 5 minutes. Serve with grated Parmesan cheese. *Serves 6 to 8.*

HEARTY HAMBURGER SOUP

A meal in itself, served with a tossed green salad.

1 pound lean ground beef (chuck or round)	2 cups diced or shredded raw vegetables—carrots, cabbage, celery, beans, etc., in any combination
2 tablespoons cooking oil	salt and pepper to taste
1 medium onion, chopped	(optional: pinch of garlic powder, basil, or curry)
3 cups stewed tomatoes—or tomato juice	2 tablespoons yeast flakes or brewers' yeast
2 cans any thick condensed soup—asparagus, pea, lentil, cream of mushroom, etc.	
1 cup vegetable water	

Brown ground beef quickly in oil. (If beef is somewhat fatty, use less oil and brown it more slowly, pouring off excess drippings.) Use a fork to prevent meat from lumping. When cooked through (about 5 minutes), remove meat and brown chopped onions lightly in the same skillet, adding a little oil if necessary. Put meat and onions in soup kettle. Make a smooth blend of tomatoes (or juice), canned soup, and vegetable water and add to kettle. Add chopped vegetables, seasonings, and yeast and simmer, covered, until vegetables are just tender—10 to 15 minutes. *Serves 6 to 8.*

LIVER SOUP

½ pound beef, pork, or lamb liver
4 cups boiling stock, vegetable water, or bouillon made with cubes
3 tablespoons butter or margarine
1 cup chopped mushrooms

1 tablespoon chopped parsley
1 teaspoon salt
⅛ teaspoon paprika
1 tablespoon whole-wheat flour
1 cup milk
2 tablespoons skim-milk solids

Drop liver into boiling stock for 2 minutes. Remove liver (reserving stock) and grind or chop fine. Sauté ground liver for 2 minutes in 2 tablespoons of the butter, stirring. Add mushrooms and sauté for 2 minutes more. Transfer to stock pot, add parsley and seasonings, and simmer, covered, for 20 minutes. Melt remaining tablespoon of butter, add flour, and blend to a smooth paste. Add a little of the soup and stir until very smooth; then pour back into the soup and stir. Bring to a boil, lower heat, add milk and milk solids, and stir over very low heat for 5 minutes. Do not boil. *Serves 6 to 8.*

OXTAIL SOUP

2 pounds oxtail, disjointed
3–4 tablespoons whole-wheat or unbleached flour
2 tablespoons cooking oil
8 cups vegetable water
1½ teaspoons salt
⅛ teaspoon black pepper
1 small bay leaf
1 tablespoon chopped parsley

½ cup chopped onion
½ cup diced carrots
½ cup chopped celery
(½ cup diced turnips or parsnips)
¼ teaspoon thyme
¼ teaspoon basil or oregano
1 teaspoon Worcestershire sauce (sherry, if desired)

Trim excess fat from oxtail joints. Dredge joints in flour and brown (in heavy soup kettle) on all sides in oil. Add vegetable water, salt, pepper, bay leaf, and parsley. Bring to boil and boil briskly for 10 minutes. Skim soup, discard bay leaf, cover kettle, lower heat, and simmer for 3 hours. Remove oxtails, separate meat from bones, and set aside. Add to kettle the chopped vegetables and herbs and simmer until vegetables are soft—about 20 minutes. Force through food mill or sieve and return to kettle. Add the reserved bits of oxtail meat and heat to serving temperature. Before serving, stir in Worcestershire sauce. Or, omit this, ladle soup into bowls or plates, and stir in up to 1 tablespoon sherry per adult serving. *Serves 6 to 8.*

117

MUSHROOM AND BARLEY SOUP

You can be old-fashioned and old-world about this and use barley, which, like all grains used in this cook book, should be whole grain; or you can be modern and new-world by substituting brown rice for the barley.

½ cup barley or brown rice
3 cups vegetable water or bouillon made with cubes
½ teaspoon salt
½ pound or more of mushrooms
2 tablespoons butter

4 cups seasoned beef stock
½ cup sliced or diced carrots
½ cup sliced or diced celery
(1–2 tablespoons brewers' yeast or yeast flakes)

Let cold tap water run over barley or rice in a strainer; then add it slowly to boiling vegetable water and season with salt. Stir, cover, then simmer over low heat until cereal is soft and water is absorbed. Stir occasionally to prevent sticking or scorching. Sauté mushrooms in butter for 2 minutes; then add them to boiling stock along with the barley or rice. Mix thoroughly, lower heat, and simmer for 20 minutes. Add carrots and celery and simmer for 20 minutes more, until vegetables are tender. The soup should then be thick enough. If you prefer it thicker, remove a few tablespoons of the barley or rice and force through a food mill or sieve, returning it to the soup. (Stir in brewers' yeast or yeast flakes before serving.) *Serves 4 to 6.*

FISH CHOWDERS

Some of the best nutrition in the world comes to us from the depths of oceans and lakes or the shallows of streams. Not only are fish high in first-rate proteins, vitamins, and minerals, but they also have another advantage peculiar to the times we live in. Nobody sprays the waterways with DDT or fertilizes them with poisonous chemicals.

FRESH OR FROZEN FISH CHOWDER

4 slices bacon, or ¼ cup very finely diced salt pork
2 cups diced raw potatoes
1 medium onion, chopped
1 tablespoon chopped celery
1 tablespoon chopped green pepper
1½ cups stock, vegetable water, or bouillon made with cubes
1 pound fish fillets cut into pieces (any variety in good supply)

2 tablespoons butter
2 tablespoons whole-wheat or unbleached flour
4 cups milk
¼ cup skim-milk solids
salt and pepper or paprika to taste
4–6 tablespoons wheat germ

Brown bacon (or salt pork) slowly until crisp. Remove from pan and in the drippings cook all of the vegetables for 5 minutes, stirring to coat them evenly. Add stock, bring to boiling point, and add fish. Lower heat and simmer, while in another pan you melt butter, blend it with the flour, and slowly add milk and milk solids. Stir until this mixture begins to thicken; then add seasonings. Cook over low heat for 10 minutes (do not boil), and add to the simmering fish-vegetable mixture. Stir; correct seasonings if necessary. Serve sprinkled with crumbled bacon or crisps of salt pork and about 1 tablespoon of wheat germ per serving. *Serves 4 to 6.*

SALMON OR TUNA FISH CHOWDER

⅓ cup diced salt pork
1 onion, finely chopped
2 cups stock, vegetable water, or bouillon made with cubes
4 medium potatoes, finely diced
½ teaspoon salt

dash of pepper
1 flat can red salmon or tuna fish
1⅔ cups milk
¼ cup skim-milk solids
2 tablespoons chopped watercress, parsley, or chives for garnish

Dice salt pork as fine as possible and render slowly in heavy soup kettle over low heat until crisp and golden brown. Remove pork bits with slotted spoon, drain them on a paper towel, and reserve. Raise heat under pork drippings to moderate and cook chopped onion until tender and light brown—4 or 5 minutes. Add stock, diced potatoes, salt, and pepper. With kettle covered, bring to a boil; then lower heat and simmer until potatoes are tender—7 or 8 minutes. Stir in drained salmon or tuna fish, milk, and milk solids. Stir over moderate heat until bubbles form around sides of pan; then remove immediately from source of heat. Do not let it boil. Pour into heated bowls and sprinkle with salt pork bits and green garnish. *Serves 6 to 8.*

PREPARING CLAMS FOR CHOWDERS

If clams in their shells come your way, put them in the bottom of a large kettle or dishpan, cover them with water, and add a handful—about ⅓ cup—of corn meal. Leave them overnight, if possible, or for at least 3 to 4 hours. They will clean themselves inside and out, although you should still scrub the shells under running water, scraping two at a time against each other to remove the patina.

Put the cleaned clams in the bottom of a dry kettle or pan and pop them in a 350° oven until they open. With a strong, sharp knife sever the muscles at both sides near the hinges. Do this over a bowl or pan to catch the juices, and use whatever juice may have escaped into the pan while the clams were in the oven. Remove the hard, dark parts of the clam meat but don't throw them away. Chop them for use in the chowder.

MANHATTAN CLAM CHOWDER

2 cups clam meat (about a quart of small ones in the shell, or 12 large ones)
¼ cup chopped salt pork—or 4 slices chopped bacon
½ cup chopped onion
2 cups diced raw potatoes
1 tablespoon chopped green pepper
2 tablespoons chopped green celery

2 cups stewed tomatoes or tomato juice
vegetable water
½ teaspoon ground pepper
pinch each of cayenne, powdered sage, and thyme
salt to taste
(2 tablespoons yeast flakes or brewers' yeast)

Wash clams in about 2 cups of clean water and save the water, straining it if it appears sandy. Brown salt pork or bacon slowly

120

in heavy soup kettle until crisp. Remove pieces and reserve. Add to the drippings the chopped onion and chopped hard parts of clams, stir, and cook for 2 minutes. Add potatoes, green pepper, and celery and cover with the water in which you washed the clams. If this does not cover sufficiently, add enough vegetable water to do so. Heat to boiling, lower heat, and simmer until potatoes are tender but not soft. Add soft parts of clams, tomatoes (or juice), seasonings, and yeast. Simmer for 3 to 5 minutes. Sprinkle reserved bits of salt pork or bacon over bowlfuls when serving. *Serves 6 to 8.*

NEW ENGLAND CLAM CHOWDER

If they are available, the large quahogs make the most flavorsome chowder. These should be chopped or ground after brief cooking.

1 quart of shucked large clams	2 tablespoons whole-wheat or un-
2 cups cold water	bleached flour
¼ pound chopped salt pork	4 cups scalded milk
½ cup chopped onion	½ cup skim-milk solids
3 cups diced raw potatoes	salt and pepper to taste
2 tablespoons butter	

Wash clams in water and save water, straining it if it appears sandy. (If you are using quahogs, boil them in the water a few minutes after washing and straining. Save the liquid.) Grind or chop hard parts of clams. Brown the chopped salt pork slowly until brown and crisp. Remove pieces and reserve. Add to drippings the onions and chopped hard parts of clams, stir, and cook for 3 minutes—a little longer if not tender by then. Add potatoes and reserved clam liquid, stir, and simmer until potatoes are tender but not soft. Add the soft parts of clams. In a separate saucepan or double boiler, melt the butter, blend with the flour, and stir in scalded milk and milk solids until mixture begins to thicken slightly. Add and stir this into the chowder and keep it hot until serving. Do not let it boil. Season to taste. Sprinkle bits of crisp salt pork over bowls when serving. *Serves 6 to 8.*

CREAMED SOUPS

If it is creamed, almost any soup can be made more meaningfully nutritious, especially for growing children and the elderly. The protein and calcium of milk are needed by young bodies and by the brittle bones of those in advancing years.

National surveys reveal that high-protein diets are particularly important to the elderly. However, because of ill-fitting dentures and a number of other reasons—economic and social—they may not eat meat in the quantities nutritionists recommend, and they frequently resent drinking milk. Creamed soups (and puddings —see index) are an excellent way of maintaining protective protein-calcium reserves among the senior set.

If overweight is a problem, creamed soups can still provide essential proteins and calcium without excessive calories. Make them with liquefied skim-milk solids instead of whole milk, using at least a third to a half more of the solids than the usual box directions specify.

BASIC RULE FOR MAKING CREAM SOUPS

3 tablespoons whole-wheat or unbleached flour

3 tablespoons butter or margarine, melted

2 cups milk plus 2 tablespoons skim-milk solids—or 2 cups liquefied skim-milk solids

2 cups any stock or soup, with or without vegetables

salt and pepper if needed

Add flour slowly to melted butter in top of double boiler, stirring to a smooth paste. Scald milk with skim-milk solids and add slowly, stirring to avoid lumps. Cook but do not boil over boiling water or very low heat until well blended—about 10 minutes. Heat stock or soup and add. Season to taste. The addition of 1 to 2 tablespoons of yeast flakes or brewers' yeast per serving will provide even better nutrition. *Serves 4.*

Individual Cream Soups

CREAM OF ASPARAGUS SOUP

2 bunches green asparagus
2 cups (vegetable) water
5 cups any stock, vegetable water, or bouillon made with cubes
1 tablespoon chopped onion
1 teaspoon chopped parsley
½ cup chopped green celery with leaves
2 tablespoons butter or margarine

2 tablespoons whole-wheat or un-bleached flour
½ cup light cream, whole milk, or liquefied skim-milk solids —warm
salt and pepper to taste
(2–4 tablespoons yeast flakes or brewers' yeast)

Remove the tender tips of the asparagus and reserve. Cut stalks into 1-inch pieces, or smaller, and boil them in the (vegetable) water for 5 minutes. Add the stalks and liquid to boiling stock along with the onion, parsley, and celery. Simmer for 20 minutes; then put through a food mill or force through a sieve. Return to low heat. In a separate saucepan melt butter, add flour, and mix to a smooth paste. Add warm cream or milk slowly, stirring to prevent lumps. Stir cream sauce into simmering stock. Add reserved uncooked tips, and simmer (do not boil) for 5 minutes, until the tips are tender. Season and stir in yeast. *Serves 6 to 8.*

CREAM OF BEET SOUP

1 cup diced raw beets
½ cup chopped onions
½ cup diced raw carrots
2 cups vegetable water
2 eggs, well-beaten

2 cups milk
¼ cup skim-milk solids
salt and pepper to taste
(1–2 tablespoons yeast flakes or brewers' yeast)

Cover vegetables with vegetable water and cook until beets are tender—about 15 to 20 minutes. You may rub the vegetables through a sieve, or let them remain in dice. Lower heat. Beat eggs with milk and milk solids and add slowly to soup, stirring over low heat until soup thickens. Season to taste (and add yeast). *Serves 4.*

123

CREAM OF GREENS SOUP

1 pound greens, individual or mixed—spinach, beet tops, and/or Swiss chard
1 average head of lettuce
4 cups stock, vegetable water, or bouillon made with cubes
3 tablespoons butter or margarine
3 tablespoons unbleached or whole-wheat flour
1¾ cups warm milk
⅓ cup skim-milk solids
½ teaspoon salt
pinch of pepper or paprika

Wash greens; then cook them in their own moisture or in very little water. While they are cooking, chop or shred lettuce and add to greens at the end of 10 minutes. Cook for another 5 minutes. Drain, reserving water; then force the greens through a food mill or sieve. Add stock and reserved water and simmer over low heat while you make cream sauce: Melt butter, blend with flour, slowly add warm milk, milk solids, and seasonings and stir over low heat until thickened. Stir cream sauce into soup pot and correct seasonings if necessary. *Serves 6 to 8.*

CREAM OF MIXED VEGETABLES

2 tablespoons chopped onion
1½ cups chopped raw vegetables, individual or mixed—carrots, beans, celery, etc.
1 cup (vegetable) water
1 cup raw or stewed tomatoes
3 tablespoons butter or margarine
1 tablespoon unbleached or whole-wheat flour
3 cups milk
½ cup skim-milk solids
salt, pepper, or paprika to taste

Cover onions and chopped vegetables with (vegetable) water and simmer until tender. Add and stir in tomatoes and keep hot over low heat while you make cream sauce: Melt butter, blend with flour, slowly add warm milk, milk solids, and seasonings, and stir over low heat until thickened. Force vegetables and water in which they cooked through food mill or sieve. Combine this purée with cream sauce; correct seasonings if necessary and heat to serving temperature. Do not boil. *Serves 4 to 6.*

PEANUT BUTTER SOUP

2 tablespoons butter or margarine
2 tablespoons whole-wheat or unbleached flour
4 cups warm milk
½ cup skim-milk solids

⅔ cup peanut butter
⅓ cup wheat germ
salt, if needed
1 teaspoon sherry per adult serving, if desired

Melt butter, add flour, and mix to a smooth paste. Slowly add milk and milk solids, stirring to avoid lumps. Add peanut butter and wheat germ, stirring constantly until soup is smooth. A wire whisk is helpful. Taste and correct seasoning if necessary. Stir in sherry just before serving. *Serves 6 to 8.*

DRY-LEGUME SOUPS

A variety of hearty, delicious, nutritious soups can be made from the dry beans, lentils, and peas so economically available in markets and so eminently storable on pantry shelves. It's a good idea to keep an assortment on hand for such times as you may have a fowl carcass, a ham bone, or the end of a smoked tongue to add flavor and nutritive value to a satisfying, popular soup.

Soaking dry legumes overnight is a strong habit, but it can and should be broken. This habit is usually accompanied by another one—discarding the water in which the legumes were soaked. When you do this, you discard a high percentage of food value. So if habit is too strong to break and you feel you must soak dry beans and the like overnight, at least restrain yourself from automatically pouring the water down the sink. Let it stay. Add more, if necessary, when you cook the soup. You'll be preserving proteins, vitamins, and minerals along with the carbohydrates.

The cause of tenderness is served when dry legumes are cooked until they are soft.

Another habit which deserves to be broken is the one of adding flour to thicken a legume soup. Nicely thick purées are achieved by putting up to half of the cooked legumes through a food mill. If you want extra body, you can achieve it—and extra nutrition —by adding a few tablespoons of wheat germ or yeast flakes to the soup after it has been puréed and returned to the stove for reheating.

Cooking times for legumes vary according to the softness of your local water and the type of legume you are using: Dry limas take less time to cook than dry navy beans, and split peas or lentils less than whole. (Some packaged brands come precooked.)

BASIC RECIPE FOR MAKING SOUP FROM DRY LEGUMES

8 cups boiling vegetable water
2 cups dry legumes (split or whole peas, lentils, black, kidney, lima, navy, or other beans)
1 bay leaf
½ cup chopped or sliced onions
a ham bone, end piece of tongue,
fowl carcass, 2-inch cube of salt pork, or 2 slices bacon
½ cup celery with leaves
½ cup chopped or diced carrots
1 teaspoon brown sugar
salt (if needed)
pepper to taste

Wash and pick over legumes, drain, and then drop slowly into boiling vegetable water. Try not to interrupt the boil. Add bay leaf, onions, whatever bone or meat you are using. Cover kettle and simmer for 2 to 3 hours, until legumes are tender and their skins crack when you blow on a few taken up in a spoon. Remove bay leaf and bone or meat. If you have time, allow soup to cool until any fat can be skimmed off top. Add celery, carrots, brown sugar. Simmer for 20 minutes. With small sieve or slotted spoon remove and reserve about half of the legumes. Put the rest through a food mill or force through a sieve. Combine purée with the unmashed legumes, bring soup to serving heat, and season to taste. If there are any bits of lean ham, tongue, or fowl clinging to the bones you removed, shred these and add them to the soup. *Serves 4 to 6.*

Serving Hints

Pea or lentil soup: Garnish with wheat germ or whole-wheat croutons.
Black bean soup: Add 1 tablespoon sherry per adult serving, along with slices of hard-cooked eggs and thin lemon wheels.

Navy bean soup: Add cubes of ham or tongue.
Kidney bean soup: Stir in ½ teaspoon chili powder 20 minutes before serving.

Any legume soup becomes a hearty one-course luncheon when you add slices or chunks of frankfurters or knockwurst. For even better nutrition, add cubes of broiled liver—or liver dumplings (page 173). Smoked brewers' yeast—½ to 1 teaspoon per portion—lends extra tang and much nutritional value to most of the hearty soups, particularly those made from legumes.

A WORD ABOUT SOYBEANS

Much nonsense has been written about soy, as a source of protein which, the public is now convinced, can replace eggs, meat, fish, fowl, and other high quality animal proteins. Soy is—for a vegetable protein—unusually efficient, but not as efficient as meat, milk, fowl and fish proteins. It lacks Vitamin B12, which is a serious deficit not encountered with animal proteins; and it is low in certain important minerals. Its chief values are: it is better quality protein than any other from a vegetable source; and it works nicely with (complements) the better proteins of animal origin. This is to say that soy makes a fine extender for hamburger or meat loaf, where its inadequacies are covered by the more efficient protein of an animal source; but it should not be used as a substitute for meat. Its amino acid balances are *not* satisfactory though they are the mainstay of poor countries where meat and milk products are scarce.

Dry soybeans are exempt from the no-soaking rule, as some form of pretreatment is desirable to neutralize their somewhat unfamiliar flavor and to shorten the cooking time. They can be soaked overnight—3 cups of water to each cup of soybeans. Or they can be covered with water, frozen solid, and kept in the freezer until used. Freezing does not detract from their nutritive value, but reduces cooking time and offers a handy way to have soybeans available on short notice.

See the index for other recipes using soybeans.

PUREE OF DRY SOYBEANS

2 cups dry soybeans soaked overnight in 6 cups water, or
frozen in 2 cups water
(4 cups vegetable water, if soybeans were frozen)
¼ cup chopped celery with leaves
2–4 tablespoons chopped onion
1 teaspoon salt
⅛ teaspoon black pepper

½ clove garlic, minced or pressed
1 cup milk
¼ cup skim-milk solids
1 tablespoon whole-wheat flour
1 cup rich stock or bouillon made
with 2 beef cubes
2 slices bacon—or 2 tablespoons
butter

If you have soaked the soybeans, bring them to just below a
boil in the soaking water, and simmer, covered, for 3 to 4 hours.
If you have frozen them, drop the frozen block into 4 cups of
boiling vegetable water. When boiling point is reached, lower
heat and simmer for 2 hours.

At the end of the cooking period, add chopped celery, onion,
salt, pepper, and garlic and simmer for 30 minutes. Force
through food mill or sieve and return to pot. Combine milk, milk
solids, and flour and stir into simmering purée. Add and stir
stock. In separate skillet fry bacon until crisp, drain, and reserve
both bacon and drippings. Taste the soup. If you find it too
dry, add some of the bacon drippings or stir in 2 tablespoons of
butter. Taste again and correct seasonings if necessary. Serve
in bowls or plates and crumble the crisp bacon over them as
garnish. *Serves 4 to 6.*

(For even better nutrition, add up to 1 tablespoon of yeast
flakes per serving and/or sprinkle with wheat germ.)

COLD SOUPS

On a hot summer day appetites may lag but nutritional requirements remain constant. A refreshing, cooling soup replen-
ishes minerals which may be lost via the pores and also provides
proteins and vitamins to compensate for spent energies.

TOMATO–COTTAGE CHEESE SOUP

1 can (10 ounces) condensed to-
    mato soup or purée
2 cups milk
½ cup skim-milk solids
1 tablespoon lemon juice
½ teaspoon salt

¼ teaspoon black pepper
dash of cayenne
½ cup fine-curd cottage cheese
2 tablespoons chopped onion
1 tablespoon chopped chives
1 teaspoon chopped parsley

Put condensed soup in mixing bowl and stir until smooth. Combine milk with milk solids and add. Stir until well blended. Add lemon juice and seasonings. Stir or beat until thoroughly mixed. Combine cottage cheese, onion, chives, and parsley and spoon into soup like dumplings. Chill in refrigerator for ½ hour or more. If desired, garnish with thin slices of unpeeled cucumbers or radishes. *Serves 4.*

CUCUMBER SOUP

2 medium-large cucumbers
1 onion
1 cup (vegetable) water
1 teaspon salt
⅛ teaspoon pepper
½ bay leaf—or 1 tablespoon
    chopped fresh dill
3 tablespoons whole-wheat or un-
    bleached flour

2 cups stock, bouillon made with
    chicken cubes, or 1 can con-
    sommé diluted with ⅔ cup
    water
1 cup sour cream
1 tablespoon chopped chives or
    parsley
(1 tablespoon grated lemon rind)

Slice unpeeled cucumbers in half lengthwise and scoop out seeds. Dice cucumbers and onion, cover with water, add salt, pepper, and bay leaf (or dill), and bring to the boiling point. (Remove bay leaf.) Make a smooth paste of the flour and about ½ cup of the stock, and stir into remainder of stock. Stir until well blended, and add to boiling cucumber and onion mixture. Simmer for 10 minutes. Cool slightly; then force through sieve or food mill and let cool to room temperature. Add sour cream, stir well, and chill in the refrigerator. Serve in chilled bowls and garnish with chopped chives or parsley (and grated lemon rind). *Serves 4.*

GREEN SOUP

1 pound greens (spinach, Swiss
    chard, beet tops)
1 quart vegetable water
2 teaspoons lemon juice
½ cup sour cream

½ cup diced mixed raw vege-
    tables (cucumber, radish,
    scallions, celery, carrots)
½ teaspoon salt
⅛ teaspoon pepper

Wash greens and put them in a saucepan without adding water; cover and cook over moderate heat until tender—about 5 minutes. Remove greens from pan, reserving water which has been extracted from them. Put greens through food mill (or electric blender) until thoroughly minced. Add vegetable water to pan in which greens were cooked and bring to a boil. Stir in puréed greens. Remove from heat in 1 minute, add lemon juice and seasonings, stir, and chill in refrigerator. Just before serving, combine sour cream and chopped vegetables. Drop this by the spoonful into soup in bowls. *Serves 4 to 6.*

PUREE OF CARROTS OR BEETS

2 cups diced or grated young car-
    rots or beets
1 tablespoon chopped onion
1 tablespoon chopped celery
½ cup shredded green cabbage
3 cups stock, vegetable water, or
    bouillon made with cubes

½ cup cooked brown rice
½ teaspoon salt
½ teaspoon brown sugar
1 cup sour cream
2 tablespoons chopped chives or
    parsley

Put vegetables in 1 cup of the stock, bring to boil, and cook only until tender. Force vegetables and brown rice through food mill or sieve. Return to heat; add remaining stock, salt, and sugar; and stir until well blended. Chill in refrigerator. Stir in sour cream before serving and garnish with chopped chives or parsley. *Serves 4 to 6.*

FRESH FRUIT SOUP

The seasonal supply of fresh fruits and berries—and your imagination—are the chief ingredients for a delightful, nutritious meal-starter.

130

4 cups mixed fresh fruits (almost
   any fruit available plus
   grapes and berries—pretend
   you are making a fruit cocktail)
cold water
2 teaspoons cornstarch

½ teaspoon salt
1 stick cinnamon
⅛ teaspoon nutmeg
(honey or brown sugar to taste)
4 tablespoons fruit wine—or
   cream

Dice fruits, carefully reserving the juices. If berries are used, mash them slightly with a fork and reserve the juices. Measure the juices and add enough cold water to yield 1 quart. Dissolve cornstarch in ¼ cup of this liquid, put in pan over low heat, and cook, stirring, until clear. Combine with fruit, remaining liquid, salt, and spices and boil for 15 minutes. Remove cinnamon, taste, and sweeten with honey or brown sugar if absolutely necessary. Chill thoroughly. For gala occasions, add 1 tablespoon of wine to each adult serving. For children, add 1 tablespoon cream. For adults wishing to gain weight, add both. *Serves 4.*

The Wonderful
One-dish Meal

7

The Wonderful
One-dish Meal

Modern home cooks take kindly to the one-dish meal for
entertaining and for family approval. Nutritionists take kindly
to it, too, especially if it is served with a green salad and a simple
dessert.

Many casseroles, stews, and skillet recipes can be prepared in
advance, requiring only last-minute heating, and this one fact
alone is enough to endear them to busy housewives. Equally busy
children also welcome the one-dish meal, for it permits them to
leave the table quickly so they can get on with their jobs as
television critics and gunslingers.

Aside from its advantages in time and convenience, the one-
dish meal provides an attractive vehicle for nutritional treasures
otherwise scorned or merely tolerated. The violent vegetable
hater somehow relaxes his prejudice when greens, yellows, or
other edible colors are absorbed into the melting pot of a hand-
some casserole or aromatic stew. The milk refuser (this may be
an older child—say, one around 60) sees no harm in a creamy,
bubbling dish brought to the table from the oven. The meat
rejecter (again, perhaps an oldster) doesn't mind meat nearly
so much when nothing has to be cut with a knife or chewed with
blunt, painful, or imitation teeth.

CASSEROLE AND SKILLET DISHES

LIVER WITH BROWN RICE

1 medium onion, chopped
3 tablespoons butter or margarine
1 pound beef, calf, or chicken liver cut into small pieces
3 tablespoons wheat germ
1½ cups stock (pages 108-112)

2 tablespoons whole-wheat flour
2½ cups cooked brown rice
1 tablespoon chopped parsley
½ teaspoon salt
⅛ teaspoon pepper
pinch of oregano or basil

Sauté onion in 1 tablespoon of the melted butter until well coated and glazed but not brown. Melt 2 tablespoons butter in same skillet. Dredge liver in wheat germ and fry, turning once, for 2 to 5 minutes (the longer time for beef liver). Combine stock with flour; add liver and all other ingredients. Mix well. Put into lightly greased casserole and bake at 350° for 20 minutes, or until piping hot. *Serves 4 to 6.*

FISH PIE

3 tablespoons butter or margarine
3 tablespoons unbleached flour
2 cups warm milk
½ cup skim-milk solids
1 teaspoon salt
⅛ teaspoon pepper
½ pound grated unprocessed yellow cheese

2 tablespoons chopped onions
1 large red or green pepper, chopped
1½ pounds any fish fillet cut into bite-size pieces
½ cup wheat germ

In saucepan, melt butter, add flour, and blend until smooth. Stir in warm milk, milk solids, salt, and pepper, and heat, stirring, until mixture is thick and smooth. Add all but ¼ cup of the grated cheese and stir until melted. Add chopped onions and peppers, lower heat, and continue to cook without boiling while you lightly grease a casserole. Sprinkle bottom of casserole with half of the wheat germ; then alternate layers of fish and sauce. Sprinkle top with remaining wheat germ and grated cheese. Bake at 350°, uncovered, until cheese melts and browns. *Serves 4 to 6.*

CASSEROLE CORNED BEEF AND CABBAGE

1 small head green cabbage, shredded
1 cup lightly salted water
2 tablespoons butter or margarine
2 tablespoons unbleached flour
1½ cups milk
⅓ cup skim-milk solids

1 pound lean cooked corned beef, cut into pieces (or 1-pound can corned beef)
½ cup grated unprocessed yellow cheese
¼ cup wheat germ

Cook shredded cabbage in salted water until barely tender—about 5 minutes. Drain and reserve cabbage. Melt butter, blend with flour, and add milk and milk solids. Stir until sauce thickens. Lightly grease casserole and arrange layers of cabbage, corned beef, and most of the cheese. Pour cream sauce over this and sprinkle with wheat germ and remaining cheese. Bake at 350° for 30 minutes, until cheese melts and browns. *Serves 4.*

SPAGHETTI GOULASH

1 pound chopped beef
½ teaspoon salt
⅛ teaspoon pepper
pinch of basil or oregano
1 cup chopped onions

1 cup chopped green peppers
2 cups cooked spaghetti * (or 1 can prepared spaghetti)
1 cup Italian meat sauce † (or 1 can prepared sauce)

Brown beef, using no extra shortening unless it is very lean. Break it with a fork as it cooks. Season with salt, pepper, and basil or oregano. Remove meat with slotted spoon and reserve. In meat drippings sauté onions and green peppers until well coated. (If necessary, add a little cooking oil.) Return meat to skillet; add and mix in spaghetti and sauce. Simmer for 10 minutes, until piping hot. *Serves 4.*

PORK AND RICE

1 pound lean pork
2 cups chopped onions
1 cup chopped celery
1 cup chopped green pepper
2 tablespoons cooking oil
4 cups stewed tomatoes

1 teaspoon brown sugar
1 teaspoon salt
¼ teaspoon pepper
1 cup uncooked brown rice
1 cup grated unprocessed yellow cheese

---

* See note, page 92.
† Page 143.

Trim pork closely and cut into small cubes. Heat fat trimmings in large skillet until bottom is coated enough to brown the meat on all sides. Remove and reserve meat, discarding the fat. In the same skillet, sauté onions, celery, and green pepper in hot cooking oil for 3 or 4 minutes. Drain vegetables and combine with tomatoes, sugar, and seasonings. Add uncooked rice and mix well. Cover bottom of casserole with half of the vegetable-rice mixture; add half of the browned pork and half of the grated cheese. Repeat these layers, topping them with the remaining cheese. Cover tightly and bake at 350° for 1½ hours. Uncover and bake 30 minutes more. *Serves 4 to 6.*

FREDERICKS' CASSEROLE

2 large sweet potatoes, or 4 small ones
3 tablespoons milk
1 tablespoon skim-milk solids
2 tablespoons wheat germ
1 tablespoon butter

salt and pepper
1 tablespoon orange juice
2 cups ground or minced cooked ham
8 slices bacon
4 eggs

Boil sweet potatoes in their jackets until soft; then peel and mash the pulp with milk, milk solids, wheat germ, butter, and seasonings to taste. Mix with orange juice. Lightly grease a casserole and line it with half of the mashed potato mixture. Spread all but 4 tablespoons of the ham over the sweet potato lining. Shape 4 cones of the remaining sweet potatoes, denting the peaks with a spoon. Put a tablespoonful of ham in each crater. Put in 325° oven while you fry bacon until it is crisp and poach the eggs. Place a poached egg on top of each potato crater and garnish with bacon. *Serves 4.*

STUFFED CABBAGE LEAVES

1 cup uncooked brown rice
4 cups boiling lightly salted water
1 cup diced lean pork
1 cup diced lean beef
1 medium onion
½ teaspoon nutmeg
1 teaspoon lemon juice

2 eggs, beaten
(1–2 tablespoons wheat germ, yeast flakes, or brewers' yeast)
12 large cabbage leaves
2 cups stewed or canned whole peeled tomatoes
1 cup sour cream

138

Cook rice in briskly boiling water for 15 minutes. Drain. Put it through the grinder with pork, beef, and onion. Add nutmeg, lemon juice, and beaten eggs (and wheat germ or yeast), and mix thoroughly. Wilt cabbage leaves until they are pliable by pouring a little boiling water over them. Remove tough core at base of leaves. Put 2 tablespoons of the meat mixture in center of each leaf and fold over the edges, starting to roll at the thick end of the leaves. Fasten securely with toothpicks. Put cabbage rolls in lightly greased baking dish or casserole and cover with tomatoes. Bake, covered, at 300° for 1 hour. Remove from oven, drain off liquid, and combine it with the sour cream for a sauce. *Serves 6.*

Note: A somewhat more nutritious but equally good-tasting recipe would be to omit the pork and substitute 1 cup of ground beef liver, kidney, or heart. Tomato sauce, soup, or purée may be used in place of the sour cream.

GOOD NUTRITION MACARONI AND CHEESE

2 cups (½ pound) enriched elbow macaroni *
2 quarts boiling water with 2 teaspoons salt
2 tablespoons butter or margarine
2 tablespoons unbleached or whole-wheat flour
2 cups warm milk
¼ cup skim-milk solids

salt, pepper, or paprika to taste
2 eggs
¼ pound chipped beef—or 1 to 2 cups any leftover cooked meat, fish, or fowl
1 cup grated unprocessed yellow cheese
½ cup wheat germ
¼ cup coarse whole-wheat bread crumbs

Drop macaroni slowly into boiling salted water and cook until tender but not soft—about 7 to 10 minutes. Drain. Melt butter in saucepan, mix into smooth paste with flour, and slowly add warm milk and milk solids. Season to taste and stir over low heat until mixture is smooth and begins to thicken. Remove from heat and cool slightly. Stir eggs with fork and beat them into the sauce. In lightly greased casserole arrange layers of cooked macaroni, sauce, meat, wheat germ, and cheese. Top with sprinkling of

* See note, page 92.

cheese and whole-wheat crumbs. Bake at 375° until cheese melts and begins to brown. *Serves 4 to 6.*

BAKED STUFFED PEPPERS

4 large, fleshy bell peppers
1 pound chopped beef—or 1 pound mixed chopped beef and country sausage
1 cup cooked brown rice
¼ cup wheat germ

¼ cup grated unprocessed yellow cheese
1 egg
½ clove garlic, minced or pressed
1 cup Italian meat sauce—your own (page 143) or canned

Cut (and save) stem ends from peppers and remove seeds. Brown chopped beef or meat mixture slowly in its own fat, pouring off excess and crumbling it with a fork as it cooks. Mix cooked meat with all other ingredients except spaghetti sauce. Stuff peppers with the mixture. Stand peppers upright in lightly greased baking dish, surround them with ½ cup of water, cap with stem ends, and bake at 350° until peppers are tender. Serve with spaghetti sauce. *Serves 4.*

SEA-FOOD POLENTA

6 cups lightly salted vegetable water
1 cup undegerminated yellow corn meal
¼ cup wheat germ
6 slices bacon
2 medium onions, chopped

¼ cup chopped green pepper
1 cup Italian meat sauce—your own (page 143) or canned
1 pound cooked shrimp, lobster, or crab meat—or 1 pound cooked fillets—or 2 cans tuna fish or salmon

Bring vegetable water to a boil and slowly add corn meal and wheat germ. Cook over low heat, stirring, until mushy. Brown bacon until almost crisp and remove from pan. Fry onions and pepper in bacon drippings for 2 minutes, remove with slotted spoon, and combine with spaghetti sauce and sea food. Line a lightly greased casserole with about two-thirds of the corn meal, fill with sea-food mixture, and top with remaining corn meal. Arrange bacon on top and bake at 350° for 15 to 20 minutes, until bacon is crisp. *Serves 4 to 6.*

ENRICHED TAMALE PIE

1½ cups undegerminated yellow
    corn meal
½ cup wheat germ
1 quart salted vegetable water
1 tablespoon olive oil
2 tablespoons minced onions
½ clove garlic, minced or pressed

1 pound chopped beef
2 cups stewed tomatoes
1 cup stock or bouillon
½ to 1 teaspoon chili powder
pinch of basil
2 eggs, lightly beaten
1 cup pitted black olives

Stir corn meal and wheat germ slowly into boiling vegetable water and cook over low heat, stirring, until mushy. Set aside to cool. Sauté onions and garlic in olive oil for 2 minutes. Add chopped beef and break with a fork as it browns. Mix meat with stewed tomatoes and stock, and season with chili powder and basil. Stir lightly beaten eggs into cooled corn-meal mush and combine with meat mixture and olives. Pour into lightly greased casserole and bake at 350° until piping hot—or keep hot in a chafing dish. If you prefer, you can press half of the corn-meal–egg mixture into the bottom of the casserole, fill with the meat mixture, and top with the remaining corn meal formed into walnut-size balls. *Serves 4 to 6.*

SEA-FOOD (OR VARIETY) RAREBIT

Welsh rarebit is a fine milk and cheese dish. The addition of eggs and your choice of sea food or organ meat makes it an exceptionally high protein recipe.

½ pound coarsely grated yellow
    cheese
2 tablespoons butter or marga-
    rine, melted
¾ cup milk
¼ cup skim-milk solids
2 eggs, lightly beaten
¼ teaspoon salt

a few grains of cayenne
1 cup or more oysters, clams,
    cooked boneless fish; or
    cooked diced liver, kidney,
    brains, heart
4 slices whole-wheat bread,
    toasted

Add cheese to melted butter over low heat. As cheese melts, gradually add milk, milk solids, lightly beaten eggs, and seasonings, stirring constantly. When smooth and hot (don't let it boil) add the sea food or diced organ meat. Serve on toasted whole-wheat bread. *Serves 4.*

141

OYSTER (OR CLAM) AND EGGPLANT CASSEROLE

Eggplant is not an especially exciting vegetable nutritionally, but it is delicious, low-calory, and nice and bulky—very fine for extending recipes. Used in combination with the high proteins, vitamins, and minerals of oysters or clams and cheese, with the vitamin C of tomatoes, and the altogether virtuous qualities of wheat germ instead of the usual bread crumbs, eggplant becomes the proud bearer of superb nutrition.

1 medium eggplant, peeled and cut in ¼-inch slices
3 large tomatoes, peeled and thinly sliced—or 2 cups canned tomatoes
2 cups grated yellow cheese

1 cup or more raw oysters or clams, coarsely chopped
½ cup wheat germ
2 tablespoons butter or margarine, melted

Alternate layers of eggplant, tomatoes, grated cheese, and chopped oysters or clams in a lightly greased casserole. Sprinkle with wheat germ and melted butter or margarine. Bake at 375° for 1 hour. *Serves 4 to 6.*

Note: This recipe can also be used with 1 cup or more diced cooked lamb instead of oysters or clams.

VEAL-EGGPLANT PARMIGIANA

Good nutrition suggests that you combine two popular items usually served separately in Italian restaurants. Note also that this recipe calls for a meat sauce instead of the usual tomato sauce.

2 eggs
2 tablespoons milk or cream
1 pound Italian style veal cutlets—very thin, very lean
1 medium eggplant, peeled and cut into ½-inch slices
½ cup wheat germ

1 clove garlic, minced
(about) 3 tablespoons olive oil
2½-3 cups Italian meat sauce (recipe follows)
½ pound Mozzarella cheese
grated Parmesan cheese

Beat eggs with milk or cream. Dip veal in beaten egg, then in wheat germ. Do the same with the sliced eggplant. Brown minced garlic in 2 tablespoons olive oil. Remove garlic. Brown prepared veal for 5 to 6 minutes on each side and remove. Add remaining

142

oil and brown prepared eggplant for 3 to 4 minutes on each side. Cover bottom of baking dish with 1 cup of sauce. Alternate veal and eggplant in layers, cover with 1 cup of sauce, and top with thin slices of Mozzarella. Pour remaining sauce over this and sprinkle with Parmesan cheese. Bake at 300° until Mozzarella melts and bubbles. *Serves 4 to 6.*

Italian Meat Sauce

1 clove garlic, minced or pressed
1 small onion, chopped
1 small green pepper, chopped
2 tablespoons olive oil
½ pound ground beef (up to half of this may be ground pork)

2 cups (1 large can) Italian tomato purée
1 small can Italian tomato paste
pinch of basil
salt and pepper to taste
(¼–½ cup dry red wine)

Sauté garlic, onion, and pepper in olive oil for 3 minutes. Add and brown ground meat, crumbling with a fork as it cooks. Pour off excess oil and drippings. Add purée, paste, and seasonings. Cover pan, lower heat, and simmer very slowly for at least 1 hour. If you have time for this to simmer longer (the secret of really good Italian sauce), you may add, if or when it seems necessary, up to a cup of tomato purée, juice, or stewed tomatoes. Just before sauce is to be served, stir in wine and simmer for 5 minutes.

FISH BAKE

4 large pieces (about 2 pounds) any fish fillet—flounder, perch, sole, swordfish
1½ cups mashed potatoes
1 cup cottage cheese
½ cup sour cream

¾ teaspoon salt
⅛ teaspoon pepper
⅔ cup milk
1 tablespoon butter
⅛ cup wheat germ

Place two slices of fish in a lightly greased casserole. Mix together the mashed potatoes, cottage cheese, sour cream, and seasonings. Spread half of this mixture over fish and repeat the layers. Pour milk over the layers, dot with butter, and sprinkle with wheat germ. Bake at 350° for 30 minutes. *Serves 4.*

CASSEROLE ESPAGNOLE

1 pound lean beef—chuck, shin, round	½ cup chopped onions
1 teaspoon unseasoned granulated meat tenderizer	3 tablespoons cooking oil
	½ teaspoon salt
1 large green pepper, coarsely chopped	⅛ teaspoon pepper
	1½ cups cooked brown rice
1 cup chopped green celery	1½ cups stewed tomatoes
	½ cup grated yellow cheese

Tenderize beef for 1 hour. Sauté chopped vegetables in 2 tablespoons of the cooking oil until wilted. Remove vegetables from skillet with slotted spoon. Add remaining tablespoon of oil to skillet. Cut tenderized beef into small cubes, season with salt and pepper, and brown quickly in the hot oil, turning frequently. Mix sautéed vegetables and beef with cooked rice and put into lightly greased baking dish. Pour tomatoes over this mixture, sprinkle with grated cheese, and bake for 40 minutes at 350°. *Serves 4 to 6.*

HIGH-PROTEIN-VITAMIN BAKE

1 pound pork sausage meat	½ cup wheat germ
4 cups milk	2 tablespoons yeast flakes
½ cup skim-milk solids	1 teaspoon salt
½ cup undegerminated yellow corn meal	1 cup grated yellow cheese
	4 eggs, separated

Shape sausage meat into flat patties and brown slowly without adding fat—5 to 6 minutes per side. Remove and drain on paper towel. Combine milk with milk solids and scald 3 cups of the mixture. Slowly stir in corn meal, wheat germ, yeast flakes, salt, and grated cheese. Mix well and cook over low heat, stirring continuously, until cheese melts and mixture thickens—about 5 minutes. Remove from heat and stir in remaining cup of (cold) milk. Allow this to cool further. Beat egg yolks until light and frothy and add them to the cereal mixture, blending thoroughly. Beat egg whites until stiff and fold into mixture. Pour into lightly greased casserole, arrange partially cooked patties on top, and bake at 350° for 40 minutes. *Serves 4 to 6.*

144

CHILI CON CARNE

2 cups (1 pound) dried kidney beans
1½ quarts rapidly boiling (vegetable) water
1 teaspoon salt
1 bay leaf
½ cup chopped onions
1 clove garlic, minced
2 tablespoons cooking oil
1 pound chopped beef

1½ cups stewed tomatoes
2 tablespoons yeast flakes
1 teaspoon salt
1 teaspoon brown sugar
2–6 teaspoons chili powder, depending on how spicy you like chili to be
½ small head lettuce, shredded
1 large onion, finely chopped
1 cup pitted ripe olives

Drop washed kidney beans slowly into boiling water, trying not to disturb the boil. Stir in salt and add bay leaf. Reduce heat to slow boil and cook until skin of bean cracks when blown on—about 1½ to 2 hours. Drain, reserving bean water. In large, heavy kettle, sauté onions and garlic in oil for 2 or 3 minutes. Add chopped beef and brown, breaking beef with a fork as it cooks. Add tomatoes and 1 cup of the bean water, and stir in yeast flakes, salt, brown sugar, and chili powder. Cook for 20 minutes. Add kidney beans and stir to mix well. If mixture seems too thick, add more bean water (or unseasoned stock). Simmer 30 minutes longer. This can be served immediately, or made ahead for reheating. The flavor intensifies on standing. If you reheat, add a little more yeast flakes to compensate for vitamin loss. Serve in bowls and garnish with shredded lettuce, chopped onions, and olives. (This is wonderful with guacamole—page 70—and tall glasses of cold milk.) *Serves 6 to 8.*

PILAF

¾ cup uncooked brown rice
3 tablespoons cooking oil
2 tablespoons chopped onion
¼ cup chopped green pepper
2½ cups stewed tomatoes
1 teaspoon salt
⅛ teaspoon paprika
½ teaspoon brown sugar

a few grains of cayenne
1 cup or more cooked shrimp, diced cooked fish, fowl, or meat of any kind
½ cup wheat germ
½ cup grated yellow cheese
2 hard-cooked eggs

Toast rice in skillet in 1 tablespoon of the oil, shaking or stirring to coat the grains. In another skillet sauté onions and

145

green pepper in remaining oil for 2 minutes. Combine with toasted rice, add tomatoes and seasonings, and simmer for 20 minutes, stirring occasionally. Remove from heat and set aside for 30 minutes so rice can absorb moisture. Mix with cooked fish or meat; bake (350°) in lightly greased casserole for 30 minutes, until rice is tender. Sprinkle with wheat germ and grated cheese and return to oven until cheese melts and starts to brown. Garnish with sliced hard-cooked egg. *Serves 4 to 6.*

CURRIED SHRIMP

3–4 quarts water
1 teaspoon salt
½ teaspoon black pepper
¼ teaspoon cayenne
1 clove garlic, minced or pressed

4 or 5 stalks celery with leaves
1 onion, sliced
2 pounds shrimp
1 tablespoon lemon juice

Boil water and seasonings together for 15 minutes. Add shrimp and lemon juice, and boil for 5 minutes. Remove from heat and let shrimp cool in cooking water. Shell and devein.

½ cup finely chopped onions
⅛ pound butter
4 tablespoons unbleached flour
1½–3 teaspoons curry powder
1 teaspoon salt
½ teaspoon brown sugar
⅛ teaspoon cinnamon
¼ teaspoon powdered ginger
2 cups hot, lightly seasoned chick-

en stock—or bouillon, omitting salt from recipe
½ cup chopped firm apple
½ cup seedless raisins (soak in cold water until used)
1 cup light cream
2 tablespoons skim-milk solids
2 cups cooked brown rice

Cook onions in butter until glazed. Using wooden spoon to stir, add and blend thoroughly the flour and all seasonings. Add hot stock slowly, stirring until smooth. Add apples, drained raisins, and cooked shrimp. Just before serving, add cream mixed with milk solids and keep the mixture hot without letting it boil. *Serves 4 to 6.*

For a company dinner, pass small bowlfuls of chutney, grated egg white, grated egg yolk, chopped peanuts or cashews, grated onion, shredded cocoanut, sweet-and-sour sauce.

This recipe can also be used with diced cooked chicken, turkey, veal, or lamb instead of shrimp.

146

SUKIYAKI

Oriental short-cooking of vegetables retains their vitamins, color, and crispness. Made at the table on a Japanese hibachi or in an American electric skillet, this dish is fun for the family as well as excellent nutrition.

4 tablespoons cooking oil
4 cups green celery, cut in ¼-inch diagonal slices
2 thinly sliced onions
1 cup young scallions, cut in 2-inch slices
1 cup coarsely cut green pepper
3 cups thinly sliced mushrooms
1 can drained bamboo shoots
2 firm, fresh tomatoes, thinly sliced
1½ cups stock, concentrated

canned consommé, or bouillon made with 2 beef cubes
½ cup soy sauce
4 teaspoons brown sugar
1 quart whole, young, tender spinach leaves torn to bite-size pieces
1½ pounds tender beefsteak sliced ⅛ inch thick (firm in freezing compartment before slicing)

Heat oil over moderate heat. Add all vegetables except spinach (tomatoes on top), and cook for only 3 or 4 minutes, stirring occasionally. Pour consommé and soy sauce over vegetables and stir. Sprinkle with sugar and stir. Add spinach and wafer-thin slices of beef. Simmer for 5 minutes and serve. *Serves 4 to 6.*

STEWS

Stews can be among the easiest, least expensive, and most nutritionally satisfying and popular one-dish meals. Men—even presidents of the United States—dote on them and occasionally take pride in making them. The recipe given here is basic and sound. Although it specifies beef, any meat the family likes—and some they think they don't like—can be used. Beef heart, for example, makes a delicious stew. Before daring to offer up a whole-hearted stew if your family is unaccustomed to this excellent food, try mixing it with beef at first. Tenderize cubes of heart by marinating them for 1 hour or more in a liquid tenderizer or by sprinkling with a granulated tenderizer.

147

FREDERICKS' BASIC BEEF STEW

2 pounds lean stew beef (chuck, round) cut into 1½-inch cubes

seasoned (salt and pepper) unbleached or whole-wheat flour for dredging

½ cup chopped onions

2 tablespoons cooking oil or rendered beef fat

2 cups boiling vegetable water or unseasoned stock

1 cup stewed tomatoes

2 cups diced potatoes

1 cup each coarsely cut carrots and green beans

½ cup thinly sliced green celery

1 green pepper, coarsely cut

1 tablespoon butter

2–3 tablespoons yeast flakes or brewers' yeast

salt and pepper to taste

(2–4 tablespoons dry red wine)

Dredge beef in seasoned flour and set aside. In large, heavy kettle sauté onions in hot oil or fat until glazed, not brown. Add beef and brown quickly on all sides.* Cover with boiling vegetable water or stock and add stewed tomatoes. Lower heat and simmer, covered, until beef is fork-tender—1 hour or more, depending on cut of beef. In separate saucepans and *very little water* parboil potatoes, carrots, and beans until tender but not soft. Add these vegetables, along with some of the water in which they were cooked, to the stew pot. Sauté celery and green pepper in butter for 3 minutes and add to stew. Stir in yeast; season to taste. Keep heat low and simmer for 20 minutes more. For adults, add dry red wine for the last 5 minutes of cooking. *Serves 4 to 6.*

Note: Vary the seasonings occasionally with your preferences in herbs. There is no limitation on the varieties of vegetables which may be used. Just remember to cook them very briefly toward the end of the beef simmering time—in a minimum of water—and add some of the water to the stew, saving the rest for future recipes.

---

* For low-fat diets, let meat cool completely before adding stock and remove all congealed fat with which it may be coated.

148

SPECIAL CHICKEN STEW

Don't waste a tender chicken on this, unless your family is so fond of what it calls "fricassee" that it pays to take the extra preparation time beyond roasting, broiling, or frying—all good ways of serving young fowl. When the markets offer "stewing" or "soup" chickens at low cost, however, this is your recipe for good nutrition.

1 stewing chicken, 4–6 pounds
3 cups vegetable water
2 teaspoons salt
¼ teaspoon black pepper
3 tablespoons chicken fat or stock
   skimmings
3 tablespoons unbleached flour
1 tablespoon brewers' yeast or
   yeast flakes

12 or more baby carrots
12 or more small white onions
1 cup fresh or frozen peas
2 egg yolks, beaten with 2 tablespoons milk and 1 tablespoon
   skim-milk solids

Disjoint chicken and put the pieces slowly into boiling vegetable water seasoned with salt and pepper. Cover pot tightly, lower heat, and simmer until chicken legs are tender—around 2 hours. Let chicken cool in the cooking water. When cool enough to handle, remove chicken, discard the skin, and cut the meat from the bones in fairly large pieces. Reserve the meat and let cooking water chill in refrigerator until fat rises to top. Skim off this surface fat, add to it enough chicken fat to yield 3 tablespoons, and melt it. Blend with flour and yeast and add to cold stock. Stir until smooth. Return to heat and simmer slowly while you cook carrots, onions, and peas in very little water until tender. To simmering stock slowly add beaten egg-milk mixture. Stir until thickened, and add boned chicken and vegetables. Serve with wheat-germ biscuits (page 203). *Serves 4 to 6.*

BEEF STROGANOFF

This sounds so fancy but is actually so simple that it is a joy to serve to family or guests even on very short notice. If budget doesn't matter, use sirloin or any other choice, tender beef. If budget does matter, use any of the lean cuts—top or bottom

149

round, chuck—and tenderize for 1 hour or more before proceeding.

1½ pounds lean beef
2 tablespoons finely chopped or grated onion
3 tablespoons butter
1 pound mushrooms, sliced—or 2 cans button mushrooms
½ teaspoon salt
sprinkling of black pepper

¼ teaspoon basil
sprinkling of nutmeg
1 tablespoon yeast flakes or brewers' yeast
1 cup warm sour cream
2 cups cooked brown or converted rice

Pound beef until it is very thin and cut into 2-inch squares or 1½- by 4-inch strips. Set aside. Sauté onion in 1 tablespoon of the butter until glazed, not brown. Add beef and sauté until tender—about 5 minutes—turning once or twice until nicely brown. Remove beef to heated plate. Sauté mushrooms in remaining 2 tablespoons of butter—2 or 3 minutes only. Return beef to pan; add and stir seasonings and yeast. Reduce heat. Just before serving, add warm sour cream and stir. Do not let this boil. Serve over rice. This is excellent with Harvard beets or glazed carrots (recipes follow). *Serves 4 to 6.*

Harvard Beets

¼ cup honey
1 tablespoon cornstarch
½ teaspoon salt
¼ teaspoon ground cloves
½ cup mild cider vinegar

½ cup orange juice
2–3 cups boiled sliced beets—or 1 large can baby beets
1 tablespoon butter

Put all ingredients except beets and butter in top of a double boiler and cook over boiling water, stirring until smooth. Taste to correct to your idea of sweet-sour combination (vinegars vary in acidity). Continue cooking and stirring until clear. Add beets; lower heat. Just before serving, add and stir in butter. *Serves 4 to 6.*

Glazed Carrots

12–18 medium carrots
2 tablespoons butter
½ teaspoon salt

dash of paprika
¼ cup dark molasses or honey

Boil unpeeled carrots in very little water until they are tender but not too soft—about 15 to 20 minutes. Remove from water (save water for other recipes) and cut lengthwise into halves. Melt butter in heavy skillet, add carrots, sprinkle with salt and paprika, and cover with molasses or honey. Cook slowly over low heat, basting with pan juice until glazed. *Serves 4 to 6.*

Note: An equally simple, delicious version of Stroganoff uses chicken livers instead of beef. The procedure is identical, except that of course you don't have to pound the livers. Just cut them into pieces and sauté very briefly until tender—seldom more than 3 minutes. Use chicken fat instead of butter.

The Best Chapter
in the Book

8

The Best Chapter
in the Book

During the course of my nutrition broadcasts, I have learned that the instant I mention organ or glandular meats as staples of diet, that is the instant I lose attention—except on the part of the truly nutrition-minded.

The average American's aversion to a long list of foods providing the most superb protective nutrition available is as deeply ingrained as it is incomprehensible. Aside from occasional condescension to calf's liver, chicken liver, cocktail pâté (goose liver), and sweetbreads, the ordinary man, woman, and child in this country goes through life with only a nodding acquaintance with the excellent, protein-rich glandular meats.

What do you suppose the vitamin manufacturers use as source material for many of the pills, tablets, and capsules which have become almost necessities for supplementing American diets? They use livers, kidneys, hearts, and brains of fish and meat animals.

It's hard to trace modern American apathy toward organ meats. Certainly our ancestors had no such apathy, nor do many of the world's current populations—both civilized and primitive. In many parts of the world an animal's vital organs are preferred over the flesh and muscles which constitute American preference.

In those parts of the world, especially if the population has not been exposed to our overprocessed, overrefined foods, the general health of the community is far better than ours.

More than one adventurer fallen into Arctic wastes or jungle tangles has been brought back to vigorous life by natives who fed him the heart, liver, or kidneys of a fresh-killed animal. Among hunting tribes in Africa and South America, the glands and organs are presented as choice prizes to the chiefs, the bravest warriors, and the pregnant women.

Properly prepared organ meats are tasty, and there are excellent reasons why they should appear more often on your dinner table. Nature is provident and protective. In her estimation, a living being's heart, pancreas, liver, kidneys, and brains are far more important than its tendons or contour. Consequently, the organs—not the muscles or flesh—are the prime depots and repositories for the best nutrients extracted from food. The organs give the best of nutrients because they get the best of nutrients—topnotch, body-repairing proteins essential aminos, natural vitamins and minerals. They are minimal in fat and almost devoid of carbohydrates. They contain agents vitally important in the metabolism of fats, the conversion of sugars, the release of essential oxygen, the building of rich blood.

If this book serves no purpose other than to induce you to serve more of the organ meats more often, its author will feel his mission almost accomplished. The "almost" is a necessary qualification. The addition of organ meats to your diet will improve it substantially. If you also reduce your intake of refined sugars and flours and accept the recommendations for breakfasts, breadstuffs, and desserts in other chapters, you will truly be on the road to optimum nutrition.

BRAINS

We might as well plunge right in and tackle first the organ that comes first in the alphabetical list of glandular meats. Steel yourself, if you're one of those who cringe at the thought or mention of brains as food. Be adventurous and courageous and try at least one of the following recipes at least once. If you do, I'm confident you will try them all. Any kind of brains available from your butcher may be used—calf, beef, lamb, or pork.

To Prepare Brains for Recipes

Wash brains quickly in about a quart of very cold water, or under running water. Remove membranes and drain.

For most recipes, brains do not require precooking. However, palates unfamiliar with their soft texture may prefer them slightly toughened by steaming or simmering. Whenever you precook them by either method, be sure to save (refrigerated) the water in which they cooked. It is teeming with B vitamins and can be added unobtrusively to soups, stews, and stocks.

To steam brains: Put them in a heavy saucepan with ¼ cup of water and 1 tablespoon of vinegar. Cover pan with a tight-fitting lid and steam for 15 minutes.

To simmer brains: Barely cover them with lightly salted water to which you have added 1 tablespoon of vinegar. Simmer gently for 20 minutes. They should never be permitted to boil violently. Their proteins should harden slowly, like the proteins of eggs.

BRAIN "OYSTERS"

1 pound brains	dash of pepper
2 eggs, slightly beaten	½ cup wheat germ
1 tablespoon milk	oil for deep frying
½ teaspoon salt	

Prepare brains by method given above. Cut drained brains into pieces about the size of small oysters. Stir beaten eggs with milk, salt, and pepper. Dip "oysters" in this mixture, then in wheat germ. Repeat. Let stand for a few minutes, or refrigerate for ½ hour. Fry in deep, hot oil until golden brown. If you like fried oysters, you'll like these. *Serves 4.*

THE BEST CHAPTER *The Carlton Fredericks Cook Book*

BRAINS A LA KING

1 pound brains
4 tablespoons butter or margarine
3 tablespoons unbleached or
    whole-wheat flour
2 cups milk
¼ cup skim-milk solids
½ cup diced green celery

½ cup chopped green pepper
2 tablespoons chopped pimiento
    or red pepper (sweet)
1 tablespoon grated onion
½ teaspoon salt
⅛ teaspoon pepper

Steam or simmer brains (page 157). Drain, and cut or separate into small pieces. Melt 3 tablespoons of butter and blend with flour into a smooth paste. Heat milk and milk solids and add to flour blend, stirring to avoid lumps. Cook over low heat until mixture thickens. Sauté vegetables for 2 minutes in remaining tablespoon of butter and add to white sauce. Season with salt and pepper. Add brains and heat thoroughly without boiling. Serve on whole-wheat toast. If you like chicken à la king, you'll like this. *Serves 4 to 6.*

Note: Timid beginners can add the precooked brains to chicken à la king recipes in any desired proportions.

WESTERN SCRAMBLED EGGS WITH BRAINS

2 tablespoons minced green or red
    pepper
1 tablespoon minced onion
2 tablespoons bacon drippings or
    ham fat

½ pound brains
4–6 eggs
¼ cup milk or cream
1 teaspoon soy sauce
salt and pepper to taste

Sauté pepper and onions in bacon or ham drippings until they are glazed and golden. Dice and add brains and sauté for 10 minutes, stirring to brown evenly. Beat eggs with milk and soy sauce, add to skillet, and scramble. Season to taste. *Serves 4 to 6.*

BRAINBURGERS

1 pound brains
3 eggs, slightly beaten
½ teaspoon salt
⅛ teaspoon pepper
3 tablespoons unbleached or whole-wheat flour

2 tablespoons wheat germ
2–3 tablespoons grated yellow cheese
oil or shortening for frying— about ¼ inch in bottom of heavy skillet

Dice or break brains into very small pieces. Add all other ingredients (except oil or fat) and blend thoroughly. Drop by the spoonful into hot oil or fat and fry until brown and crisp— about 5 minutes per side. Serve on whole-wheat bread or wheat-germ biscuits (page 203) and pass sliced onions, tomatoes, pickles, relish, chili sauce, or catsup—everything you'd reach for when you order a hamburger. *Makes 6 to 12 patties, depending on size.*

BRAINS ITALIAN STYLE

Preheat oven to 400°.

1 pound brains
2 tablespoons olive oil
½ teaspoon salt
⅛ teaspoon pepper

1 tablespoon capers
1 cup pitted black olives
½ cup wheat germ or whole-wheat bread crumbs

Simmer brains (page 157) 30 minutes and cut into 4 or 6 pieces. Coat bottom and sides of baking dish with 1 tablespoon of olive oil. Spread brains over bottom of dish, season with salt and pepper, and sprinkle with capers and olives. Top with wheat germ (or bread crumbs) and sprinkle with remaining olive oil. Bake at 400° for 15 minutes. *Serves 4 to 6.*

BRAIN CANAPES

Cold:

1 pound brains	2–4 tablespoons chili sauce or cat-
¼ cup each minced onion,	sup
chopped green or red pepper,	1 tablespoon mayonnaise
chopped green celery	1 teaspoon horse-radish
3 hard-cooked eggs, chopped	salt, pepper, cayenne to taste

Simmer brains (page 157) and chop or mash with fork. Add and blend in all other ingredients, seasoning to taste. (For variety, add also a dash each of curry powder and powdered ginger.) Serve on whole-wheat crackers or toast rounds. *Makes enough for a fairly large cocktail party.*

Hot:

1 pound brains	whole-wheat bread cut into small
2 eggs, slightly beaten	rounds
2 tablespoons wheat germ	deep oil or fat for frying
½ teaspoon salt	sliced pimiento-filled olives
⅛ teaspoon pepper	

Steam or simmer brains (page 157) and grind or chop. Add beaten eggs, wheat germ, and seasonings. Spread on whole-wheat rounds and fry in hot oil or fat until bread is crouton-crisp— about 1 minute. Drain on paper towels and top with slices of stuffed olives. *Makes enough for a fairly large cocktail party.*

HEART

Heart, which is a large muscle as well as an organ, has a texture similar to lean beef, veal, or lamb; but it is far richer than any of these in essential protein, vitamins, and minerals.

Because it is comparatively inexpensive many housewives who are pet lovers are accustomed to buying and preparing heart for their dogs or cats but not for their families. Mama, Papa, and the kids partake of an animal's rump, shoulder, or pelvic area while Fido gnaws happily on its nutrient-filled heart. It may or may not be coincidence that in such families the doctor is usually a more familiar figure around the house than the veterinarian.

160

Heart is prepared for cooking by washing in cold water and removing the veins and arteries, if the butcher hasn't already removed them.

SWEET AND SOUR BEEF HEART STUFFED WITH BROWN RICE

1 beef heart (select a small one, about 2½–3 pounds)
1½ cups cooked brown rice
2 tablespoons butter or margarine, melted

¼ cup cooking oil or melted shortening
salt and pepper
1 cup water

Wash and trim heart. Combine cooked rice with melted butter and fill heart cavity. Fasten with skewers. In chicken fryer or other deep covered heavy pan, brown heart, turning frequently, in hot cooking oil or shortening. When nicely and evenly browned, add 1 cup of water (be prepared to add more later) and season lightly with salt and pepper. Cover closely and simmer over low to moderate heat until tender—allow 3 to 3½ hours. Peek once in a while and add a little water if necessary. Don't worry about adding water—you'll be using it later for the sauce. When heart is tender, remove it from the pan and keep it warm while you make the sweet and sour sauce:

2 tablespoons butter
2 tablespoons whole-wheat flour
liquid in which heart was cooked plus enough stock or vegetable water to yield 2 cups
4 tablespoons vinegar

1 tablespoon honey
1 tablespoon brown sugar
1 bay leaf
2 whole cloves
⅛ teaspoon thyme
salt and pepper

Melt butter and blend with flour until smooth. Gradually add the pan liquid, stirring constantly. Cook over low heat until thickened. Add vinegar, honey, sugar, and seasonings and simmer for 15 minutes. Remove bay leaf and cloves. Return heart to pan and reheat. *Serves 4 to 6.*

BRAISED HEART WITH APPLES

½ average beef heart—or 3 pork
    hearts, 4 lamb hearts, or 2
    veal hearts
salt and pepper
(about) 1 cup unbleached or
    whole-wheat flour
2 tablespoons cooking oil

4 hard, sweet apples
¼ cup honey
8 whole cloves
2 small bay leaves, crushed
1 small lemon, thinly sliced
½ cup water

Wash and trim heart. Season with salt and pepper, and roll in flour. Brown in hot oil. Quarter and core apples, but do not peel them. Put heart in lightly greased baking dish, surround with apples, and sprinkle with honey, cloves, and crushed bay leaves. Top with slices of lemon, add water, cover tightly, and bake at 300° until heart is tender—beef, 4 hours; others from 2 to 2½ hours. *Serves 4 to 6.*

HEART FRICASSEE

1 small or ½ large beef heart—or
    3 pork, 4 lamb, or 2 veal
    hearts
(about) 1 cup whole-wheat flour
¼ cup cooking oil
1 teaspoon salt

¼ teaspoon pepper
½ cup chopped or sliced onion
2 cups stewed tomatoes
1 cup coarsely diced carrots
½ cup coarsely cut green peppers

Wash and trim heart. Slice across the grain, dredge pieces in flour, and brown in hot oil. Season, add chopped or sliced onions, and sauté until onions are glazed. Add tomatoes, bring to boiling point, lower heat, and simmer, covered, until heart is tender— about 2¼ hours for beef heart, 1¼ to 1½ hours for others. Parboil carrots in very little water for 5 or 6 minutes, then add them —and the water—along with the green peppers. Simmer for 15 minutes more. *Serves 4 to 6.*

VEAL HEARTS BRAISED IN BUTTERMILK

2 veal hearts
2 cups buttermilk
2 tablespoons unbleached flour

¾ teaspoon salt
⅛ teaspoon black pepper
¼ cup cooking oil

Wash and trim hearts, cut into ½-inch slices, and soak in buttermilk overnight or for several daytime hours in the refrigera-

162

tor. Without draining them, dip heart slices in flour mixed with salt and pepper. Brown in hot oil, turning to brown completely and evenly. Lower heat and add buttermilk in which heart was soaked. Cover closely and simmer until tender—about 1 hour. *Serves 4 to 6.*

HEART AND BEEF MEAT LOAF

1 pound any kind of heart
1 pound chopped beef, or beef trimmings
1 medium onion
1 medium green pepper
½ cup wheat germ
2 slices crustless whole-wheat bread soaked in ½ cup skim milk

½ cup cottage cheese
1 large or 2 small eggs, stirred
2 teaspoons salt
¼ teaspoon black pepper
pinch of cayenne or paprika
1 cup vegetable water, stock, tomato juice, or stale beer for basting

Put heart, beef, onion, and pepper through meat grinder. In large bowl, mix these with all other ingredients in turn—except basting liquid. (The best way to blend meat loaf ingredients is with the hands, in a kneading motion.) Form into a high loaf and center on a lightly greased shallow baking dish. Bake at 325° for 1 hour, basting frequently with liquid. *Serves 6 to 8.*

KIDNEYS

The people who savor kidneys are usually those with gourmet palates who also appreciate such foods as venison, wild duck, and other bagged fowl—the stronger-tasting, gamy meats. The people who scorn kidneys are usually those who, for example, eat only the breast of chicken or turkey, will try domesticated rabbit (but not any brought home by a hunter) on a dare or to be polite, and, as a rule, don't care too much for lamb.

In order to overcome the prejudice of dainty eaters, kidneys should not taste strong. People with robust tastes will eat them anyway, and presumably the ones who need their nutrients most are the ones who say they'd rather starve—which, in a sense, they do, for their eating preferences are likely to lean toward bland, overstarchy foods.

Kidneys need not taste strong, and they need never be anything but tender. The secret of mildness and tenderness is threefold:

1. Fat-trimming and careful, thorough removal of tubes before putting kidneys into or near water.

2. A little vinegar somewhere in the recipe to neutralize taste —or a marinade of French dressing for about an hour or so before proceeding with a recipe.

3. Short cooking.

To Prepare Kidneys for Cooking

Before washing, split kidneys lengthwise and remove tubes. Trim fat. Wash quickly in cold water and remove membranes. Drain or pat dry.

BEEFSTEAK AND KIDNEY STEW

1 pound beef kidneys	2 cups boiling vegetable water
1 tablespoon vinegar	or stock
1 pound lean stew beef cut into 1-inch cubes	1½ cups coarsely cut carrots
seasoned unbleached flour for dredging	1½ cups diced potatoes
	½–1 cup any other vegetables, individual or mixed—beans,
4 tablespoons cooking oil	turnips, celery, etc.
½ chopped onions	salt and pepper
½ cup coarsely cut green peppers	

Prepare kidneys (see above) and cut into ½-inch slices or 1-inch cubes. Sprinkle with vinegar, or marinate in French dressing, and set aside while you make the beef stew: Dredge beef in seasoned flour and brown quickly on all sides in 2 tablespoons of the oil. Add and glaze onions and green peppers. Pour boiling vegetable water or stock over these ingredients, lower heat, and simmer until beef is tender—1 to 1½ hours. Parboil vegetables separately in very little water until not quite tender and add to stew along with some of the cooking waters. Season to taste—a pinch of basil or oregano may be added, if you like these herbs. Now dredge the marinated kidney pieces in seasoned flour, brown quickly in remaining 2 tablespoons of oil, add to stew pot, and simmer for 10 minutes. *Serves 6 to 8.*

Note: This can be converted into a beefsteak and kidney pie by transferring the cooked beef stew to a casserole dish, adding kidneys when they have been browned, topping with biscuit dough (page 203), and baking at 425° until dough is done—about 12 to 15 minutes.

KIDNEY DIABOLO

1 pound beef kidneys
1 tablespoon vinegar
½ cup chopped onions
2 tablespoons cooking oil
½ cup whole-wheat or unbleached flour
2 tablespoons wheat germ

½ cup boiling water or unseasoned stock
1 teaspoon salt
¼ teaspoon black pepper
1½ teaspoons dry mustard
½-¾ cup warm sour cream

Prepare kidneys (page 164) and cut into small pieces. Sprinkle with vinegar and let stand for 1 hour in refrigerator. Glaze onions in oil, roll kidneys in mixture of flour and wheat germ, and brown on top of onions for 2 or 3 minutes, turning to brown evenly. Add boiling liquid and seasonings and stir. Simmer for 10 minutes, lower heat, and stir in sour cream. Do not let it boil. *Serves 4.*

KIDNEY LOAF

1 pound beef, veal, pork, or lamb kidneys
1 tablespoon vinegar
1 green pepper
1 onion
2 or 3 carrots
4 slices whole-wheat bread without crusts, soaked in ½ cup skim milk

½ cup wheat germ
2 eggs, lightly beaten
1 teaspoon salt
¼ teaspoon pepper
¼ teaspoon powdered sage
1 cup vegetable water, stock, tomato juice, or stale beer for basting

Prepare kidneys (page 164), cut into random pieces, and sprinkle with vinegar. Let stand for 1 hour in refrigerator. Put kidneys and vegetables through medium blade of meat grinder. Combine with soaked bread, wheat germ, eggs, and seasonings and blend well. Form into loaf and place in center of lightly greased baking dish and bake at 350° for 1 hour, basting occasionally with liquid. *Serves 4 to 6.*

KIDNEY AND MEAT LOAF

1 pound beef, veal, pork, or lamb
    kidneys
1 tablespoon vinegar
½ cup chopped onions
¼ cup chopped green pepper
1 tablespoon cooking oil
1 pound mixed chopped beef,
    veal, and pork
2 slices crustless whole-wheat
    bread soaked in ½ cup skim
    milk

½ cup wheat germ
1 egg
1 teaspoon salt
¼ teaspoon black pepper
⅛ teaspoon powdered sage or
    thyme
pinch of cayenne
1 cup vegetable water, stock, to-
    mato juice, or stale beer for
    basting

Prepare kidneys (page 164), sprinkle with vinegar, and let stand in refrigerator. Glaze onions and green pepper in oil. Add mixed chopped meats, and brown, breaking with a fork as meat cooks. Put kidneys through medium blade of meat grinder and mix with browned meat, soaked bread, wheat germ, egg, and seasonings. Blend well. Form into loaf and put in center of lightly greased baking dish. Bake at 350° for 1 hour, basting occasionally with liquid. *Serves 6 to 8.*

KIDNEYS A LA KING

1 pound veal or lamb kidneys
1 tablespoon vinegar
½ pound sliced mushrooms
5 tablespoons butter or marga-
    rine
¼ cup chopped onions
¼ cup chopped green, red, or
    mixed peppers

¼ cup chopped green celery
3 tablespoons unbleached or
    whole-wheat flour
1 cup warm milk
1 cup warm stock
2 egg yolks, lightly beaten
salt and pepper to taste
(2–3 tablespoons sherry)

Prepare kidneys (page 164), dice, sprinkle with vinegar, and let stand in refrigerator while you proceed. In large, heavy skillet, sauté mushrooms in 2 tablespoons of the butter or margarine for 2 minutes. Remove from skillet. Sauté vegetables for 2 minutes. Add diced kidneys to skillet and brown, stirring, for 3 minutes. Remove from heat and add mushrooms. Melt remaining 3 tablespoons of butter or margarine in saucepan or double boiler, blend in flour to a smooth paste, and slowly add warm milk and stock, stirring to prevent lumps. Season to taste. When sauce is smooth and hot, reduce heat and stir in lightly beaten egg yolks. Stir as sauce thickens. Add kidney-vegetable mixture, stir thoroughly, and heat without boiling. Just before serving, add 2 or 3 tablespoons of sherry if desired, for adults. Serve on whole-wheat toast or biscuits (page 203). *Serves 4 to 6.*

KIDNEY CREOLE

1 pound beef, veal, pork, or lamb
    kidneys
1 tablespoon vinegar
3 tablespoons whole-wheat flour
3 slices bacon, chopped
½ cup chopped onions
½ cup chopped green peppers

½ teaspoon salt
¼ teaspoon black pepper
1 small garlic clove, finely
    minced
1½ cups stewed tomatoes
½ cup tomato juice or purée

Prepare kidneys (page 164), dice, and sprinkle with vinegar. Let stand for 1 hour in refrigerator. Roll diced kidneys in flour. Fry chopped bacon until almost crisp and drain off drippings. Add diced kidney, chopped vegetables, and seasonings. Stir well and sauté for 5 minutes. Add canned tomatoes and juice, and simmer for 10 minutes. Serve on brown or enriched rice, enriched noodles, or whole-wheat toast or biscuits (page 203). *Serves 4 to 6.*

CURRIED KIDNEYS

1 pound veal or lamb kidneys
1 tablespoon vinegar
½ teaspoon salt
sprinkling of black pepper
2 tablespoons oil or bacon drippings
2 tablespoons unbleached flour
2–4 teaspoons curry powder (de-

pending on how much you
    like curry)
2 tablespoons butter or margarine, melted
½ teaspoon salt
dash of cayenne
1 cup warm milk
2 tablespoons skim-milk solids

Prepare kidneys (page 164), dice, and sprinkle with vinegar. Let stand for 1 hour in refrigerator. Season kidneys with salt and pepper, and brown in oil or bacon drippings for 3 minutes, stirring often. Remove from heat while you make curry sauce: Mix flour and curry powder; blend with melted butter or mar-

167

garine in top of double boiler to a smooth paste. Add seasonings. Mix warm milk with milk solids and add slowly, stirring until smooth and thickened. Add diced kidneys and heat without boiling. *Serves 4 to 6.*

LAMB KIDNEYS GOURMET

1 pound lamb kidneys
1 tablespoon vinegar
salt and pepper
2 tablespoons cooking oil
3 tablespoons butter
1 pound sliced mushrooms
1 tablespoon chopped chives or onion

3 ounces dry red wine (Burgundy, claret, etc.)
½ cup rich beef stock
½ cup stewed tomatoes or tomato purée
2 tablespoons dry white wine (sherry or Madeira—for a gamy taste, use Marsala)

Prepare kidneys (page 164) and cut again, into quarters. Sprinkle with vinegar, season with salt and pepper, and sauté in oil for 2 or 3 minutes, turning frequently until golden brown. Remove from pan and drain on paper towels. Discard oil from pan, wipe with paper towel, melt 2 tablespoons of the butter, and sauté mushrooms for 2 minutes. Add chopped chives or onion and red wine. Cook over low heat until half of the wine evaporates. Add beef stock and tomatoes, and heat. Below boiling point, swirl remaining tablespoon of butter and white wine into sauce. Return kidneys to pan; bring sauce to boiling point. Serve with a sprinkling of chopped parsley. *Serves 4.*

KIDNEY SAUSAGE BAKE WITH BROWN RICE

1 pound beef, veal, or lamb kidneys
1 tablespoon vinegar
½ cup uncooked brown rice
4 cups vegetable water
½ pound pork sausage meat
1 large or 2 small carrots

2 small onions
1 small garlic clove, minced
2 tablespoons chopped parsley
⅛ teaspoon powdered sage
2 tablespoons whole-wheat flour
1 tablespoon yeast flakes or brewers' yeast

Prepare kidneys (page 164), sprinkle with vinegar, dice, and let stand in refrigerator while you prepare rice. Soak rice for 1 hour in vegetable water; then cook it in the same water for 1 hour. Drain, reserving both rice and water. Cook sausage meat slowly over low heat, adding no grease, until enough fat has

168

accumulated in the pan to sauté kidneys. Remove and reserve sausage meat and brown the kidneys for 3 minutes, stirring frequently. Reserve pan liquid. Put kidneys, sausage meat, and vegetables through meat grinder. Mix with parsley and sage. Put cooked rice in lightly greased baking dish, cover with meat mixture, and bake at 350° for 30 minutes. Add flour and yeast to pan liquid, stir until smooth, and add 1 cup of the water in which rice was cooked. Stir until hot and thickened and serve over meat and rice. *Serves 6 to 8.*

LIVER

Please remember that other meat animals besides calves have livers. Calf's liver is very nice, and it provides generous amounts of the vitamins, minerals, and protein for which it is rightly acclaimed. However, the livers of other animals are likely to contain *more* of these essential nutrients per serving—usually because other animals have been permitted to live longer and therefore have had more time to accumulate and store in this vital organ of their bodies the life-preserving, healing, blood-building, health-giving elements it is the liver's function to accumulate and store.

LIVER FRICASSEE

1 pound beef, calf, pork, or lamb liver, sliced	2 cups canned tomatoes
½ teaspoon salt	2 medium green peppers, chopped
⅛ teaspoon pepper	½ cup sliced onions
¼ cup whole-wheat flour	½ teaspoon celery salt
¼ cup bacon drippings or cooking oil	½ teaspoon poultry seasoning

Dredge liver with seasoned flour and brown on both sides in bacon drippings or oil. Add tomatoes, peppers, onions, and seasonings. Cover and simmer for 30 minutes. (Serve with brown rice.) *Serves 4 to 6.*

169

LIVER PAPRIKA

½ cup chopped onions
3 tablespoons butter, margarine,
    or cooking oil
1 pound beef, calf, pork, or lamb
    liver

1 heaping teaspoon paprika
salt and pepper to taste
3 egg yolks, lightly beaten
1 cup warm sour cream

Sauté onions in butter until golden. Dice and add liver, and stir in seasonings. Cook over low heat with frequent stirrings until just fork-tender—from 3 to 10 minutes, depending on which kind of liver you are using. Beat eggs into warm sour cream and stir over low heat to bubbling point. Do not boil. Combine with liver and onions. *Serves 4 to 6.*

LIVER WITH THYME AND ORANGE

4 slices of bacon, chopped
1 pound beef, calf, pork, or lamb
    liver, sliced
2 tablespoons whole-wheat or un-
    bleached flour

1 teaspoon powdered thyme
⅛ teaspoon salt
2 oranges, peeled and sliced

Fry chopped bacon until crisp. Remove bacon bits and drain. Pour off all but 2 tablespoons of the bacon drippings. Combine flour and seasonings, and dredge liver slices. Brown liver in bacon drippings on both sides. Cover with orange slices, cover skillet, and cook over low heat for 15 minutes. *Serves 4.*

STUFFED LIVER ROLLS WITH VEGETABLES

1 pound beef or calf liver
2 cups diced crustless whole-
    wheat bread
½ cup grated yellow cheese
1 tablespoon chopped parsley
¾ teaspoon salt
dash of pepper
¼ teaspoon powdered sage
¼ cup vegetable water

4 tablespoons butter, margarine,
    cooking oil, or bacon drip-
    pings
2 tablespoons whole-wheat flour
2 cups stock or bouillon
1 pound small white onions—or
    sliced yellow onions
4–6 carrots, coarsely cut

Have butcher cut liver so that you have 4 to 6 thin slices. Combine diced bread, cheese, parsley, and seasonings. Sprinkle with ¼ cup vegetable water and 2 tablespoons of melted or liquid

170

shortening. Spread liver slices with this dressing and roll each slice, fastening with toothpicks or skewers. Dust lightly with flour, salt, and pepper. Brown the liver rolls quickly in remaining 2 tablespoons of shortening, turning to brown evenly. Add stock or bouillon and vegetables. Simmer, covered, until vegetables are just tender—20 minutes or so. *Serves 4 to 6.*

To make gravy: Pour off pan liquid and thicken with whole-wheat flour, stirring to prevent lumps. Add seasonings if necessary and simmer for 5 minutes.

LIVER CASSEROLE NO. 1

1 pound beef, calf, pork, or lamb liver
2 cups boiling vegetable water
2 tablespoons butter or margarine
2 tablespoons unbleached or whole-wheat flour
2 tablespoons thinly sliced green celery

½ cup sliced stuffed olives
1 teaspoon salt
¼ teaspoon paprika
1 tablespoon Worcestershire sauce
½ cup wheat germ
2 hard-cooked eggs, chopped

Drop liver into boiling vegetable water, lower heat, and simmer for 5 minutes. Drain (reserve liquid) and cut into small dice. Melt butter and blend with flour to a smooth paste. Gradually add 1½ cups of water in which liver was simmered, stirring until sauce is smooth and thickened. Add liver, celery, olives, and seasonings. Pour into lightly greased casserole, sprinkle wheat germ over top, and bake, uncovered, at 350° for 20 minutes. Garnish with chopped hard-cooked eggs. *Serves 4 to 6.*

LIVER CASSEROLE NO. 2

½ cup fine whole-wheat bread crumbs
½ cup wheat germ
½ teaspoon poultry seasoning
2 tablespoons finely chopped parsley
1 pound beef, pork, or lamb liver
1 tablespoon lemon juice

1 cup chopped onions
⅔ cup chopped green celery with leaves
2 tablespoons bacon drippings or cooking oil
1 cup seasoned stock, vegetable water, or bouillon
1 tablespoon butter

171

Mix bread crumbs, wheat germ, poultry seasoning, and parsley and place half of this mixture in a well-greased casserole. Slice liver very thin and spread over crumb mixture. Sprinkle with lemon juice and let stand while you sauté onions and celery in bacon drippings or cooking oil until onions are glazed. Drain these vegetables and spread them over the liver. Pour seasoned stock over these ingredients, top with remaining crumb mixture, and dot with butter. Bake at 350° for 1 hour. *Serves 4 to 6.*

DEVILED LIVER

1½–2 pounds beef, pork, or lamb liver
½ cup unbleached or whole-wheat flour
3 onions, sliced
2 tablespoons bacon drippings or cooking oil

2 teaspons dry mustard
1 teaspoon salt
⅛ teaspoon pepper
½ cup stock or vegetable water
½ cup warm sour cream

Cut liver into small pieces and dredge with flour. Sauté onions in bacon drippings or oil until glazed. Add floured liver, and brown, turning, until tender and cooked through. Stir seasonings into stock and add to pan. Bring to boiling point, stirring constantly. Reduce heat to below boiling point, stir in sour cream, and heat to serving temperature without boiling. *Serves 4 to 6.*

LIVERBURGERS

1 pound beef, pork, or lamb liver
2 small onions
⅔ teaspoon salt
⅛ teaspoon pepper

2 tablespoons wheat germ
1 egg, lightly beaten
2 tablespoons cooking oil

Put liver and onions through medium blade of meat grinder. Mix with seasonings, wheat germ, and lightly beaten egg. Form into patties and brown on both sides in cooking oil—or pan-broil without oil for 2 minutes on each side. Serve on toasted wholewheat or wheat-germ biscuits (page 203). Top with tomato slices. *Makes 4 to 6 patties.*

VITAMIN B PROTEIN LOAF

1 pound pork liver
1 pound lean boneless pork
2 eggs, lightly beaten
½ cup soft whole-wheat bread crumbs
½ cup wheat germ
1½ teaspoons salt

1 tablespoon chopped parsley
1 tablespoon chopped green celery
¼ teaspoon black pepper
⅛ teaspoon each sage and thyme
1 large clove garlic, minced or pressed

Put liver and pork through fine blade of your meat grinder. Combine with all other ingredients. Form into a loaf, or press into a baking dish, and set dish in a shallow pan of hot water. Bake at 300° for 2 hours. *Serves 4 to 6, with leftovers for cold sandwiches.*

LIVER DUMPLINGS

These may be used to hearten further a hearty soup such as tomato, pea, or lentil—or as a satisfying luncheon or supper course.

1 pound beef, pork, or lamb liver
2 small onions
1 teaspoon salt
⅛ teaspoon pepper
pinch of basil, oregano, or marjoram
2 eggs, lightly beaten
1½ tablespoons butter or margarine, melted—or bacon drippings
1½ cups soft whole-wheat bread crumbs
½ cup wheat germ
1 quart boiling vegetable water (or soup)

Put liver and onions through fine blade of your meat grinder. Add all other ingredients and blend thoroughly. Drop by the tablespoonful into boiling vegetable water or soup, lower heat, cover, and simmer for 15 minutes. *Serves 4 to 6.*

LIVER IN SWEET AND SOUR SAUCE

4 large, thin slices of beef liver
4 tablespoons unbleached or whole-wheat flour
1 egg, beaten
4 tablespoons wheat germ

4 tablespoons butter, margarine, or cooking oil
4 teaspoons honey
4 teaspoons lemon juice

Dredge liver slices in flour, dip in beaten egg, and roll in wheat germ. Brown on both sides in 3 tablespoons of shortening—

173

about 3 or 4 minutes per side. Remove to heated serving dish and keep warm. Add remaining tablespoon of butter and the honey to skillet, and heat thoroughly but do not boil. Remove pan from heat, add lemon juice, and mix well. Return liver to skillet over low heat, and turn in the sweet and sour sauce until the slices are well coated on both sides. *Serves 4.*

MEXICAN LIVER

1½ pounds beef, pork, or lamb liver, thinly sliced
¼ cup bacon drippings
2 large onions, sliced
4 tomatoes, diced

2 cups vegetable water or stock
2 teaspoons chili powder
1 teaspoon salt
pinch of black pepper or cayenne
¼ teaspoon curry powder

Brown liver slices on both sides in hot drippings. Remove from heat, drain on paper towel, and cut into ½-inch strips. Return liver to pan and add all other ingredients. Stir to mix well. Cover and simmer over low heat for 30 minutes. *Serves 4 to 6.*

Note: If fresh tomatoes are not available, use 1½ cups of stewed tomatoes and only 1 cup of vegetable water or stock.

CHICKEN LIVERS *

People who absolutely refuse to eat organ meats usually make an exception of chicken livers—possibly because of their delicate taste and texture, possibly because their higher cost puts them in the luxury class.

Nutritionally, chicken livers are not quite so desirable as the other varieties, but they are nevertheless quite good. So if chicken liver is the only liver your family will eat, I suggest you serve it as often as the budget permits.

Chicken livers are delicious sautéed very briefly in a little chicken fat or butter until they are just cooked through—a matter of 2 or 3 minutes. They may be scrambled with eggs, used in omelets, substituted for chicken in à la king recipes. (See chicken liver variation of Beef Stroganoff, page 151.)

Because very little "doctoring" is necessary to make chicken

---

* See footnote, Page 71.

livers acceptable to family palates, only a handful of fancy recipes is given here, chosen chiefly for their accompanying ingredients which are rich in the high-quality proteins which non-organ-meat eaters may lack in their customary diets.

Several of the recipes to follow are especially recommended for the elderly, who as a class get all too little protein. These dishes are easy to chew and digest, are full of good nutrition—and their tastiness tempts lagging appetites.

CREAMED CHICKEN LIVERS

½ pound chicken livers
1 cup chicken stock, bouillon, or vegetable water
2 tablespoons butter or margarine
2 tablespoons unbleached or whole-wheat flour

½ cup milk or skim milk, scalded
1 tablespoon yeast flakes or brewers' yeast
salt and pepper (or paprika) to taste

Drop chicken livers into boiling stock, reduce heat, cover, and simmer for 7 or 8 minutes, until tender. Drain, reserving stock. Melt butter or margarine and blend with flour to a smooth paste. Slowly stir in scalded milk and stock and cook over low heat until thickened. Add yeast and seasonings, stir, and return livers to sauce. Do not boil. Serve over brown or enriched rice or wheat-germ biscuits (page 203). *Serves 2.*

CHICKEN LIVER CUSTARD

½ pound chicken livers
1 tablespoon melted chicken fat or butter
3 eggs, slightly beaten
2 tablespoons finely chopped parsley or chives

1 teaspoon salt
¼ teaspoon nutmeg
⅛ teaspoon paprika
2 cups milk or skim milk

Sauté chicken livers in melted fat for 2 minutes. Drain, cut into small pieces, and put in greased casserole or divide equally and put in greased custard cups. Combine beaten eggs, chopped parsley or chives, and seasonings. Scald milk and stir into egg mixture. Pour over chicken livers and set casserole or custard cups in shallow pan of hot water. Bake at 350° for 1 hour. *Serves 4.*

CHICKEN LIVERS PAPRIKA

1 large onion, chopped
2 tablespoons melted chicken fat,
    butter, or margarine
¾–1 pound chicken livers

1 heaping teaspoon paprika
salt to taste
1 cup sour cream
3 egg yolks

Glaze onions in melted fat or butter. Add chicken livers and seasonings, and stir over low heat for 5 minutes, turning the livers often. In a separate saucepan scald sour cream and beat in egg yolks. Continue to beat over low heat until mixture begins to bubble. Combine with liver-onion mixture. Serve over brown rice cooked in chicken stock or consommé, or on whole-wheat toast. *Serves 4 to 6.*

CHICKEN LIVERS WITH APPLES

1 pound chicken livers
4 tablespoons whole-wheat flour
1 teaspoon salt
½ teaspoon paprika

4 tablespoons butter or margarine, melted
3 or 4 firm apples
1 tablespoon brown sugar

Dredge livers in mixture of flour, salt, and paprika and sauté in 2 tablespoons of the melted butter, turning to brown both sides evenly. Remove from pan; add remaining 2 tablespoons of butter. Wash and core apples; then slice them thickly (about ½-inch slices). Dredge apple slices with brown sugar and sauté in melted butter until tender, turning to glaze both sides. *Serves 4.*

Note: This recipe is also good with the addition of ½ cup sliced glazed onions.

SWEETBREADS

I sometimes wonder whether it is semantics, relative scarcity, or high price which accounts for sweetbreads' place on fashionable menus which never include brains. If sweetbreads were called by their physiological name—thymus glands—would they be as desirable? On the other hand, if brains were given a more poetic and concealing name, would they suddenly become popular? Sweetbreads' delicacy, texture, and flavor are greatly appealing to many a person who wouldn't dream of lifting a forkful of brains—whose delicacy, texture, and flavor are so similar as to be undistinguishable in most recipes.

To Prepare Sweetbreads for Recipes

Wash quickly under running cold water and remove connective membranes.

Or: Barely cover with lightly salted water to which you have added 1 tablespoon of vinegar. Simmer gently for 15 minutes. Cool, and remove membranes. Simmering makes it a little easier to handle the sweetbreads, but a percentage of their nutrients is now in the water—so save it to use in stocks, soups, stews, and other recipes calling for water.

CREAMED SWEETBREADS

1 pound sweetbreads
3 tablespoons butter or margarine, melted
3 tablespoons unbleached flour
1 cup warm milk

¼ cup skim-milk solids
1 cup sweetbread stock
salt and pepper to taste
(sherry)

Simmer sweetbreads (see above) and separate into small pieces, reserving 1 cup of the water. Blend butter and flour in saucepan until smooth, and add warm milk, milk solids, and sweetbread stock, stirring to prevent lumps. Season to taste and add sweetbreads. If you like, add 1 or 2 teaspoons of sherry for each adult serving. Serve on whole-wheat toast or wheat-germ biscuits (page 203). *Serves 4 to 6.*

BREADED SWEETBREADS

1 pound sweetbreads
1 egg, beaten with 1 tablespoon milk (or cooled sweetbread stock)
½ cup wheat germ or fine whole-wheat bread crumbs

½ teaspoon salt
⅛ teaspoon pepper
2 tablespoons butter or margarine, melted

Separate washed or simmered (see above) sweetbreads into 4 serving pieces. Roll in egg mixture and wheat germ or bread crumbs seasoned with salt and pepper. Brown in hot butter or margarine. *Serves 4.*

SWEETBREAD SCALLOP

1 pound sweetbreads
½ pound mushrooms, sliced
¼ cup chopped onions
2 tablespoons butter or margarine, melted
2 tablespoons unbleached flour
½ cup sour cream
2 cups stock or vegetable water

(1 cup may be sweetbread stock)
¼ cup chopped green celery
1 tablespoon chopped parsley
salt and pepper (paprika) to taste
3 tablespoons wheat germ
1 tablespoon grated yellow cheese

Simmer sweetbreads (page 177), drain, and reserve stock. Sauté mushrooms and onions in butter or margarine for 3 minutes. Sprinkle flour over them and cook over low heat, stirring, for 3 minutes more. Heat sour cream and stock, and add to pan, stirring briskly to prevent lumps. When sauce is smooth, add celery and parsley, and season to taste. Simmer sauce for 10 minutes, stirring occasionally; then add sweetbreads and mix well. Transfer to a lightly greased baking dish and sprinkle with wheat germ and cheese. Bake at 350° for 20 minutes. *Serves 4.*

Note: This recipe can be extended to serve 6 or more by adding diced cooked chicken, turkey, or veal—1 or more cups. Add and fold into the sweetbread mixture just before it is transferred to the baking dish.

Note also: If your family loves sweetbreads but not brains, try combining the two for this recipe.

SWEETBREAD KABOBS

1 pound sweetbreads
8–12 slices of bacon
8–12 fairly large mushroom caps

8–12 large stuffed olives
1 tablespoon oil or melted butter

Prepare sweetbreads (page 177) and separate into pieces about the size of large walnuts. Wrap each piece with a strip of bacon. Thread wrapped sweetbreads, mushrooms, and olives on skewers and sauté, turning often, in large skillet or on a griddle —for about 5 minutes. When bacon begins to melt and become transparent, transfer the kabobs to the broiler, arranging the skewers across the top of an empty metal bread or cake pan. Broil, turning from time to time, until bacon is crisp. *Serves 4 to 6.*

SWEETBREADS GOURMET

1 pound sweetbreads	yolks of 4 eggs, well beaten
1½ cups heavy cream, sweet or sour	(2 tablespoons brandy)
½ cup coarsely chopped nuts—walnuts, pecans, cashews, almonds	¼ cup sherry
	½ teaspoon salt
	pinch of curry powder

Simmer sweetbreads (page 177) and cut into small dice. Heat cream in top of double boiler—or, if you have one, a chafing dish or electric skillet at the table. Add all other ingredients in order, stirring over low heat until sauce thickens. Serve on whole-wheat toast or wheat-germ biscuits (page 203). *Serves 4 to 6.*

SWEETBREAD SALAD

You are not bound by the ingredients suggested below. Use any cooked or raw vegetables you like, and/or mix in ½ cup of diced apples or pears.

1 pound sweetbreads—or ½ pound sweetbreads and 1 cup diced cooked chicken	¾ cup mayonnaise
1 cup thinly sliced green celery	1½ teaspoons lemon juice
1 cup cooked or canned green peas or cut green beans	salt and pepper
	lettuce

Simmer sweetbreads (page 177), break into small pieces, and combine with all other ingredients. Add the mayonnaise gradually, until the salad is moistened to your liking. Chill and serve on bed of lettuce. *Serves 6 to 8.*

SWEETBREADS A LA KING

See recipe on page 158 for brains à la king. Substitute sweetbreads for brains, and follow recipe step by step.

TONGUE

All animals have edible tongues. The pampered princesses of fairy tales dined delicately on hummingbirds' tongues, and very possibly some of the gourmet food shops still stock them along with the fried baby bees, sautéed grasshoppers, smoked rattlesnake meat, and marinated ants they provide for the limited but enthusiastic audience which dotes on spooky foods. More practical sizes of tongues are available for main meat courses, but they are neglected far too much except in enlightened households, especially those with European backgrounds. Here again, as with brains and sometimes kidneys, the objection to tongue seems to be a matter of philosophy rather than taste. Few dishes are as delicious as well-prepared tongue.

Tongue is not properly an organ meat. It is, rather, a well-exercised muscle which means that it requires longer cooking for tenderness. Remember the lesson repeated throughout this book that long cooking in water liberates essential vitamins and minerals. When you cook tongue for the sake of its taste as well as its excellent protein, make it a habit to save part of the cooking water as the basis of dried legume soups or to add to stews.

SIMMERED TONGUE, FRESH OR SMOKED

1 fresh or smoked beef tongue— or 2 veal, or 8 lamb tongues
water to cover
(1 teaspoon salt per quart of water for fresh tongue only; omit salt for smoked tongue)

1 bay leaf
3 or 4 cloves
1 teaspoon peppercorns
1 onion, sliced
a few celery tops with leaves—or 1 tablespoon celery flakes

Special note for smoked tongue: Depending on the type you purchase, smoked tongue may or may not require soaking in cold water for 3 hours or more to remove some of the saltiness. If no soaking is required, the label on its wrapping will say so. If there is no label—soak it.

Cover tongue with water, add all other ingredients, and bring to boiling point; then lower heat and simmer, covered, until tender. You'll find that from 50 to 60 minutes per pound of beef

180

tongue will do it—somewhat less for smaller ones. To be sure, stick a fork into the tip end. If this is tender, so is the rest. Let tongue cool in the cooking water. When it can be handled, remove the skin and roots, which can be used to add flavor to legume soups. See recipes at the end of this section for sauces. *Serves 6 to 8.*

HONEYED TONGUE

1 fresh beef tongue
½ cup honey
½ cup brown sugar
1 cup stewed fruit or berries—
    any kind

2 teaspoons whole cloves stuck
    into slices of ½ lemon
    slices of ½ lemon

Simmer tongue (page 180). Blend all remaining ingredients with 1 cup of liquid reserved from cooking water, and simmer the tongue in this mixture for 15 minutes. Slice tongue and serve with its own sauce. Garnish with cloved lemon slices. *Serves 6 to 8.*

COLD JELLIED BEEF TONGUE WITH RAW VEGETABLES

1 smoked beef tongue
3 cups of water in which tongue
    is cooked
1½ tablespoons unflavored gela-
    tin
¼ cup lemon juice
1 tablespoon brown sugar

1 cup chopped green celery
½ cup shredded carrots
½ cup chopped green peppers
½ cup shredded cabbage
½ cup raisins
2 or 3 hard-cooked eggs
fresh parsley

Simmer tongue (page 180). Dip out ½ cup of the tongue liquid and cool in refrigerator. Measure 2½ cups more of the liquid and simmer. Stir 1½ tablespoons unflavored gelatin into the cold tongue liquid, and add this to the simmering tongue liquid. (You may add 2 beef or chicken bouillon cubes, or 1 cube and 1 teaspoonful of Worcestershire sauce, if you like.) Stir in lemon juice and sugar, and remove from heat. Remove to refrigerator until mixture thickens. Stir in vegetables and raisins. Moisten an aspic mold or bread pan with cold water and cover the bottom with a few spoonfuls of the gelatin mixture. Add a layer of sliced hard-cooked egg. Place the trimmed tongue on this

181

and cover with the rest of the gelatin mixture. Chill thoroughly in the refrigerator. Turn upside down on a bed of lettuce to unmold, and garnish with remainder of hard-cooked eggs and with parsley. *Serves 6 to 8.*

Sauces for Fresh or Smoked Tongue

SOUR CREAM AND HORSE-RADISH SAUCE

1 firm, tart apple
1½ cups sour cream
½ cup white horse-radish
1 teaspoon brown sugar

½ teaspoon grated lemon or orange peel
⅛ teaspoon paprika
dash of cayenne

Peel apple and grate it immediately into sour cream. Add remaining ingredients and blend thoroughly. This may be served cold, or heated through without boiling.

VEGETABLE SAUCE

3 tablespoons unbleached or whole-wheat flour
1 tablespoon yeast flakes or brewers' yeast
1½ cups liquid in which tongue was cooked

1 cup diced or shredded carrots
½ cup chopped onions
½ cup diced green celery
½ teaspoon salt
¼ teaspoon pepper

Make a smooth paste of flour, yeast, and a little of the tongue water. Add remaining liquid gradually, stirring to prevent lumps. Add vegetables and seasonings, and simmer until vegetables are tender.

CURRY SAUCE

3 tablespoons butter or margarine, melted
3 tablespoons unbleached flour
1 cup water in which tongue was cooked
1 cup milk or skim milk

1 teaspoon onion juice or minced onion
1-2 teaspoons curry powder
1 teaspoon lemon juice
salt, pepper, and paprika to taste

Blend melted butter and flour to a smooth paste. Gradually add warm tongue liquid and milk, and stir to prevent lumps. Cook over low heat until sauce begins to thicken; then stir in remaining ingredients.

MUSTARD SAUCE

3 tablespoons butter or margarine, melted
3 tablespoons unbleached flour
1 cup tongue liquid

1 cup milk or skim milk
1–2 tablespoons table mustard
salt to taste

Blend butter and flour to a smooth paste. Gradually add warm tongue liquid and milk, and stir to prevent lumps. Cook over low heat until sauce begins to thicken. Stir in mustard and salt (if needed).

CREOLE SAUCE

2 tablespoons chopped onion
¼ cup chopped green pepper
1 clove garlic, minced
2 tablespoons cooking oil
3 tablespoons unbleached flour
1 cup liquid in which tongue was
   cooked

1½ cups stewed tomatoes
1 small bay leaf
¼ teaspoon black pepper
½ teaspoon salt
1 teaspoon brown sugar
dash each of paprika and cayenne

Sauté onion, green pepper, and garlic in hot oil until onion is glazed, not brown. Sprinkle flour over these ingredients and stir well. Add and stir in remaining ingredients. Simmer over low heat for 5 minutes.

OXTAILS

For want of a better classification, oxtails are grouped among the organ meats, although, like tongue, the oxtail is not an organ. They are deserving of inclusion here, however, because they are nutritious, tasty, fairly economical, and far too seldom used.

DEVILED OXTAILS

4 pounds oxtails, cut into 2-inch
   pieces
1 large onion, coarsely chopped
½ cup each diced celery and carrots
1 clove garlic, cut in half
2 tablespoons chopped parsley
1 bay leaf

2 quarts water
1½ tablespoons dry mustard
1 tablespoon Worcestershire sauce
1 tablespoon sour cream
2 tablespoons butter or margarine, melted
½ cup (about) wheat germ or
   whole-wheat bread crumbs

183

Trim excess fat off oxtails and put them in a large kettle with vegetables, garlic, parsley, and bay leaf. Cover with water and bring to a boil. Reduce heat and simmer, covered, for 3 hours. Cool and skim off surface fat. Drain the oxtails. (Put liquid through a food mill and save in refrigerator as a base for soup or stew.) Blend mustard, Worcestershire sauce, sour cream, and melted butter or margarine to a smooth paste and brush it over the oxtail pieces. Roll them in wheat germ or crumbs and broil, turning once, for about 5 minutes. *Serves 6 to 8.*

OXTAIL PIE

4 pounds disjointed oxtails
4 tablespoons unbleached or whole-wheat flour
4 tablespoons cooking oil
½ cup mushrooms, thinly sliced
½ cup each diced carrots, celery, onions
1 cup stock or vegetable water
2 cups canned whole peeled or stewed tomatoes

1 clove garlic, minced
1 bay leaf
1 teaspoon salt
¼ teaspoon black pepper
⅛ teaspoon grated nutmeg
1 recipe whole-wheat pie crust (page 278)
2 tablespoons milk

Trim excess fat from oxtails and dredge with flour. Heat oil and glaze mushrooms, onions, carrots, and celery for 3 minutes, stirring. Add oxtails and turn in this mixture for 3 minutes. Add all other ingredients (except pie crust and milk) and mix well. Bring to a boil, lower heat, and simmer, covered, for 3 hours. Either skim off surface fat or allow kettle to cool and remove congealed fat. Pour mixture into a round casserole. Roll pie crust ⅛ inch thick and cover the casserole with it. Be sure to cut vents in the crust to permit steam to escape. Brush crust with milk and bake at 400° for 15 minutes. *Serves 6 to 8.*

OXTAILS ITALIAN STYLE

3 pounds disjointed oxtails
3–4 slices bacon, chopped
½ cup chopped onion
½ clove garlic, minced
1 large carrot, sliced or diced
1 teaspoon chopped parsley
½ teaspoon salt

⅛ teaspoon pepper
(1 cup dry red wine)
2 cups canned tomatoes
vegetable water for adding, if necessary
1 small bunch green celery, coarsely cut

184

Trim excess fat from oxtails. Fry chopped bacon until there are enough drippings to glaze onions, garlic, carrot, and parsley. When these are glazed, add and brown oxtails quickly. Season with salt and pepper. Add wine at this time, if you are using it, and cook over low heat until wine is almost all absorbed. Add canned tomatoes and continue cooking over low heat, covered, for 3 hours until oxtail meat is fork-tender. If necessary, add enough vegetable water to keep meat covered. When meat is tender, add coarsely cut celery, cover pan again, and continue to simmer for 20 minutes more. *Serves 4 to 6.*

OXTAIL STEW

4 pounds disjointed oxtails	3 or 4 whole cloves
2 tablespoons whole-wheat flour	pinch of basil or oregano
3 tablespoons cooking oil	1 cup coarsely chopped vegetables
½ cup chopped onions	—green pepper, string beans,
1 clove garlic, minced	carrots, celery (your choice
1 teaspoon salt	or mixture)
⅛ teaspoon pepper	1 cup diced potatoes
1 cup canned tomatoes	1 tablespoon lemon juice
2 cups stock or vegetable water	(2 tablespoons dry red wine)
1 bay leaf	

Dredge oxtail joints with flour and brown on all sides in cooking oil. Remove meat and glaze onions and garlic in pan until golden. Return meat to pan, season with salt and pepper, and cover with tomatoes and stock (or vegetable water). Add bay leaf, cloves, and herb, and cover pan and simmer over low heat for 2½ hours. Add more vegetable water if necessary to keep the meat covered with liquid. At end of cooking time, stir mixture, add chopped vegetables and diced potatoes, and continue to simmer until vegetables are tender. Five minutes before serving, add lemon juice (and wine) and stir. *Serves 4 to 6.*

Using Leftovers
Nutritionally

9

Using Leftovers Nutritionally

Leftovers are inevitable in even the best-run households, and it is a temptation to serve them up again in their original, if slightly tired, form. Remember, however, that previously cooked foods suffer a certain amount of nutrient loss with the passage of time, unless they have been quickly frozen and held at protectively low temperatures. This is especially true of vegetables, whose volatile vitamins—already in jeopardy from their exposure to heat and air—continue to escape into the never-never land even when refrigerated. Cooked meats, whose proteins may remain more or less constant, also give up the ghosts of their shy vitamins when exposed again to heat or moisture.

The conscientious housewife, intent on feeding her family good nutrition, will do something about leftovers other than merely disguise them with garnishes calculated to appease the beloved critics gathered around her table. What she will do is bolster their nutritive values by adding vitamins and minerals—and protein, of which there rarely is enough in the average diet.

Using slices of cold roasts and fowl as sandwich filling is traditional and nutritionally acceptable, provided the bread is whole grain to compensate for loss of B vitamins. Diced cold cooked meats appear advantageously in hearty salads. But leftovers should seldom if ever be heated in or over water, or popped into warming ovens, or mixed with devitalized, starchy extenders whose nutritive contributions are skimpy or negligible.

Adding good nutrition to leftovers is not difficult, as the following recipes will demonstrate.

LEFTOVER BEEF, VEAL, OR LAMB CASSEROLE

1 medium eggplant, peeled and thinly sliced
2 onions, chopped or sliced
4 or 5 tomatoes, thinly sliced (reserve several slices for topping)
½ cup string beans, limas, or peas
½ small head of cabbage, coarsely shredded
2½ cups cooked sliced or diced beef, veal, or lamb

1 cup cooked brown or enriched rice
1 cup stock, vegetable water, or bouillon
1 tablespoon brewers' yeast or yeast flakes
2 teaspoons olive oil
¼ teaspoon oregano
¼ cup wheat germ

In lightly greased baking dish, alternate layers of vegetables and meat. Spread cooked rice over these ingredients. Combine stock, vegetable water, or bouillon with yeast and pour over the layers. Lay reserved slices of tomatoes on top; sprinkle with olive oil and oregano, and then with wheat germ. Bake at 325° for 1 hour. *Serves 4 to 6.*

Note: If stock or vegetable water is unseasoned, lightly salt the layers before adding liquid.

LEFTOVER-PORK CASSEROLE

½ cup chopped onions
2 tablespoons cooking oil
2½ cups diced cooked pork
salt, pepper, pinch of marjoram
1 cup diced carrots
1 large green pepper, chopped
1 large firm apple, peeled, cored, and diced
2 cups cooked brown rice—or diced parboiled sweet potatoes

3 tablespoons butter, margarine, or bacon drippings
3 tablespoons whole-wheat flour
½ tablespoon salt
1 teaspoon dry mustard
2 cups stock or vegetable water
grated yellow cheese
wheat germ

190

Glaze onions in oil. Season pork lightly with salt, pepper, and marjoram and brown over glazed onions. Combine pork and onions with diced vegetables, apple, and rice (or parboiled potatoes), and mix well. Melt butter or other shortening and blend with flour, salt, and mustard to a smooth paste. Add liquid, stir smooth, and add salt and dry mustard. Cook over low heat until sauce thickens. Put meat-vegetable-rice mixture in lightly greased casserole and pour sauce over it. Sprinkle with grated yellow cheese and wheat germ and bake at 350° for 1 hour. *Serves 4 to 6.*

LEFTOVERS A LA KING

3 tablespoons bacon or ham drippings
3 tablespoons unbleached or whole-wheat flour
2 cups warm milk
¼ cup skim-milk solids

2 cups diced cooked meat or poultry
¼ cup minced pimientos
¼ cup minced green peppers
½ cup thinly slivered green celery

Melt drippings and blend with flour to a smooth paste. Add warm milk and milk solids, and stir over low heat until smooth and thickened. Add remaining ingredients and stir over low heat to serving temperature. Vegetables will be crisp. Serve over brown rice, whole-wheat toast, or wheat-germ biscuits (page 203). *Serves 4 to 6.*

LEFTOVERS A LA NEWBURG

2 cups cooked brown rice
2 cups diced cooked meat, poultry, or fish
1 can condensed cream of mushroom, celery, or chicken soup
½ cup milk

2 tablespoons skim-milk solids
2 tablespoons sherry
½ cup wheat germ
1 tablespoon butter or margarine, melted

Cover bottom of lightly greased baking dish with cooked rice and spread with diced leftovers. Heat condensed soup, adding milk and milk solids slowly and stirring until smooth. When hot (not boiling), remove from heat and stir in sherry. Pour sauce over leftovers and rice; sprinkle with wheat germ and melted butter or margarine. Bake 30 minutes at 350°. *Serves 4 to 6.*

191

CURRIED LEFTOVERS

3 tablespoons butter or margarine, melted
3 tablespoons whole-wheat flour
1 cup vegetable water
1 cup milk
2 tablespoons skim-milk solids
1 tablespoon yeast flakes or brewers' yeast
2–4 teaspoons curry powder
salt to taste

dash of cayenne
dash of powdered ginger
½ cup chopped onions
2 tablespoons cooking oil
1 small, tart apple, peeled and chopped
1 teaspoon brown sugar
1 cup or more diced leftover meat, poultry, or fish

Blend melted shortening with flour to a smooth paste. Add vegetable water, milk, and milk solids, and stir until smooth. Cook over low heat as you stir in yeast and all seasonings. In separate skillet glaze onions in oil until golden. Add chopped apple and sugar and cook for 1 minute more. Add these ingredients and the leftovers to the sauce. Mix well. Serve when hot, or pour into lightly greased baking dish and bake at 350° until bubbly. Serve over brown rice or enriched noodles. *Serves 4 to 6.*

CROQUETTES

½ cup butter or margarine
½ cup whole-wheat flour
1½ teaspoons salt
1 teaspoon poultry seasoning
⅛ teaspoon pepper
2 cups milk
¼ cup skim-milk solids

4 cups finely chopped or minced leftover meat or poultry
1 tablespoon chopped parsley
2 eggs
4 tablespoons cold water
1 cup wheat germ
shortening or oil for deep frying

Melt butter, blend in flour and seasonings, and stir to a smooth paste. Add milk and milk solids, stirring to prevent lumps, and cook over low heat until sauce thickens. Add and stir in leftovers and parsley. Pour into a fairly shallow pan and chill this mixture in the refrigerator for 1 hour or more. Beat eggs with cold water lightly. Form chilled meat mixture into balls or cones and dip first into the egg mixture, then in wheat germ, rolling to coat completely. You may refrigerate the croquettes again, or prepare them immediately for serving. Heat shortening in deep fryer until a cube of bread turns brown while you count to 20. Fry croquettes (2 or 4 at a time) until golden brown— about 3 or 4 minutes. Drain on paper towel. *Serves 4 to 6.*

LEFTOVER-BEEF PARMIGIANA

Use leftovers from roast beef or pot roast for this recipe.

2 eggs
2 tablespoons milk
1 teaspoon salt
1 teaspoon dry mustard
¼ teaspoon pepper
½ cup wheat germ
¼ cup grated Parmesan cheese

4 large or 8 smaller slices of
   cooked beef
¼ cup melted shortening
1 cup Italian spaghetti sauce—or
   1 can Italian tomato paste
sliced Mozzarella or yellow cheese

Beat eggs lightly with milk, add seasonings, and blend thoroughly. Mix wheat germ and Parmesan cheese together. Dip meat slices into egg mixture, then into wheat germ and cheese mixture. Brown in hot shortening, 5 minutes per side. Spoon about one-third of the spaghetti sauce or paste over bottom of flat baking dish. Spread meat over this, top with slices of cheese, and cover with the remaining sauce or tomato paste. Bake at 350° for 10 minutes, or until cheese melts. Move dish close to broiler for the last minute or so and brown the cheese. *Serves 4.*

HASH FROM LEFTOVERS

6 medium potatoes
1½–3 cups chopped cooked meat
3 tablespoons sour cream or stock
½ cup chopped onion

1 cup wheat germ
3 tablespoons bacon drippings or
   oil
4–6 eggs, to be poached

Boil potatoes in their jackets; then peel and dice them. Combine all ingredients except drippings or oil. Heat drippings in heavy skillet and spread hash evenly. Brown slowly over low heat until bottom is crusty. Turn carefully and brown other side. Serve topped with poached eggs. *Serves 4 to 6.*

LEFTOVER-POULTRY CASSEROLE

½ cup chopped onions
¼ cup chopped green pepper
⅓ cup thinly slivered green celery
3 tablespoons butter or margarine
3 tablespoons unbleached flour
2 cups milk
¼ cup skim-milk solids
½ cup diced carrots

1 tablespoon chopped parsley
1½ cups diced leftover chicken
   or turkey
½ teaspoon salt
⅛ teaspoon pepper or paprika
1 small head of cauliflower
¼ pound sliced Swiss or unprocessed yellow cheese

193

Glaze onions, green pepper, and celery in melted butter or margarine. Stir in flour. Combine milk with milk solids and add, stirring. Cook over low heat until slightly thickened. Add carrots, parsley, poultry, and seasonings, and simmer for 15 minutes. Stir occasionally. Break cauliflower into flowrets and boil in very little water until tender but not soft. Add cauliflower to chicken mixture. Pour into lightly greased casserole, top with cheese slices, and bake at 350° until cheese melts. *Serves 4 to 6.*

HAM AND CHEESE PIE

1 double recipe crisp pie crust
   (page 278)
½ pound bacon
½ cup or more diced cooked ham
3 eggs, lightly beaten
2 cups milk

¼ cup skim-milk solids
¼ pound yellow, Swiss, or Gru-
   yère cheese, crumbled
1 teaspoon salt
dash of pepper or paprika

Fry bacon slowly until crisp. Crumble and reserve. Line 9-inch pie pan with 1 crust and cover it with mixed bacon and ham. Combine eggs, milk, milk solids, cheese, and seasonings, and pour over bacon-ham mixture. Cover with top crust and bake at 400° for 35 to 40 minutes, until crust browns. *Serves 4 to 6.*

LEFTOVERS IN ASPIC

1 envelope unflavored gelatin
½ cup vegetable water
1 cup hot stock or bouillon
1 teaspoon onion juice
¼ teaspoon salt
1 tablespoon lemon juice
1 cup chopped leftover meat,
   poultry, or fish
¼ cup cooked peas

¼ cup cooked carrots
2 tablespoons finely chopped celery
2 tablespoons chopped green pepper or pimiento
½ cup wheat germ
2 hard-cooked eggs
lettuce leaves

Soak gelatin in cold vegetable water for 10 minutes; then dissolve the mixture in the hot stock. Add onion juice, salt, lemon juice. Stir until well mixed and refrigerate until mixture begins to thicken. Stir in all of the remaining ingredients except the hard-cooked eggs and lettuce. Pour into wet molds and chill until completely firm. Unmold on lettuce leaves and garnish with slices of hard-cooked eggs. *Serves 4 to 6.*

LEFTOVER MEAT AND VEGETABLE SALAD

2 cups diced leftover meat
1 cup diced potatoes (cooked in their jackets, then peeled)
½ cup diced cooked carrots
½ cup cooked green beans
½ cup diced green celery

¼ cup chopped sweet pickles
⅓ cup any good-nutrition salad dressing (pages 101-103)
2 or more hard-cooked eggs, sliced

Combine in large salad bowl all ingredients except salad dressing and eggs. Pour dressing over this mixture, and toss to coat well. Garnish with egg slices. *Serves 4 to 6.*

LEFTOVER-VEGETABLE SCALLOP

3 tablespoons bacon drippings
3 tablespoons whole-wheat flour
1 cup vegetable water
1 cup milk
¼ cup skim-milk solids

½ cup grated yellow cheese
salt and pepper to taste
2 cups or more leftover vegetables—individual or mixed
½ cup wheat germ

Blend bacon drippings and flour to a smooth paste. Add vegetable water, milk, and milk solids, and stir over low heat until lumps disappear. Stir in grated cheese and seasonings, and cook slowly until smooth and hot. Add vegetables and pour mixture into lightly greased baking dish. Top with wheat germ and bake at 350° until bubbly. *Serves 4.*

LEFTOVER LOAF

1 can condensed cream soup (any kind)
½ cup milk
¼ cup skim-milk solids
2 eggs
1 cup or more chopped leftover meat, poultry, or fish

½–1 cup mashed or chopped leftover vegetables
½ cup wheat germ
1 tablespoon minced onion
1 tablespoon chopped parsley
1 tablespoon yeast flakes or brewers' yeast

Blend soup, milk, and milk solids together until smooth, without cooking. Beat in eggs and add all remaining ingredients, mixing thoroughly. Spread evenly in lightly greased baking dish and bake at 350° until heated through—about 15 to 20 minutes. *Serves 4 to 6.*

LEFTOVER GRILLED SANDWICHES

1 cup ground or finely chopped cooked meat
1 cup grated yellow cheese
2 tablespoons any good-nutrition salad dressing (pages 101-103)
1 teaspoon prepared mustard
½ teaspoon salt
dash each of pepper, cayenne, and chili powder
8 slices whole-wheat bread
2 eggs
½ cup milk
1 tablespoon skim-milk solids
3 tablespoons bacon drippings

Mix together the meat, cheese, salad dressing, mustard, and seasonings. Make sandwiches with whole-wheat bread and press together firmly. Beat eggs with fork, beat in milk and milk solids, and dip sandwiches in this mixture, turning to coat both sides well. Brown slowly on both sides in bacon drippings. *Serves 4.*

The Staff of Life

10

The Staff of Life

On the modern American scene, much if not most of that which poses as bread is a tribute to engineering ingenuity, advertising cleverness, and packaging artistry. It is also an insult to human intelligence.

The Egyptians are credited with having invented bread, as we know it. That was back in the time of the ancient Pharaohs, several thousands of years B.C. Ever since then, it seems, there has been a conspiracy afoot to see just how much nutrition could be taken out of bread and still have people willing to buy and eat it. That this conspiracy was brilliantly successful is implicit in recent government action which enjoins bakers and millers to put back into bread and flour some of the nutrients they remove. Note, I said "some." According to the best of calculations, about four times more vital nutrients are removed from wheat processed into white bread flour than are replaced in the current "enrichment" program. This makes about the same kind of sense as rice refinement, which polishes off the grain's true nutrients. The pretty white rice is sold to people and the polishings to the vitamin industry. The vitamin industry sells supplements made from rice polishings to people who need them because they've been eating white rice.

Most commercial flour used by the bakeries or at home is beautiful to behold and scrupulously sanitary. It's as white as snow, as fine as silk, as pure as a sterile hospital gown—and approximately as nourishing.

There was a time when the flour milled from wheat contained all of wheat's goodness—its protein, enzymes, amino acids, vitamins, and minerals. Modern milling processes have almost entirely done away with most of wheat's truest nutrient value—its germ. If you could examine a single grain of wheat under a microscope, cutting it into thin slices to show a cross section, you would see a demonstration of nature's way of concentrating life in a speck. The outer skin is familiar to you as bran. It is made up of a fibrous carbohydrate substance we call cellulose, and it contains a few minerals and vitamins as well. The bran, valuable in diet as roughage, accounts for about 14 per cent of the grain.

Working toward the center, the next mass visible in the cross section is the kernel, called endosperm or middlings, and it is composed of starch and a little gluten. Gluten, a protein, holds bread dough together when you add water and yeast. The kernel is the bulkiest part of the grain—85 per cent of it.

Thus far, the miscroscope reveals, we have 14 per cent bran and 85 per cent carbohydrate kernel in a grain of wheat. What about the remaining 1 per cent? This is the germ or embryo, the heart of wheat, the reservoir for vastly important vitamins, unsaturated fatty acids, and other vital nutrients.

Wheat germ contains protein, unsaturated fat, thiamin, niacin, and most of the other B Complex vitamins. It also contains precursors of arachidonic acid, a type of fatty acid important to the functioning of the brain. In wheat-germ oil is a 25-carbon waxy alcohol, used for such degenerative disorders as multiple sclerosis. It is also the richest natural source of a vitamin largely removed from our carbohydrate foods: Vitamin E, which—contrary to popular thinking—is more important to slowing down aging than it is in reproduction.

200

In almost all store-bought white bread, the wheat germ has been ruthlessly sacrificed on the altar of modern milling processes because of certain problems raised by storage and transportation. Wheat germ, containing the oil-soluble vitamin E, becomes rancid if stored too long. Moreover, it attracts mice and other vermin who won't bother with refined flour if they can help it because they know instinctively it is not nourishing enough to ensure natural life span, freedom from disease, and continuation of their species.

If you look for it in the right places, it is possible to buy 100 per cent whole-wheat bread with the wheat germ intact. Similarly, it is possible to buy 100 per cent whole-wheat or whole-rye flour for home baking, and unbleached white flour which has escaped at least some of the superrefining of most commercial flours or which has had wheat germ restored to it.

Also available in modest mills springing up all over the countryside in response to mounting interest in good nutrition are cracked wheat, graham, peanut, potato, rice, bean, cottonseed, flaxseed, and soybean flours, along with whole-cereal grains.

If you are, as I hope, in a mood to embark on a bake-your-own-bread program for good nutrition, it is worthwhile looking into some of these sources for carefully milled flours and grains. They are likely to be somewhat more expensive than ordinary commercial grades, unfortunately, because they are produced in lesser quantities and by small mills rather than by the big combines. Moreover, because of widespread faddism which labels some foods as "health foods" and sells them in "health food stores," the prices of natural grains and flours from these sources are too often inflated beyond justice.

In the pages to follow, you will find a few recipes calling for some of these less easily obtained flours and grains. However, I face the reality that time, budget considerations, convenience, and the line of least resistance will inevitably lead all except the most zealous to the supermarket shelves. Therefore, the greatest number of recipes given here make the best of the more readily available whole wheat, unbleached, and vitamin-enriched flour in the happy knowledge that there are also readily available wheat germ, brewers' yeast, yeast flakes, and skim-milk solids to permit your bread to emerge from the oven with considerably more virtue than most of the stuff you're used to.

Using Commercial Mixes

The best advice in buying commercial biscuit and cake mixes is: don't. In bygone years, one could in good conscience tell the hard-pressed housewife how to improve the nutritional value (and the palatability) of these concoctions, by using wheat germ, soy flour, and nonfat milk. Now their labels read like prescriptions, and there are no nutritious additions that offset the undesirability of preservatives like BHA and BHT, or artificial flavors and colors. BHT has been found to have so profound an impact on the animal brain and animal behavior that a leading American University asked FDA to ban these chemicals from use as food additives. If you can locate mixes which are innocent of such chemicals, you can improve them nutritionally by the addition of nutritious yeast—1 teaspoonful per cup, and wheat germ in the same quantity. Even then you are still serving less nutritious food than your own baked recipes, made with yeast, for yeast recipes are always superior to those made with baking powder.

GOOD-NUTRITION BISCUITS
Baking Powder Biscuits
WHEAT-GERM BISCUITS

2½ cups whole-wheat or unbleached flour
1 teaspoon salt
2½ teaspoons double-acting baking powder
¼ cup skim-milk solids

1 cup wheat germ
3 tablespoons chilled solid shortening, lard, margarine, or
  bacon grease
¾ cup milk

Mix all dry ingredients together. Cut in shortening with pastry blender or two knives until mixture is coarsely granular. Add milk all at once and stir with a fork until moistened. Turn out on a floured board or waxed paper and knead lightly until fairly smooth. Pat or roll out to ¾ inch thickness and cut with floured biscuit cutter. Place on greased baking sheet and bake at 425° for 15 to 18 minutes. *Makes 16.*

Dropped Biscuits

Increase the milk by an additional ¼ cup. Drop by the spoonful onto greased baking sheet or into greased muffin tins.

Sour Cream or Sour Milk Biscuits

Substitute sour cream or sour milk for fresh for either of the preceding methods.

Vitamin C Biscuits

For the liquid, use half milk and half fruit juice—orange, pineapple, apricot, apple—anything you happen to have open, even tomato juice, whose vitamin C is protected in cooking by the natural acidity of tomatoes.

BRAN BISCUITS

1 cup whole-wheat, unbleached, or enriched flour
1 cup whole bran—or ½ cup each whole bran and wheat germ
½ teaspoon salt
¼ cup skim-milk solids

2½ teaspoons double-acting baking powder
4 tablespoons chilled solid shortening, lard, margarine, or bacon grease
½ cup milk

Mix all dry ingredients together. Cut in shortening with pastry blender or two knives. Add milk and stir with a fork. Dough will be soft. Pat it on waxed paper to ½ inch thickness, cut with floured biscuit cutter, and place on greased cookie sheet—or add a little more milk and drop by the spoonful onto sheet or into greased muffin tins. Bake at 425° for 15 to 18 minutes. *Makes 16.*

CHEESE BISCUITS

2 cups sifted enriched, unbleached, or whole-wheat flour
2½ teaspoons double-acting baking powder
¾ teaspoon salt

1 cup grated sharp yellow cheese
4 tablespoons solid shortening, lard, margarine, or bacon grease
¾ cup milk

Mix all dry ingredients together, including cheese. Cut in shortening with pastry blender or two knives. Add milk and stir with fork until well blended. Turn out onto lightly floured board or waxed paper and knead lightly. Pat or roll dough to ½ inch thickness, cut with floured biscuit cutter, and place on greased cookie sheet. Or—add ¼ cup more milk, mix well with dry ingredients, and drop by the spoonful onto sheet or into greased muffin tins. Bake at 450° for 12 to 15 minutes. *Makes 16.*

MASHED POTATO BISCUITS

Use either white or sweet potatoes.

1 cup whole-wheat, unbleached, or enriched flour
¼ cup wheat germ
1 tablespoon yeast flakes or brewers' yeast
1 tablespoon skim-milk solids
2½ teaspoons double-acting baking powder

1 teaspon salt
1 cup mashed potatoes
4 tablespoons melted butter or margarine, or oil
½ cup milk

204

Mix dry ingredients together. Stir melted shortening and milk into mashed potatoes, blending thoroughly, and add to flour mixture. Work dough with fork until well blended. Turn out onto lightly floured board or waxed paper, and knead only a few times, until fairly smooth. Roll or pat to ½ inch thickness. Cut with floured biscuit cutter, place on greased cookie sheet, and bake at 450° for 15 to 18 minutes. *Makes 12 to 15.*

BUCKWHEAT BISCUITS

A little on the heavy side, but very good—and reminiscent of Grandma's kitchen on a Sunday morning in winter.

1 cup whole-buckwheat flour
1 cup sifted unbleached, whole-wheat, or enriched flour
2½ teaspoons double-acting baking powder
1 teaspoon salt
¼ cup skim-milk solids
4 tablespoons lard or solid shortening
(about) ½ cup milk

Mix all dry ingredients together, and cut in shortening with pastry blender or two knives until well distributed. Add milk gradually, using only enough to make a soft dough which can be handled easily. Turn out onto a floured board or waxed paper and roll to ½ inch thickness. Cut with floured biscuit cutter, place on greased baking sheet, and bake at 450° for 12 to 15 minutes. *Makes 8 to 10.*

PEANUT BUTTER BISCUITS

2 cups whole-wheat or unbleached flour
¾ teaspoon salt (less, if peanut butter is very salty)
¼ cup skim-milk solids
3 teaspoons double-acting baking powder
1 tablespoon brewers' yeast or yeast flakes
3 tablespoons butter or margarine
4 tablespoons peanut butter
1 cup milk
1 tablespoon dark molasses or honey

Mix dry ingredients together. Cream butter or margarine with peanut butter; then cut this blend into the dry ingredients with a pastry blender or two knives. Add milk and molasses (or honey), and mix briskly with a fork. Drop by the spoonful onto greased cookie sheet or into greased muffin tins. Bake at 450° for 15 minutes. *Makes 12 to 15.*

SHORTCAKE BISCUITS

1¾ cups sifted unbleached or enriched flour	¼ cup skim-milk solids
2½ teaspoons double-acting baking powder	3 tablespoons chilled butter
1 teaspoon salt	¾ cup cream (try sour cream)
	1 tablespoon honey
	2 tablespoons butter, melted

Resift flour with other dry ingredients. Cut in chilled butter with pastry blender or two knives. Add cream and honey and stir well with a fork. Turn out onto lightly floured board or waxed paper, and divide dough into 2 unequal parts—roughly, ⅔ and ⅓. Pat or roll larger quantity into desired shapes or cut with floured biscuit cutter; then brush with melted butter. These are the bottom halves of shortcakes. Pat or roll remaining dough into similar but thinner shapes, and cover bottom halves. Bake on greased cookie sheet at 450° for 12 to 15 minutes. When slightly cooled, these biscuits are easily separated into halves. *No quantity given:* These may be made small, for dainty desserts, or large, for family servings.

Soybean Biscuits

If you've never tasted soybean flour biscuits—or soybean anything, for that matter—it might be wise for you to start out with either of the lesser quantities of soybean flour and the corresponding greater quantity of regular flour given in the following recipe. Unlike the grain flours, soybean has a distinctive taste of its own. Many people like this taste, others do not. In the lesser quantities it is not pronounced, yet it still provides excellent high-quality proteins lacking in grain. If you find that you and your family like the taste, increase the quantity of soybean flour in future recipes, ending up cup for cup with wheat flour. In a protein-needy nation, the more you can get the better.

SOYBEAN BISCUITS

2 cups flour, comprising ¼, ½, or 1 cup soybean flour and 1¾, 1½, or 1 cup whole-wheat or unbleached flour

2½ teaspoons double-acting baking powder

4, 3, or 2 tablespoons solid shortening (more if you are using less soybean flour, which has fat content)

⅔ cup skim-milk

Sift dry ingredients together, cut in shortening with pastry blender or two knives, and add milk quickly. Mix well, and knead lightly on a floured board or waxed paper. Roll or pat to ½ inch thickness, place on greased cookie sheet, and bake at 425° for 15 to 20 minutes. *Makes 12 to 18, depending on size.*

Note: If you recognize the value of soybean flour's protein content and wish to use it in maximum quantities but are not crazy about the taste, try using peanut butter and shortening, half and half. Cream them together and cut into the dry ingredients.

Yeast Biscuits

Make either of these recipes when you're expecting a crowd, or if you own a freezer. The use of yeast means a little more time and work than you ordinarily care to devote to mere biscuits—but, then, these aren't mere. The yields are large to permit you to make an impression at a party, or to freeze however many the family doesn't consume at one sitting. Freeze biscuits wholly baked, when cool, in plastic bags. To serve, put them into a 400° oven without thawing and remove them when heated through.

SOUTHERN RAISED SPLIT BISCUITS NO. 1

Eggless, single-rising, made with dry yeast.

1 package dry yeast

2 cups lukewarm milk, skim milk, or vegetable water

1 teaspoon salt

(about) 5 cups sifted enriched, unbleached, or whole-wheat flour

1 tablespoon brown sugar

¼ cup skim-milk solids

½ cup solid shortening or margarine—or ¼ cup each of shortening and butter

¼ cup butter or margarine, melted

207

Sprinkle yeast over lukewarm liquid and let it rest for 5 minutes while you sift dry ingredients together. Cut in the solid shortening with pastry blender or two knives. When thoroughly blended, add yeast-liquid solution and mix briskly with a fork until dough is soft. You may add a little more flour if necessary to make dough easy to handle. Turn out on floured board or waxed paper, and roll to ¼ inch thickness. Cut with floured cutter. Brush half the rounds with melted butter or margarine and top with the remainder. Place on greased cookie sheet, cover lightly with a clean cloth or towel, and let rise in a warm place (80 to 85°) for an hour or more, until double in bulk. Bake in (preheated) 425° oven for 10 to 12 minutes. *Makes 3 dozen.*

SOUTHERN RAISED SPLIT BISCUITS NO. 2

Triple-rising sponge method with eggs, potatoes, compressed yeast.

6 medium potatoes
1 compressed yeast cake
1 tablespoon brown sugar
2 cups lukewarm milk, skim milk, or vegetable water
½ cup solid shortening
½ cup butter
2 eggs

2 teaspoons salt
(about) 11 cups enriched or unbleached flour (up to 5 cups of total may be whole-wheat)
½ cup skim-milk solids
2 tablespoons brewers' yeast
½ cup butter or margarine, melted

While potatoes are boiling in their jackets, crumble yeast and sugar over the lukewarm milk or other liquid. When potatoes are soft, peel and mash them fine while they are still hot. Add shortening and butter, and mash again. Beat eggs with salt and beat into the hot potatoes. Add and stir in the yeast-liquid mixture. Stir in enough of the flour to make a soft sponge—about 3 cups. Let the sponge rise in a warm place until double in bulk. Sift together the remaining flour, milk solids, and brewers' yeast, and work this mixture into the sponge until the dough is easily handled. Knead lightly in the bowl until smooth, form into a tight ball, cover with clean cloth or towel, and let rise again until double. Punch down, roll on floured board to ½ inch thickness, and cut with floured biscuit cutter. Brush tops of half of the rounds with melted butter or margarine, top with the remaining rounds, cover, and let rise again until double on greased cookie sheets. Bake at 400° for about 15 minutes. *Makes 4 to 5 dozen.*

MUFFINS

If you can find commercial muffin mixes without the usual preservatives—and it is more of a possibility than with cake mixes—you can give them greater nutritional values by these steps:

When the box recipe calls for 1 cup of mix, add 1 or 2 teaspoons of wheat germ before filling the cup with mix.

When the box recipe calls for water, use vegetable cooking water.

When it calls for milk, put ⅛ cup of skim milk powder in a measuring cup, fill the cup with whole milk, and beat or blend until thoroughly dissolved.

Instead of sugar, use dark molasses or honey. With honey— which is not really more desirable than any other form of sugar —you will at least use less, for it is sweeter. The molasses at least gives a bit of iron and another useful nutrient.

But if you're going to be a c.g.n. cook (creative, good-nutrition) make your own muffins from scratch.

GOOD-NUTRITION PLAIN BAKING POWDER MUFFINS

2 cups whole-wheat, unbleached, or enriched flour
¼ cup wheat germ
2½ teaspoons double-acting baking powder
½ teaspoon salt
¼ cup skim-milk solids
1 egg

1¼ cups milk
2 tablespoons butter or margarine, melted
2 tablespoons bacon drippings or melted chicken fat
2 tablespoons dark molasses or honey

Combine dry ingredients and mix well. Beat together the egg, milk, melted shortenings, and sweetener. Pour these into the dry ingredient mixture all at once and stir briskly until batter is moist. Don't overwork. The batter will have a lumpy appearance, and that's how it should be. Fill greased muffin tins about ⅔ full and bake at 425° for 25 minutes. *Makes 12 to 15.*

BETTER-NUTRITION PLAIN YEAST MUFFINS

2 cakes compressed yeast—or 2 packages dry yeast

1 cup lukewarm milk, buttermilk, or skim milk

2 tablespoons butter or margarine, melted

2 tablespoons bacon drippings or chicken fat

2 tablespoons dark molasses or honey

1 egg, lightly beaten

1 cup whole-wheat, unbleached, or enriched flour

1 teaspoon salt

¼ cup skim-milk solids

½ cup wheat germ

Add yeast to warm milk and let stand for 10 minutes. Add shortenings, sweetener, and lightly beaten egg, and stir until well mixed. Sift together the flour, salt, and milk solids. Stir wheat germ into this mixture and add to the liquid. Stir briskly with a fork until moist and lumpy, and drop by the spoonful into greased muffin tins. These may be prepared an hour or so in advance of baking, if you wish them to rise. After they have doubled in bulk, bake at 425° for 15 minutes. Or—bake immediately at 350° for 20 minutes. *Makes 12 to 15.*

Special Note: Substituting Yeast for Baking Powder in Muffin Recipes

MOST OF THE RECIPES WHICH FOLLOW CAN BE MADE WITH YEAST INSTEAD OF BAKING POWDER—FOR BETTER NUTRITION, AND WITH VERY LITTLE EXTRA TROUBLE.

TO MAKE MUFFINS WITH YEAST: OMIT BAKING POWDER. USE 1 OR 2 CAKES OF COMPRESSED YEAST, OR 1 OR 2 PACKAGES OF DRY YEAST PER RECIPE. HEAT MILK (OR OTHER LIQUID SPECIFIED) TO LUKEWARM AND COMBINE WITH YEAST (AND SWEETENER, IF RECIPE CALLS FOR ONE). LET THIS MIXTURE STAND FOR 10 MINUTES. COMBINE REMAINING INGREDIENTS CALLED FOR IN RECIPE YOU ARE USING AND ADD TO THE YEAST MIXTURE. STIR BRISKLY WITH A FORK UNTIL MIXTURE IS MOIST AND LUMPY, AND DROP BY THE SPOONFUL INTO GREASED MUFFIN TINS. FILL THE CUPS TO THE HALF-WAY MARK. YOU MAY LET MUFFINS RISE IN A WARM PLACE UNTIL DOUBLE IN BULK AND THEN BAKE THEM AT THE OVEN TEMPERATURE AND BAKING TIME SPECIFIED IN THE RECIPE; OR—YOU MAY BAKE THEM IMMEDIATELY IN A 350° OVEN, INCREASING THE SPECIFIED BAKING TIME BY 5 TO 10 MINUTES.

210

OATMEAL MUFFINS

1½ cups sifted unbleached, whole-
  wheat, or enriched flour
⅓ cup oatmeal
¼ cup wheat germ
½ teaspoon salt
1 tablespoon brown sugar
1 tablespoon dark molasses or
  honey

¼ cup skim-milk solids
2½ teaspoons double-acting baking powder *
1 egg, beaten
1 cup milk
3 tablespoons melted margarine
  or oil

Combine all dry ingredients. Mix together the egg, milk, and melted shortening, and pour all at once into the dry ingredients. Stir briskly until moist but somewhat lumpy. Fill greased muffin tins ⅔ full and bake at 425° for 25 minutes. *Makes 12 to 15.*

FRUITED BROWN RICE MUFFINS

2¼ cups whole-wheat, unbleached,
  or enriched flour
¼ cup wheat germ
1 teaspoon salt
¾ cup chopped pitted dates, seedless raisins, or chopped cooked
  prunes

3 teaspoons double-acting baking
  powder *
1 cup milk
1 egg, beaten
¾ cup cooked brown rice
2 tablespoons oil or melted shortening

Sift together flour, baking powder, and salt, and stir in wheat germ. Add fruit, milk, beaten egg, rice, and shortening, and blend briskly. Fill greased muffin tins ⅔ full and bake at 425° for 30 minutes. *Makes 15 to 18.*

BANANA-BRAN MUFFINS

1 cup sifted whole-wheat, unbleached, or enriched flour
2 tablespoons skim-milk solids
½ teaspoon salt
1 cup whole bran
1 egg, beaten
3 tablespoons dark molasses

2½ teaspoons double-acting baking powder *
¼ cup milk
1 cup mashed ripe banana
2 tablespoons oil or melted shortening

---

* See note regarding yeast, page 210.

211

Sift together the flour, baking powder, milk solids, and salt. Stir in bran and distribute well. Combine egg, molasses, milk, banana, and shortening, and add all at once to dry ingredients. Stir briskly to blend. Fill greased muffin tins ⅔ full and bake at 400° for 20 to 25 minutes. *Makes 12 to 15.*

FRUIT-NUT BANANA FLAKE MUFFINS

½ cup enriched flour
½ cup whole-wheat flour
⅓ cup skim-milk solids
½ cup wheat germ
1 cup milk or buttermilk
2 tablespoons dark molasses, honey, or brown sugar
1 egg, beaten
3 tablespoons melted butter or margarine, or oil

1 teaspoon salt
2½ teaspoons double-acting baking powder *
½ cup seedless raisins
½ cup finely chopped or ground nut meats
⅛ cup banana flakes

Sift together the flours, milk solids, salt, and baking powder. Add and stir in wheat germ. Combine milk, sweetener, egg, and melted shortening, and add to dry ingredients, stirring just enough to mix. Fold in the nut meats, raisins, and banana flakes, distributing well. Fill greased muffin tins ⅔ full and bake at 425° for 12 to 15 minutes. *Makes 12 to 15.*

SOYBEAN MUFFINS

½ cup sifted soybean flour
1¼ cups sifted whole-wheat or unbleached flour
1 teaspoon salt
2 tablespoons dark molasses or honey
¾ cup milk or buttermilk

2 tablespoons skim-milk solids
2 teaspoons double-acting baking powder *
1 egg, beaten
2 tablespoons oil or melted shortening

Resift dry ingredients together. Combine sweetener, milk, egg, and shortening, and add all at once to dry ingredients, mixing

---

* See note regarding yeast, page 210.

only enough to moisten and blend. Fill greased muffin tins ⅔ full and bake at 400° for 25 minutes. *Makes 12 to 15.*

SOYBEAN-BRAN YEAST MUFFINS

2 cakes compressed yeast, or 2 packages dry yeast
1 cup warm milk, buttermilk, or vegetable water
2 tablespoons oil or melted shortening
½ cup whole-wheat flour

½ cup soybean flour
1 teaspoon salt
⅓ cup skim-milk solids
1 cup bran or bran flakes
(½ cup raisins or chopped nuts, optional)

Crumble or sprinkle yeast over warm liquid and let stand 10 minutes; then stir in the oil or shortening. Sift together the flour, salt, and milk solids, and stir into them the bran. Add liquid to dry ingredients (add raisins or nuts) and stir until moist and blended. Fill greased muffin tins ½ to ⅔ full. Either let rise until almost double in bulk and bake at 425° for 15 minutes, or bake immediately at 350° for 20 minutes. *Makes 12 to 15.*

APPLESAUCE MUFFINS

2 cups whole-wheat, unbleached, or enriched flour
¼ cup skim-milk solids
½ teaspoon salt
2 tablespoons dark molasses or honey
1 cup milk

2½ teaspoons double-acting baking powder *
1 egg, beaten
4 tablespoons oil or melted shortening
1 cup applesauce **

Sift together the flour, baking powder, skim-milk solids, and salt. Combine sweetener, milk, egg, and shortening, and add all at once to dry ingredients, stirring briskly until just moist and blended. Cover bottoms of greased muffin tins with a tablespoonful of batter; then add a scant tablespoonful of applesauce. Fill cups to ⅔ mark with remaining batter and bake at 400° for 20 minutes. *Makes 12 to 15.*

---

* See note regarding yeast, page 210.
** In the supermarket you should be able to find applesauce without added sugar, thereby 50 percent lower in carbohydrate calories.

DAY-OLD BREAD CRUMB MUFFINS

2 cups crustless day-old whole-wheat bread crumbs (coarse)
1 cup milk
¼ cup skim-milk solids
½ teaspoon salt
¼ cup wheat germ

2 eggs, beaten
¾ cup whole-wheat flour
2½ teaspoons double-acting baking powder *
2 tablespoons oil or melted shortening

Soak bread crumbs in milk for 10 minutes. Sift together milk solids, flour, baking powder, and salt. Combine with bread crumb and milk mixture and stir in wheat germ, beaten eggs, and shortening. Mix well and fill greased muffin tins half full. Bake at 400° for 20 minutes. *Makes 12 to 15.*

BERRY MUFFINS

1 cup naturally sweet berries of any kind
2⅔ cups whole-wheat, unbleached, or enriched flour
¼ cup skim-milk solids
2 tablespoons dark molasses, honey, or brown sugar

½ teaspoon salt
2½ teaspoons double-acting baking powder †
¼ cup butter, margarine, or solid shortening ‡
1 egg, beaten
1 cup milk

Toss berries lightly in about ½ cup of the flour and let them stand for at least 30 minutes. Sift remaining flour with salt, baking powder, and milk solids. Cream together the shortening and sweetener, and cut this into the flour mixture with a pastry blender or two knives. Stir beaten egg with milk and add to dry mixture, stirring only enough to moisten and blend. Fold in the floured berries. Fill greased muffin tins ⅔ full and bake at 400° for 20 minutes. *Makes 12 to 15.*

---

* Yeast can be used instead of baking powder. Toss bread crumbs in ½ cup of the milk and let stand for 10 minutes. Heat remaining ½ cup of milk to lukewarm and combine with 1 package dry yeast. Let stand for 10 minutes. Omit baking powder and proceed as directed, adding the yeast-milk mixture when you combine all ingredients.

† See note regarding yeast, page 210.

‡ You can, if you prefer, use melted shortening or oil, eliminating the creaming and cutting in. Mix milk with sweetener and liquid shortening, add to beaten egg, and add all at once to dry ingredients. Fold berries in last and bake as directed.

CUP-FOR-CUP CORN-MEAL MUFFINS

1 cup undegerminated corn meal
1 teaspoon salt
2 teaspoons brown sugar
2 tablespoons cooking oil
1¼ cups milk
¼ cup skim-milk solids

1 egg, beaten
1 cup whole-wheat, unbleached,
   or enriched flour
2½ teaspoons double-acting baking powder *
1 tablespoon brewers' yeast or
   yeast flakes

Put corn meal, salt, sugar, oil, and milk in top of double boiler, stir, and cook over boiling water for 10 minutes. Let cool. When cool, add beaten egg and stir. Sift together flour, baking powder, milk solids, and yeast, and stir into milk and corn-meal mixture. Fill greased muffin tins ⅔ full. Bake at 400° for 5 minutes, reduce heat to 350°, and bake 15 minutes more. *Makes 12 to 15.*

CORN-MEAL-BACON MUFFINS

4 slices bacon
2 cups undegerminated corn meal
½ teaspoon salt
¼ cup skim-milk solids
2 cups boiling vegetable water

1 cup cold milk
2 eggs
2½ teaspoons double-acting baking powder
2 tablespoons bacon drippings

Fry bacon crisp, drain, crumble, and reserve. Also reserve bacon drippings. Combine corn meal, salt, and milk solids in mixing bowl, and pour boiling vegetable water over the mixture. Immediately add cold milk; stir well to prevent lumps. Beat eggs into this mixture, add baking powder and bacon drippings, and blend well. Stir in crisp bacon bits. Pour into greased muffin tins and bake at 475° for 25 minutes. *Makes 15 to 18.*

RAISED GRIDDLE-BAKED ENGLISH MUFFINS

Caution: If English muffins are a favorite at your house, I advise you not to make these unless you resign yourself to repeating often. Freezer owners can make up several batches at a time to store for a month or two of Sundays. They'll keep

---

* See note regarding yeast, page 210.

longer than that in the freezer (up to a year), but not if the family knows where to find them.

¾ cup milk
½ cup water
¼ cup warm water
3 tablespoons shortening, melted (try chicken fat)
1 egg, beaten
1 tablespoon honey
4 cups sifted whole-wheat, unbleached, or enriched flour

1 cake compressed yeast, or 1 package dry yeast *
⅛ cup skim-milk solids
1½ teaspoons salt
2 tablespoons butter or margarine, melted
(about) ½ cup undegerminated corn meal or wheat germ

Scald milk with ½ cup of water, remove from heat, and cool to lukewarm. Crumble or sprinkle yeast over ¼ cup warm water and let stand 10 minutes. When scalded milk is lukewarm, add the dissolved yeast, melted shortening, beaten egg, and honey. Resift flour with milk solids and salt. Combine dry and liquid ingredients, mixing to a soft dough. Turn out onto a floured board and knead for about 5 minutes, adding a little more flour if necessary to make handling easy. Dough should remain soft, however. Put dough in greased bowl, brush top with melted butter or margarine, cover with clean cloth, and let stand until double in bulk—about 1 hour. Roll out on floured board to about ⅓ inch thickness and let rest for 3 minutes. Cut with floured biscuit cutter, rekneading the scraps gently and rolling similarly. Pick muffins up carefully with pancake turner and place them on baking sheets or trays liberally covered with corn meal or wheat germ. Sprinkle corn meal or wheat germ on top of muffins. Let rise for 30 minutes. Heat ungreased griddle until drop of water bounces on it; then reduce heat to low. With pancake turner, carefully move muffins to griddle and bake over low heat for about 5 to 7 minutes. Turn and bake other side for same length of time. *Makes 15 to 20.*

Note: Unless you have a really first-class pretreated griddle, it might be wise to rub the griddle lightly with an oiled rag before each batch of muffins to prevent scorching.

---

* For yeastier, faster muffins, use 2 cakes or packages of yeast. Reduce first rising time to 40 minutes, second rising to 20 minutes.

ROLLS

While any of the bread doughs in the section immediately following this one can be shaped into plain or fancy rolls, a few separate roll recipes are given here for new home bakers. (See discussion on enriching commercial mixes on page 202.)

Shaping Rolls

Dinner rolls: Pinch off pieces of dough the size of ping-pong balls. Roll into cylinders or balls. Bake about 2 inches apart.

Pan rolls: Follow directions for dinner rolls, but place rolls so that they touch each other, in a round, square, or oblong pan.

Finger rolls: Pinch off smaller pieces of dough, roll into cylinders, and place touching each other in a square or oblong pan.

Clover-leaf rolls: Roll dough on a floured board into a 1 inch thick rope. Cut into 1-inch slices. Roll each slice into a round ball and place three balls in each cup of a greased muffin tin.

Crescents: Roll dough on floured board into 12-inch circles about ¼ inch thick. Cut each circle into 6 pie wedges. Roll each wedge from outside in to the point. Curve slightly.

Braids: Divide dough into equal parts and roll each part into a long, thin rope. Roll ropes ¼ inch thick. Pinch together the tips of 3 strips and braid them like a pigtail. Cut into 2-inch or 3-inch lengths.

ELECTRIC MIXER ROLLS

1 cake compressed yeast, or 1 package dry yeast
1 cup warm milk, buttermilk, or vegetable water
4 tablespoons butter or margarine, melted
1 egg, lightly beaten

½ cup wheat germ
2¾ cups whole-wheat, unbleached, or enriched flour
¼ cup skim-milk solids
1½ teaspoons salt
(melted butter or margarine for brushing)

In large mixer bowl, crumble or sprinkle yeast over warm liquid and let stand for 10 minutes. Add melted butter or margarine and lightly beaten egg to bowl and stir until well mixed. Add and stir in wheat germ. Sift in the flour, milk solids, and salt. Beat at low speed for 5 minutes, cleaning sides of bowl often with rubber spatula. Let rise in warm place until double in bulk—about 1 hour. Punch down and form into rolls of desired shape, and let rise again until double in size, on oiled baking sheet or in oiled muffin tins. Brush with melted butter or margarine and bake at 425° for 10 to 15 minutes, the lesser time for smaller rolls. *Makes 12 to 18, depending on size and shape.*

RAISED CORN-MEAL ROLLS

½ cup undegerminated yellow corn meal
2 tablespoons brown sugar
1 teaspoon salt
2 cups milk
3 tablespoons melted butter, margarine, or bacon drippings

1 cake compressed yeast, or 1 package dry yeast
¼ cup warm water
2 eggs, lightly beaten
4½ cups sifted whole-wheat, unbleached, or enriched flour
⅓ cup skim-milk solids

Combine corn meal, sugar, and salt in top of double boiler. Add milk slowly, stirring until mixture is smooth. Add shortening, stir, and cook over boiling water until thick, stirring often to prevent lumps. Lower heat and continue to cook over hot water for 20 minutes. Remove from heat and let cool to lukewarm. Crumble or sprinkle yeast over warm water and let stand for 10 minutes; then add to corn-meal mixture. Stir in beaten eggs. Sift flour with milk solids and add, working in with hands to a soft, easily handled dough. Put dough in lightly greased bowl, cover with clean cloth, and let rise in a warm place until double in bulk—about 1 hour. Punch down, form into rolls, place on greased baking sheet or in greased muffin tins, and let rise again until nearly double in bulk. Bake at 425° for 15 minutes. *Makes 3 to 4 dozen, depending on size and shape.*

RAISED OATMEAL ROLLS

1 cake compressed yeast, or 1 package dry yeast
1¼ cups lukewarm milk
¾ cup dry oatmeal
1 tablespoon butter or margarine, melted

2 tablespoons dark molasses—or 1 each of molasses and honey
1 teaspoon salt
2 cups sifted whole-wheat, unbleached, or enriched flour
¼ cup skim-milk solids

218

Crumble or sprinkle yeast over warm milk and let stand for 10 minutes. Combine oats, shortening, sweetener, and salt in mixing bowl. Add yeast-milk mixture and beat by hand or with electric mixer until thoroughly blended. Sift flour with milk solids into the bowl and mix thoroughly into a fairly heavy batter. Drop by the spoonful into greased muffin tins, cover with a clean cloth, and let rise in a warm place until double in bulk—about 1 hour. Bake at 375° for 15 to 20 minutes. *Makes 15 to 18.*

RAISED HERB ROLLS

1¾ cups milk
3 tablespoons butter, margarine, bacon drippings, or chicken fat
1 tablespoon brown sugar
1 tablespoon dark molasses or honey
2 teaspoons salt
1 teaspoon ground nutmeg
½ teaspoon ground sage
½ teaspoon ground thyme
2 teaspoons caraway seeds
1 cake compressed yeast, or 1 package dry yeast
¼ cup warm water
2 eggs, beaten
6 cups whole-wheat, unbleached, or enriched flour
½ cup skim-milk solids
½ cup wheat germ

Scald milk; add shortening, sweeteners, salt, and herbs; stir, and set aside to cool to lukewarm. Crumble or sprinkle yeast over warm water and stir until dissolved. When milk is lukewarm, stir in yeast mixture. Add beaten eggs and about half of the flour to the liquid mixture. Beat thoroughly with rotary or electric mixer. Sift remaining flour with milk solids, mix with wheat germ, and add to beaten mixture, kneading in bowl or on floured board for about 3 minutes, until dough is smooth and springy. Place in greased bowl, cover with clean cloth, and let rise in warm place until double in bulk—about 1 hour. Punch down, shape into rolls, place on greased baking sheet, cover, and let rise again until double in bulk. Bake at 400° for 20 minutes. *Makes 2 dozen.*

BREAD

When you reach the point of baking your own bread for the sake of good nutrition, let's not have any nonsense about "quickie" loaves tossed together with one hand tied behind your back while the other hand measures out baking powder or baking soda. If speed is what you want, make biscuits. But if real, honest, body-and-soul-satisfying, praiseworthy *bread* is your goal, approach its creation as lovingly as an artist and be prepared to let it rise nobly and leisurely. For the most part you'll be working with yeast in the following recipes—or, rather, yeast will be working with you—and yeast insists on time in which to accomplish its leavening process.

Don't begrudge the time it takes to convert flour, liquid, shortening, and yeast into the aromatic poetry which emerges from your oven. Much of that time will not concern you directly. While the dough rests and rises you can be shopping, or doing chores, or watching television.

If you time your baking preparations strategically, you will have popped the loaf pans into the oven a half hour or so before your mate opens the front door to be greeted by the maddening perfume of hot, fresh, home-baked bread. This experience makes the term "breadwinner" less a cliché than an honorable title. (A nutritionist is not a marriage counselor, but I'm willing to bet that the ratio of divorces might just possibly drop in proportion to the number of households where home-baked bread is part of family enjoyment.)

Bread baking is neither mysterious nor difficult. Follow directions carefully. A few baking terms with which you should become familiar follow.

Baking Terms and Directions

Scald: Put cold liquid in a pan over moderate to high heat, and heat to just below the boiling point. When small bubbles appear around the edges where liquid meets pan, the proper scalding temperature has been reached.

Mix: Unless directions tell you to make a "sponge," which means to add only enough flour to form a loose, batterlike dough to which more flour will be added later, mixing requires you to use a rather large bowl in which you can begin to stir ingredients with a heavy spoon or fork. As they thicken, mix the ingredients by working them with your clean hands until well blended.

Knead: When dough is turned out on a floured board, it is likely to be a little sticky, clinging to your fingers and the board. Kneading means that you continually fold the dough over toward you, pressing down with the palms of your hands, turning it slightly, and folding and pressing again, until it becomes smooth and elastic.

Rise in a warm place: On warm summer days or evenings, just set the dough in a bowl on the counter in your warm kitchen. Yeast likes a temperature of from 80 to 85°. On cool or cold days, this temperature can be achieved by setting the bowl in your *unlighted* oven over a pan of hot (110°) water and closing the oven door. You may also place a covered bowl near a radiator or heat register.

Double in bulk: Yeast will usually cause dough to double its bulk in from 45 minutes to 2 hours, depending on how much yeast is used, its proportion to the other ingredients, and the warmth of the surroundings. Double or nearly double bulk is the size to aim for. Less will mean a heavy, unbread-like bread. More will mean a dry, coarse crumb because when yeast dough blows up beyond its desirable size it almost invariably deflates and falls down of its own accord. If you don't trust your eye to tell you when the dough has actually and accurately doubled, poke it in the center with your fingertips. If it is ready for the next step, it won't bounce back but will retain the imprint of your fingers.

Baking times are given in the recipes, but some ovens are "faster" than others. Bread is done when the loaf shrinks inward a little from the sides of the pan. When it is removed from the oven, remove it immediately from the pan and let it cool on a rack before slicing and eating.

Always preheat oven to indicated temperature before baking bread.

221

GOOD-NUTRITION WHITE BREAD

Rising time about 2 hours. *Makes 3 loaves.*

3 cups whole or skim milk
2 cakes compressed yeast, or 2
    packages dry yeast
2 tablespoons honey
6 cups sifted unbleached flour
½ cup soybean flour or unde-
    germinated corn meal
¾ cup skim-milk solids

4 teaspoons salt
3 tablespoons brewers' yeast
3 tablespoons wheat germ
2 tablespoons liquid or melted
    shortening—oil, bacon drip-
    pings, chicken fat, butter, or
    margarine

Scald milk and cool to lukewarm. Crumble or sprinkle yeast over lukewarm milk, add honey, and let stand for 5 minutes. Resift flour with soybean flour, milk solids, salt, and brewers' yeast. Stir in wheat germ (and corn meal, if you are substituting this for soybean flour) and distribute well. Stir yeast-milk mixture, and, while stirring, add half of the flour mixture. Beat vigorously with rotary or electric beater until smoothly blended, add shortening, and beat again to mix well. Add remaining flour mixture, stirring first with a heavy spoon and then working with your hands. Turn dough out on a floured board and knead for about 5 minutes, until dough is smooth and elastic. (Use up to 1 cup more of unbleached flour if necessary.) Grease a large bowl, put dough in, and then turn dough upside down to grease all surfaces. Cover bowl with a slightly dampened clean cloth, and let dough rise in a warm place (80 to 85°) free of draughts until nearly double in size. This takes about 45 minutes, usually.

Punch dough down, fold edges in, and replace in bowl to rise 20 minutes more.

Turn out on a lightly floured board and divide dough into 3 equal parts. Fold each portion in toward its center to make smooth, tight balls. Cover with cloth and let rest on board for 10 minutes.

Shape 3 loaves to fit 3½- by 7½-inch tins and let rise in the tins until dough again doubles in size—about 45 minutes. Bake in preheated oven at 350° for a total of about 50 minutes. If loaves begin to brown within 15 or 20 minutes, reduce oven temperature to 325°. Remove from tins and put on rack or cloth to cool.

GOOD-NUTRITION YELLOW BREAD

Rising time about 3 hours. *Makes 2 loaves.* (This a substantial, compact, somewhat heavy bread—a stick-to-your ribs loaf especially good when toasted.)

1 cake compressed yeast or 1 package dry yeast
¼ cup warm vegetable water
2 cups milk
3 tablespoons dark molasses or honey
3 tablespoons brown sugar
⅛ cup liquid or room-temperature shortening

2½ teaspoons salt
6 cups unbleached or enriched flour
2 eggs, lightly beaten
1 cup undegerminated yellow corn meal
½ cup wheat germ

Crumble or sprinkle yeast over warm vegetable water and let stand for 5 minutes. Scald milk and combine with sweeteners, shortening, and salt. Mix well, and let cool to lukewarm. When lukewarm, add softened yeast, lightly beaten eggs, and 3 cups of the flour. Beat until smoothly blended with rotary or electric mixer. Add corn meal, wheat germ, and remaining flour, mixing first with a heavy spoon and then with your hands to make a soft dough.

Turn out on lightly floured board and knead for 10 minutes. Place in a greased bowl, turning once to grease all surfaces. Cover with slightly dampened clean cloth and let rise in a warm place until double in bulk—about 1½ to 2 hours. Punch down and let rest for 10 minutes. Divide dough in half and shape into 2 loaves. Place them in greased tins. Cover and let rise again until almost double—about 1 hour. Bake at 375° for 40 to 45 minutes.

100 PER CENT WHOLE-WHEAT BREAD

Rising time about 2 hours. *Makes 2 loaves.*

1 cake compressed yeast, or 1 package dry yeast
½ cup lukewarm vegetable water
1 tablespoon brown sugar or honey
2 cups milk or skim milk
2 tablespoons any oil or room-temperature shortening (try bacon or ham grease or chicken fat)
1 tablespoon salt
6 tablespoons dark molasses
5½ cups whole-wheat flour
(½ cup wheat germ)

Crumble or sprinkle yeast over warm water; add honey and stir. Scald milk, remove from heat, and stir in shortening, salt, and dark molasses. Combine yeast water with milk mixture and beat with rotary or electric beater until well blended. Add liquid to flour (mixed with wheat germ), mix well, and knead in bowl for 2 or 3 minutes * (add a little vegetable water or milk if dough is stiff). Put dough in large greased bowl, turning once to grease all surfaces. Cover with a slightly dampened cloth and let rise until double in bulk—about 1 hour. Divide in equal parts without punching dough down, and form gently into 2 loaves which fit easily into greased bread pans. Cover and let rise again in warm place until double in bulk—about 1 hour. Preheat oven to 375° and bake for 20 minutes. Reduce heat to 325° and bake for 50 minutes to 1 hour, until bread shrinks away from sides of pans.

WHEAT-GERM BREAD

Rising time 2½ to 3 hours. *Makes 1 loaf.*

1 cup milk
1½ teaspoons salt
1 tablespoon brown sugar
1 tablespoon oil or melted shortening
1 cake compressed yeast, or 1 package dry yeast
(about) 3 cups sifted whole-wheat or unbleached flour
1 cup wheat germ

---

* If you prefer a smoother grain, knead for 5 minutes. After first rising, punch down and knead again for 2 or 3 minutes before forming loaves.

224

Scald milk. Combine salt, sugar, and shortening and pour over these ingredients ¾ cup of the scalded milk. When remaining ¼ cup of scalded milk is lukewarm, crumble or sprinkle yeast over it and let stand. Combine 2½ cups of the flour with all of the wheat germ. Add dissolved yeast to milk mixture, beating with rotary or electric beater until thoroughly blended. Add to flour and mix thoroughly. Turn out onto board floured with remaining ½ cup of flour and knead for about 5 minutes, until dough is smooth and elastic. Put dough in greased bowl, turning to grease all surfaces. Cover with dampened cloth and let rise in a warm place until double in bulk. Knead again, lightly, on floured board. Cover (on board) with dampened cloth and let rise again until double in bulk. Punch down, shape into loaf, and put in greased bread tin. Cover and let rise again until double in bulk. Bake at 350° for 35 to 40 minutes.

WHEAT-GERM FRENCH BREAD (WHITE OR WHOLE-WHEAT)

Rising time about 2 hours, 40 minutes. *Makes 2 loaves.*

1¼ cups vegetable water
1 cake compressed yeast, or 1 package dry yeast
1½ teaspoons salt
1 tablespoon softened shortening

1 tablespoon sugar
2½ cups sifted enriched, unbleached, or whole-wheat flour
1 cup wheat germ

Heat vegetable water to lukewarm. Crumble or sprinkle yeast over vegetable water and stir until dissolved. Stir in salt, shortening, and sugar. Combine flour with wheat germ and add liquid. Mix well. On lightly floured board, knead from 8 to 10 minutes, until dough is smooth and elastic. Put dough in greased bowl, turning to grease all surfaces. Cover with slightly dampened cloth and let rise in a warm place until double in bulk—about 45 minutes. Punch down and let rise again, covered, until almost double in bulk—about 30 to 35 minutes. Punch down again, turn out onto lightly floured board and divide dough into 2 equal parts. With floured rolling pin, roll each part out into an oval, or uneven circle, about 10 inches long. Roll each oval tightly, starting at the wider side and rolling toward you. Roll back and forth to stretch to desired length, putting more pressure on both ends to taper them. Put loaves on greased baking sheets and, with sharp scissors or knife, cut diagonal slits across tops. Let rise in warm place until almost double in bulk—from 1 to 1½ hours. In preheated 400° oven, put a shallow pan of boiling water. On rack above water, bake loaves for 15 minutes. Reduce heat to 350° and bake for 30 minutes more.

If you want your loaves to be shiny, brush them about 5 or 10 minutes before they are due to come out of the oven with one of the following glazes:

1 egg white beaten with 1 tablespoon water, or
1 teaspoon cornstarch mixed with 1 teaspoon cold water and then with ½ cup boiling water, cooked until smooth and clear and slightly cooled

NO-FAT, NO-KNEAD BREAD

Rising time, in oven, 1 hour. *Makes 1 large or 2 small loaves.* This is not the most exciting loaf in the book, but it's tasty and satisfying—as low in calories as it's possible for decent bread to be—and very easy to make. It would be a kindness to spend the little time required to bake a week's supply at a time for household members on reducing or low-fat, low-salt diets.

Note: Be sure to follow directions carefully. If dough is allowed to rise too high, or if pans are too full, the loaves will be difficult to remove.

1 teaspoon honey (molasses if you're using whole-wheat flour)
2½ cups warm vegetable water; or skim milk, scalded and cooled to lukewarm
1 cake compressed yeast, or 1 package dry yeast

4 cups sifted flour (try in rotation whole-wheat, unbleached, or enriched)
½ cup wheat germ
1–2 teaspoons salt, depending on rigor of diet

Stir sweetener into 1 cup of the warm liquid; then crumble or sprinkle yeast over it and let stand for 5 minutes. Combine flour, salt, and wheat germ. Stir liquid mixture into flour and add the remaining warm liquid slowly, stirring until you have a moist, well-blended dough. With a spatula scrape the dough into 1 or 2 very well greased bread pans (for strict dieters, use a no-fat pan spray), filling less than half full. Level the dough with spatula. Let rise at 100° for 1 hour or less. (A pan of hot water in an unlighted oven will provide a sufficiently warm rising place.) When dough has almost doubled, remove pan of water. Raise oven temperature to 450° and bake for 5 minutes. Reduce heat to 350° and bake for 40 to 50 minutes, until loaf pulls away from sides of pan.

MRS. LATHROP'S OATMEAL BREAD

Rising time 2 to 2½ hours. *Makes 4 loaves.*

2¼ cups old-fashioned (not quick-cooking) oatmeal
4 teaspoons salt
1 cup molasses (all dark, or half dark and half light)
8 tablespoons oil (or 4 oil, 4 bacon drippings)
1 cup wheat germ

4 cups boiling vegetable water (potato water is excellent)
2 packages dry yeast
⅔ cup warm water
⅓ cup brewers' yeast
10 cups unbleached flour (1 cup of this may be soybean flour)
1½ cups skim-milk solids

In your largest mixing bowl combine oatmeal, salt, molasses, oil, and wheat germ. Stir to distribute thoroughly. Pour over this 4 cups of boiling vegetable water and let stand while you do the following: Sprinkle yeast over ⅔ cup of warm water and let stand. Sift together the brewers' yeast, flour, and milk solids. Stir yeast-water mixture into oatmeal mix; then add flour, mixing first with a heavy spoon and then with your hands. If dough seems too sticky, add a little more flour until it is easy to work with. Turn out onto floured board and knead for 5 minutes. Return to the bowl, now washed and well greased, cover with slightly dampened cloth, and let rise until double in bulk—about 1 hour. Punch down, separate into 4 equal parts, and shape loaves, putting them into 4 greased bread tins. When double in bulk—about 1 hour—bake at 375° for 40 to 45 minutes.

SWEET RYE BREAD

Rising time 8 hours. Set it overnight, if you don't sleep more than 6 hours. *Makes 2 loaves.*

2 cups milk	¼ cup lukewarm water
½ cup skim-milk solids	2 tablespoons caraway seeds
¼ cup shortening	7¾ cups rye flour
½ cup dark molasses	4 tablespoons brewers' yeast
⅓ cup honey	(about) ½ cup regular flour for
2 teaspoons salt	the board
1 cake compressed yeast or 1 package dry yeast	

Scald milk and milk solids together and pour over shortening, molasses, honey, and salt in a large bowl. Stir until dissolved and let cool to lukewarm. Soften yeast in ¼ cup lukewarm water and stir into the milk mixture. Add caraway seeds. Combine flour and brewers' yeast and work into the liquids, mixing first with a heavy spoon and then with the hands. Turn out on floured board and knead for 10 to 15 minutes, until dough is smooth and springy but not too stiff. Put dough in a greased bowl, turn dough upside down to grease the top, cover with a clean cloth, and let rise in a warm place until double in bulk. This will take about 6 hours. Punch down, knead again for 3 or 4 minutes on floured board, and shap into 2 round or oval loaves. Put them closely together on a greased baking sheet, cover, and let rise again until double in bulk—about 2 hours this time. Bake at 400° for 15 minutes, reduce heat, and bake at 350° for 35 to 40 minutes more.

DR. CLIVE McKAY'S TRIPLE RICH CORNELL BREAD

This is a high-protein, high-vitamin, high-mineral bread, restoring many of the nutritional values depleted in the milling of white flour, and vastly improving on ordinary white bread. Moreover, it is perfectly acceptable to the majority of white-bread devotees, many of whom will not accept whole-wheat bread. The Cornell mix itself is simple: in an 8-ounce measuring cup, put in 1 tablespoon of soy flour, 1 teaspoon of wheat germ, and 1 tablespoon of nonfat dry milk powder. Now fill the cup with white flour, preferably unbleached. Thoroughly stirred, this is now used to make a bread which closely resembles ordinary white bread in appearance, but is flavorful and nutritious. It is a perfect way to outflank the family who as yet will not accept whole grains, though its lack of bran keeps it from being a complete substitute for whole wheat. (The bran has unique values in the human diet, but you can work it in in other ways—bran muffins, for instance [see Soybean-Bran Yeast Muffins, page 213].) To make the bread, use about 6 cups of well-mixed and sifted Cornell mix. Have on hand:

2 tablespoons vegetable oil (without additives)
1 tablespoon sea salt
2 tablespoons dry yeast (granule form—available at health food stores)
2 tablespoons honey
3 cups warm water

Soften two tablespoons of the yeast in 3 cups of water. Add the honey. Mix the sea salt with 3 cups of the Cornell mix. When the yeast-honey-water mixture bubbles, gradually add to it the 3 cups of Cornell mix, beating it by hand about 70 or 80 times. You can use an electric mixer, but hand-beaten, it somehow turns out better for me. Now add the 2 tablespoons of oil, and enough of the remaining Cornell mix to form it into a dough which is moderately stiff. Knead this on a flour board, until its texture is smooth and elastic. Then shape it into a ball, place it in a bowl greased with a little oil, and oil the top of the ball.

You are now ready to let it rise: just cover it and put it in a warm place—which doesn't mean oven heat—until it rises to about double the original size. That should take about 45 minutes.

Now use your fist to deflate the ball, fold the edges in, and turn it upside down, letting it rise again for another 20 minutes. Now turn the dough out on the board (which should still be floured). Split the dough into 3 approximately equal parts, and fold each one inward until it is a smooth and tight ball.* Cover these with a cloth, and wait 10 minutes. You are now ready to shape each of the 3 into loaves, and put them in oiled bread pans.

---

* One of these can be used to make rolls, if you wish, as a pleasant change of pace for breakfast.

In about 45 minutes, the loaves should double in bulk, and you are now ready for baking—325° for 45 minutes, or so. (Vague, because ovens differ in characteristics. 50 minutes may be necessary. The appearance of the loaves will tell you, when you have gained a little experience.)

The recipe should be called: "How to attract small children and keep the wandering husband at home." That isn't theory—this is the special bread we baked for the children at our summer camps. They enjoyed it, and never discovered that we were infiltrating their defenses, and feeding them better nutrition.

STEAMED WHEAT-GERM BROWN BREAD

Makes two 1-quart molds.

2 cups milk or buttermilk
2 cakes compressed yeast, or 2 packages dry yeast
¾ cup dark molasses
1 egg, lightly beaten
1 cup wheat germ
1 cup undegerminated yellow corn meal

1 cup whole-wheat flour
¼ cup skim-milk solids
1 teaspoon salt
(½ cup seedless raisins or chopped nut meats—or both)

Scald milk and let cool to lukewarm. Crumble or sprinkle yeast over milk and let stand for 5 minutes; then stir in molasses and beaten egg. Combine dry ingredients and stir into liquid, blending well. (Fold in raisins and/or nut meats.) Pour into greased molds or tins (clean coffee or fruit juice cans will do). Fill them half full. Cover closely with lids, cheesecloth, or aluminum foil, and set on a rack or trivet in a large kettle over 1 inch of boiling water. Steam, with kettle tightly covered, for 2 hours. Lift tins from kettle with tongs, remove covers, and dry in 350° oven for 15 minutes.

Good-nutrition Desserts

11

Good-nutrition Desserts

Contrary to a popularly held unpopular belief, "dessert" is
not a forbidden word in the nutritionist's vocabulary. It merely
requires definition. Unfortunately, even a conscientious homemaker who makes honest attempts to feed her family sensibly is
likely to boggle at a decision about dessert. Should she infuriate
her loved ones by serving raw fruit—and raw fruit only? Should
she risk alienation, divorce, or runaway children by withholding
dessert entirely? Or should she succumb to family brainwashing
techniques, toss discretion and nutrition to the winds, and go
hog-wild with—oh, dear—sugar?

Needless to say, the author of this cookbook is not going to en-
courage you to stuff your family with empty calories and nutri-
ent-sabotaging goo. Nor is he going to say, in paraphrase of what
might be your rationalizations, "Well, you've virtuously fed
your folks a good substantial breakfast, supervised a nutritious
lunch, and crammed plenty of vitamins, minerals, and proteins
into dinner's main courses. Go ahead—satisfy the yearnings of
their sweet little teeth."

On this point I am inflexible. Living and eating should be fun
—but not at the expense of health. Rich, sugary desserts in the
quantities they are consumed by the American public indict

233

themselves, sooner or later. Along with candy, soda pop, and overstarchy diets, they account in part for this nation's appalling record of obesity, tooth decay, skin disturbances, and a long list of minor to serious illnesses. They do this by direct attack—and more subtly by ruining the appetite for foods which feed the hungry body.

Although the reward-dessert habit can be broken—by feeding larger portions of real food, and sometimes by drastic scenes in which the housewife screams back at her screaming children (including Papa), these are not ideal solutions. In the first place, children (including Papa) who can't possibly finish their vegetables because they're too full, miraculously find room for a 500-calory half-pound dessert. In the second place, anyone old enough to open the front door unaided is likely to run, not walk, to the nearest candy store to buy a little something sweet to sustain him. So let's not have any delusions. If Mama makes too much fuss without voluntary family cooperation or the honor system, she may breed a houseful of candyholics.

Ingenious and loving ways can be found to pamper a sweet tooth, of course, but the ideal in nutrition is to extract such a tooth from the oral cavity—or at least to deaden its nerve. A sweet tooth does not grow naturally in the mouth. It is an acquisition, useless and often harmful, but nevertheless present in many people for a variety of reasons. (An inordinate craving for sweets should be investigated by the family physician. It may betoken the presence of functional or organic disease, such as hypoglycemia or diabetes.)

It is hardly any wonder that multitudes of Americans grow up to be dessert fetishists. As children they were repeatedly warned—"No dessert until you eat all your spinach," thus making spinach a hateful punishment and dessert a shining reward. The reward image persists in adulthood and gets all mixed up with the emotions. Some people take to drink when their problems (which often include nutritional ones) get too much for them. Others find some satisfaction in stuffing themselves with sweets—"rewards" to compensate for their frustrations, fears, insecurity, and privately suspected inadequacies. Still others use sweets to serve a kind of self-bolstering competitiveness—a way of keeping up with the Joneses. Their reasoning seems to be, "Well, I can't afford a fancy new car, but I *can* eat rich."

Except in rare instances the nutrition-minded American wife and mother is totally unable to convert her family to the ideal and typical European dessert—fresh fruit and cheese, which supply natural sugar and vitamins plus a desirable amount of milk proteins. Oddly enough, a husband may rave about Madame La Parisienne's fruit bowl and cheese tray when invited to this glamorous lady's dinner table. He may smile expansively over his cigar smoke when being entertained by the company's sales manager at a continental restaurant where fruit and cheese are brought to the table with the demitasse and cognac. But try to serve this as a home dessert! The wife who does is usually flattened by husbandly sarcasm or told, not for the first time, that *Mother* thought enough of her boy to bake seven-layer cakes and whipped cream pies every single day.

It does very little good, many a housewife wails, to explain the food facts of life to her household. Her husband, for the most part, is stunned and outraged by the idea that food has any function beyond tasting good and filling his stomach. The children, with wide-eyed innocence and irrefutable logic, are prone to remarks like, "But we're not *hungry* for broiled grapefruit. We're hungry for marshmallow-fudge sundaes—like Tommy's mother gives us."

The nutrition-conscious homemaker should remember that chocolate layer cake usually means 12 to 14 teaspoons of sugar per portion; that baked apples prepared by old-fashioned methods carry more calory value from sugar than from apples and may mean the loss of about 70 per cent of the fruit's vitamin C content. She should remember that the easy-to-use puddings and desserts on supermarket shelves (except on the higher-priced "dietetic" list) are filled with overprocessed starch and sugar, and that even so-called "slimming" prepared gelatin desserts may be up to 85 per cent sugar. She should remember, moreover,

235

that the anticipation of a gooey dessert frequently prompts her domestic dinner companions to bypass another helping of foods which do have nourishing qualities.

The end-of-the-meal stumbling block is not insurmountable. Acceptable desserts need not compromise with standards of good nutrition. They need not be dull, and they need not be peculiar. A sweetening agent is usually unavoidable, but all that sweetens is not sugar. There is honey, and there is dark molasses, both of which contain a certain goodness which sugar lacks, even though they are about equal in calories, spoon for spoon, and as injurious to teeth if allowed to remain in the mouth without rinsing. There are also on the market a few satisfactory man-made sweeteners in granular, tablet, or liquid form which contain no sugar —or nutrients either, for that matter. However, they may be used on occasion in place of sugar, either entirely or in part, following the manufacturers' recommendations for proportions.

Despite my reputation as a stormy critic of overprocessed foods, it is not sugar itself (or alone) which is my target. It is, rather, the public's avid consumption of unbelievably excessive quantities of sugar which rouses my ire—and sympathies. Sugar is no nutritional bugaboo when it is used as a condiment in discreet amounts or even, sometimes, in amounts which seem to exceed discretion, provided the rest of the day's meals have supplied adequate intake of nutrients and provided also that the dessert which includes sugar includes also elements which contribute to total nutrition.

GELATIN DESSERTS

SUGARLESS WHIPPED GELATIN DESSERT

1 envelope unflavored whole gelatin
¼ cup cold water
½ cup skim-milk solids
hot water

1 cup sugar-free carbonated soda —any favorite fruit or berry flavor
1 egg white
½ teaspoon vanilla

Soften gelatin in ¼ cup cold water. Put skim-milk solids in a measuring cup and stir in enough hot water to yield a cupful of

milk. Dissolve softened gelatin in milk and add 1 cup of sugar-
free carbonated soda. Stir to blend well; then chill in refrigerator until firm. Add vanilla and whip mixture until frothy.
Beat egg white until stiff and fold into the whipped gelatin. Return to refrigerator until firm. Serve as is, or with topping of
fresh or frozen fruit or berries—unsweetened. *Serves 4.*

HOMEMADE GELATIN DESSERT

2 tablespoons unflavored gelatin	if necessary with sugarless
½ cup cold water	sweetener, honey, or brown
½ cup boiling water	sugar
3 cups fresh, frozen, or canned	(1 cup sliced fresh, frozen, or
fruit juice sweetened to taste	canned fruit or berries *)

Soften gelatin in cold water; then add the solution to boiling
water and stir until dissolved. Add fruit juice, blend thoroughly,
and pour into molds or cups which have been rinsed with cold
water. Firm in refrigerator. If this is to be served plain, let it set
thoroughly. If you are going to add fruit, do so when the jelly is
only half firm. *Serves 4 to 6.*

CUSTARDS

GOOD-NUTRITION "BOILED" CUSTARD

4 egg yolks	⅛ teaspoon salt
2 tablespoons brown sugar	2 cups milk
2 tablespoons dark molasses or	⅓ cup skim-milk solids
honey	flavoring (see end of recipe)

Stir egg yolks with a fork until blended but not frothy. Add
sweetener and salt, and stir. Scald milk and milk solids together,
add slowly to egg mixture, and stir or beat until all ingredients
are well blended. Pour mixture into a heavy-bottomed saucepan
and stir over low heat until it thickens—5 to 7 minutes, depending on how you interpret "low heat." There are two ways to
determine when custard has cooked enough: (1) when it coats

---

* Fresh or frozen-fresh pineapple (not canned) must be boiled for 2 or
3 minutes before it is added to gelatin.

the spoon or (2) when a cooking thermometer reads 175°. When one of these two things happens, remove pan from stove, allow custard to cool slightly, and then chill it in refrigerator. A few minutes before serving, flavor custard by stirring in your choice of:

1 teaspoon vanilla, maple, or rum flavoring	1 teaspoon lemon juice ½ teaspoon almond extract

If you like, add also ½ cup grated or shredded cocoanut. This is a soft custard, not firm, and may be served alone or mixed with fresh, frozen, or canned fruit, or it may be spooned over small servings of ice cream or good-nutrition puddings or cake. *Serves 4.*

Note: For a coffee-flavored custard, add 1 tablespoon instant coffee or instant coffee substitute to scalded milk before beating.

GOOD-NUTRITION BAKED CUSTARD

3 cups milk	⅛ teaspoon salt
½ cup skim-milk solids	butter or margarine for greasing custard cups
4 whole eggs or 6 egg yolks	nutmeg, cinnamon, shredded cocoanut, or finely ground nuts for garnish
2 tablespoons brown sugar	
2 tablespoons dark molasses or honey	
1 teaspoon vanilla (or ½ teaspoon almond extract)	

Scald milk and milk solids together. Beat eggs or yolks with a fork and add sweeteners, vanilla or almond extract, and salt. Pour scalded milk over these ingredients slowly, stirring constantly. Do not beat. Pour into lightly greased custard cups to within ¼ inch of top, and sprinkle with garnish. Set cups in large, flat baking pan partly filled with hot water. Cups should rest in water to the halfway mark. Bake at 300° for 35 to 40 minutes, until a stainless steel knife, inserted in the center of one cup, comes out clean. Serve warm or chilled in cups—or inverted on dessert plates and surrounded with fresh, frozen, or canned fruit. *Makes 4 large or 6 small servings.*

Note: For better nutrition and a pleasantly nutty taste, add 4 to 6 tablespoons of wheat germ to the mixture before you pour it into the custard cups, stirring to distribute evenly.

PUDDINGS

FRUIT TAPIOCA PUDDING

Processed tapioca is no prize, but the addition of eggs, skim-milk solids, and fruit can make nutritional sense out of this old favorite.

½ cup skim-milk solids
2¾ cups whole or skim milk
2 eggs, separated
4 tablespoons quick-cooking tapioca
2 tablespoons brown sugar—or 1

teaspoon sugarless liquid
  sweetener
⅛ teaspoon salt
½ teaspoon vanilla
1–2 cups diced fresh, frozen, or
  canned fruit—or berries

Add milk solids to either whole or skim milk and scald. Beat egg yolks slightly with a fork and add to scalded milk. Stir in tapioca, sweetener, and salt. Cook over moderate heat or in double boiler for about 10 minutes, stirring frequently. Do not let it boil. Remove from heat and let cool slightly. Stir in vanilla. Beat egg whites until stiff and fold into tapioca mixture. Chill and serve topped with fruit. *Serves 4 to 6.*

OLD-FASHIONED CUSTARDY RICE PUDDING

2 eggs
½ cup skim-milk solids
1⅔ cups whole milk
2 tablespoons each of dark molasses and honey—or 4 of
  brown sugar
¼ teaspoon salt

1 teaspoon vanilla
1 cup seedless raisins
1¼ cups cooked rice (preferably
  brown, but at least converted)
¼ teaspoon mixed cinnamon and
  nutmeg

Beat eggs. Combine milk solids with milk, add eggs, and beat again. Add sweetener, salt, vanilla, raisins, and rice, and stir until sugar is dissolved (if you're using sugar) or until molasses and honey are well distributed. Pour into a greased casserole and sprinkle top with mixed spices. Put casserole in a shallow pan of hot water; bake at 325° until a stainless steel knife, inserted at the center, comes out clean—about 30 minutes. *Serves 4.*

BROWN RICE AND MOLASSES PUDDING

1 cup skim-milk solids	1 cup brown rice
5 cups milk	¼ cup wheat germ
2 egg yolks	2 tablespoons butter or margarine
½ teaspoon salt	½ teaspoon vanilla
4–6 tablespoons dark molasses	1 cup chopped dates, chopped mixed dried fruits, or raisins
½ teaspoon ginger	

Dissolve milk solids in milk, and beat in egg yolks, salt, molasses, and ginger. Heat in top of double boiler until hot—not boiling—and slowly add rice and wheat germ. Stir, cover, and steam over simmering water for 1 hour, until rice is tender. Stir in butter and vanilla. Drop chopped fruit into 1 cup of boiling water, reduce heat, and simmer for 5 minutes. Drain and stir fruit into rice mixture. Serve hot or cold, with or without crushed fruit or sauce (pages 249–251). *Serves 6 to 8.*

BROWN RICE APPLE PUDDING

2 cups cooked brown rice	½ cup raisins
2 eggs, separated	4 medium-sized sweet apples
¼ teaspoon salt	3 tablespoons butter or margarine, melted
¾ teaspoon cinnamon	
⅓ cup brown sugar	

Combine cooked rice with beaten egg yolks, salt, cinnamon, sugar, and raisins. Slice or chop unpeeled apples very fine and add to mixture. Fold in beaten egg whites. Stir in melted butter and pour pudding into well-greased baking dish. Bake at 350° for 30 minutes. *Serves 4 to 6.*

GOOD-AS-GOLD VEGETABLE PUDDING

2 cups peeled, diced raw sweet potatoes, carrots, winter squash, or pumpkin	½ cup skim-milk solids
	¾ cup dark molasses
	½ teaspoon salt
3 cups salted water (½ teaspoon salt)	1 tablespoon butter or margarine
	¼ teaspoon each cinnamon, ginger and nutmeg
½ cup undegerminated yellow corn meal	⅛ teaspoon ground cloves
3 cups milk	½ cup seedless raisins

Cook diced vegetables in salted water until soft. Drain, reserving water, and mash. Bring 2 cups of the vegetable water to boil and slowly add corn meal, stirring. Reduce heat and cook, stirring, until thickened. Add and mix well the mashed vegetables, milk with milk solids, molasses, salt, butter, spices, and raisins. Pour into a greased baking dish and bake at 325° for 1 hour. *Serves 6 to 8.*

BREAD PUDDING

5 cups diced crustless fresh (or 4 cups stale) whole-wheat (or your own home-baked) bread
3 cups warm milk
½ cup skim-milk solids
2 whole eggs, or 4 egg yolks
2 tablespoons wheat germ

2 tablespoons brown sugar
4 tablespoons dark molasses
1 teaspoon vanilla
¼ teaspoon nutmeg
¼ teaspoon cinnamon
½ cup seedless raisins

Moisten bread in warm milk with milk solids. Beat eggs or yolks, combine with remaining ingredients, and add to moistened bread, tossing with fork until well blended. Pour into greased baking dish and set dish in pan of hot water. Bake at 325° for 1 hour. Serve hot or cold with crushed fruit, applesauce, or custard sauce (page 237). *Serves 4 to 6.*

FRUIT SOUFFLE BREAD PUDDING

2½ cups diced fresh crustless whole-wheat (or your own home-baked) bread
1½ cups milk
¼ cup skim-milk solids
juice of 2 oranges—or 1 jar apricot or peach baby purée

rind of 1 orange, grated
2 tablespoons wheat germ
¼ teaspoon salt
2 eggs, separated
⅛ cup honey

Soak bread in milk mixed with milk solids. Add juice or purée and stir with a fork. Add and blend in grated rind, wheat germ, and salt. Beat egg yolks with honey and add. Beat egg whites until stiff and fold into mixture. Pour into greased baking dish, set dish in pan of hot water, and bake at 325° for 40 minutes *Serves 4.*

INDIAN PUDDING

Not authentic Indian, but a good way to get eggs, whole grains, and wheat germ into your papooses.

4 slices crustless whole-wheat bread	2 eggs
2 tablespoons butter or margarine	¼ teaspoon salt
4 tablespoons wheat germ	4 tablespoons dark molasses
	2½ cups milk
	¼ cup skim-milk solids

Spread bread with butter or margarine. Put slices in greased baking dish and sprinkle generously with wheat germ. Beat together all remaining ingredients and pour over the bread. Bake at 300° for 1 hour. *Serves 4.*

PEANUT BUTTER PUDDING

1½ cups diced crustless whole-wheat bread	2 cups milk
½ cup wheat germ	2 tablespoons skim-milk solids
4 tablespoons peanut butter	2 egg yolks
1 tablespoon brown sugar	⅛ teaspoon salt

Combine diced bread and wheat germ, and spread over bottom of well-greased baking dish. In a saucepan, blend peanut butter and sugar. Combine milk and milk solids, and stir slowly into pan. Cook over low heat, stirring until smooth. In a bowl, beat eggs lightly with salt. Pour hot mixture over beaten eggs, stirring to blend thoroughly. Pour liquid over bread-crumb mixture in baking dish, place dish in pan of hot water, and bake at 350° for about 45 minutes, until a stainless steel knife blade inserted in the center comes out clean. *Serves 4 to 6.*

COTTAGE CHEESE SOUFFLE PUDDING

3 tablespoons butter or marga-
    rine, melted
3 tablespoons whole-wheat or un-
    bleached flour
½ teaspoon salt
1 cup warm milk
2 tablespoons skim-milk solids

3 eggs, separated
4 tablespoons brown sugar
2 tablespoons lemon juice
1 teaspoon grated lemon rind
½ cup seedless raisins
1 cup cottage cheese
2 tablespoons wheat germ

Blend butter, flour, and salt to a smooth paste. Combine milk with milk solids and add slowly, stirring until no lumps remain. Cook in top of double boiler until thickened and smooth, and remove from heat. Beat egg yolks; add sugar, lemon juice, and rind; and stir. Add egg mixture to sauce and stir; then add raisins and cottage cheese, and stir or beat until very smooth. Beat egg whites stiff and fold into mixture. Pour into well-greased baking dish, sprinkle with wheat germ, place dish in pan of hot water, and bake at 350° until set—about 30 to 40 minutes. *Serves 4 to 6.*

GOOD-NUTRITION FRUIT DESSERTS

BROWN BETTY

Apples are traditional for this pudding, but it may be made with other fruits—either alone or combined. Frozen, stewed, or canned apricots or peaches are nice, using the fruit juice in place of the lemon juice and water called for in the following recipe.

1 cup whole-wheat bread crumbs
    or graham cracker crumbs
½ cup wheat germ
¼ cup butter or margarine,
    melted
2½ cups sliced apples (with or
    without peels)
½ cup seedless raisins

2 tablespoons honey
⅓ cup brown sugar
¾ teaspoon cinnamon
¼ teaspoon nutmeg
⅛ teaspoon cloves
½ teaspoon salt
1 tablespoon lemon juice in ¼
    cup water

Combine crumbs, wheat germ, and melted butter. Cover bottom of a lightly greased baking dish with about one-third of this mixture. Sprinkle apples and raisins, combined, with honey and toss lightly to distribute evenly. In another bowl combine sugar with spices and salt, mixing well. Put half of the honeyed apple-raisin mixture over crumbs in baking dish, and sprinkle with half of the sugar-spice mixture and half of the lemon water. Cover with another layer (one-third) of the crumb mixture, then with the rest of the apples. Sprinkle with remaining sugar-spice mixture and again with lemon water. Top with final one-third of crumbs. Cover baking dish and bake at 350° for 35 minutes. Remove cover, increase oven heat to 400°, and brown for 10 to 15 minutes. Serve hot with custard sauce (page 237), cream, or sour cream. *Serves 4 to 6.*

TOP-OF-THE-STOVE BROWN BETTY

4 slices crustless whole-wheat bread
2 tablespoons butter or margarine
4 tablespoons wheat germ
2 tablespoons honey
2 cups sweet sliced or crushed fruit—apples, peaches, apricots, berries

Dice bread into ½-inch cubes and brown in butter or margarine in skillet. Sprinkle with wheat germ and stir in the honey and fruit. Cover skillet and cook over low heat until fruit is tender—about 6 to 7 minutes. Serve hot or cold, with custard sauce (page 237) or sweet or sour cream. *Serves 4.*

BLENDER "BETTY"

If you have an electric blender, you can whip up a delicious, nutritious, low-calory dessert in a few minutes. Quantities are omitted (except for the suggested proportions of wheat germ) because much depends on the type and size of the fruit used.

Into the blender put, a little at a time, cut-up pieces of fresh, sweet, unpeeled fruit—apples, pears, peaches, nectarines, plums. Run the blender at low speed until fruit is puréed. To each cupful of purée add enough wheat germ to give a pudding consistency (some fruits will take as much as 6 tablespoons of wheat germ per cup of purée). If you like, you may stir in raisins,

244

chopped dates or figs, or broken nuts. Because this dessert supplies so many nutrients at moderate calory cost, you may—if you want to—top it with custard sauce (page 203) or whipped cream.

Lacking a blender, a similar dessert can be made by using baby fruit purées or your own or canned applesauce, mixed with wheat germ.

FRUIT PAN DOWDY

2 cups sliced naturally sweet apples, peaches, apricots, or nectarines
2 tablespoons brown sugar
¼ teaspoon each salt, nutmeg, and cinnamon

½ cup hot fruit juice
½ recipe wheat-germ biscuit dough (page 195) or shortcake biscuit dough (page 206)

Spread sliced fruit over bottom of well-greased baking dish. Mix sugar with seasonings and sprinkle over fruit. Pour hot fruit juice over this and bake at 400° for 10 to 15 minutes, until fruit is tender. Remove from oven. Pat or roll biscuit dough to proper size and cover fruit. Return to 400° oven and bake 15 to 20 minutes, until dough rises and browns. *Serves 4 to 6.*

GOOD-NUTRITION BAKED APPLES

4 large, firm apples
2 tablespoons honey
2 tablespoons wheat germ

1 tablespoon butter, melted
1 tablespoon orange or lemon juice

Scrub and dry apples. Core them carefully without cutting through the bottoms, and peel only the tops—removing about 1 inch of the peel. Put them in a baking dish. Combine honey, wheat germ, melted butter, and juice, and fill hollows of the apples with this mixture. Sprinkle with cinnamon or nutmeg. Preheat oven to 400°. Add ¼ cup of boiling water to the baking dish and bake the apples only until they are tender, basting occasionally. They should not bake for more than 30 minutes, and some varieties will be tender in 15 minutes. Serve hot or cold, with or without cream, sour cream, whipped cream, or whipped topping (page 249). *Serves 4.*

STEAMED PUDDINGS

Because of the comparatively long time it takes to steam something, and the traditional use of baking powder or soda, you might as well say farewell to the vitamin C content of whatever it is you're steaming, along with a sizable portion of the water-soluble B vitamins.

But there's a holiday excitement about a steamed pudding, and there aren't too many holidays when you're willing to go to the trouble of making one—so go ahead. Just be sure to use whole-grain or unbleached flours; add wheat germ whenever possible; use little or no sugar; fortify the milk with skim-milk solids—and avoid undoing all the good of these loving precautions when it comes to the sauce. (The vitamins, I trust, appear elsewhere in the day's menus and in supplements.) Recipes for sugarless or sugar-minimum pudding sauces start on page 249.

Steaming Rules

Lacking a special steamer, you can improvise one with a tight-lidded Dutch oven or heavy kettle and a rack or trivet that will raise the molds about an inch from the bottom. Instead of molds as such you can use cans (coffee, baking powder, etc.) which have fitted covers. Even ovenproof bowls will do—stainless steel, ovenproof glass, or ceramic. These you can cover with cheesecloth and aluminum foil, tied around with string.

Water must be boiling in the bottom of your steaming vessel when the recipe is ready to be cooked, and the water must remain boiling throughout the steaming process. This usually means that you must add water—boiling water. It is not necessary to keep the vessel over high heat. Once the water has begun to boil, heat may be reduced to moderate and the water will continue to boil gently.

Fill molds ½ to ⅔ full.

CARROT PUDDING

1 cup whole-wheat bread crumbs	1 cup dark molasses
½ cup wheat germ	½ cup seedless raisins
¼ teaspoon salt	½ cup ground nuts
1 teaspoon baking powder	½ cup chopped dates
1 tablespoon butter or margarine, melted	2 tablespoons lemon juice
1 cup grated carrots	1 teaspoon grated orange or lemon rind

Combine bread crumbs, wheat germ, salt, and baking powder, and mix thoroughly. Add remaining ingredients in turn, stirring after each addition. Fill well-greased molds ⅔ full, cover, and steam according to directions on page 246 for 3 hours. *Serves 4 to 6.*

OATMEAL PUDDING

¾ cup rolled oats	2 eggs
½ cup wheat germ	½ cup dark molasses
1 tablespoon skim-milk solids	⅔ cup milk
½ teaspoon baking soda	1 tablespoon orange or lemon juice
¼ teaspoon salt	

Combine dry ingredients, mixing to distribute evenly. Beat eggs and mix with molasses, milk, and juice. Stir dry mixture into liquid, blending thoroughly. Pour into greased molds, filling ½ full; cover and steam according to directions on page 246 for 2½ hours. *Serves 4 to 6.*

STEAMED WHOLE-WHEAT PUDDING

1½ cups whole-wheat flour	1 cup raisins, chopped dates, chopped figs, chopped pitted prunes, or other dry fruit
½ cup wheat germ	½ cup dark molasses
¼ cup skim-milk solids	1 cup milk
½ teaspoon salt	
½ teaspoon baking soda	

Combine dry ingredients, mixing thoroughly. Toss raisins or other fruit in molasses until well coated and combine with dry mixture. Combine both of these mixtures and add milk, stirring to blend well. Pour into greased molds, filling ½ to ⅔ full; cover and steam according to directions on page 246 for 2 hours. *Serves 6 to 8.*

CRANBERRY PUDDING

1½ cups sliced raw cranberries
2 tablespoons brown sugar
1½ cups whole-wheat or unbleached flour
2 teaspoons baking powder

½ teaspoon salt
¼ cup wheat germ
2 eggs
½ cup molasses
⅓ cup milk

Toss cranberries in brown sugar and let stand. Sift together flour, baking powder, and salt, and mix in the wheat germ, distributing well. Beat eggs with molasses and milk. Combine flour mixture and liquid, stir well, and then fold in the sweetened cranberries. Pour into greased molds, filling ½ full; cover and steam according to directions on page 246 for 1½ hours. *Serves 6 to 8.*

BLUEBERRY PUDDING

1½ cups blueberries
1 cup whole-wheat or unbleached
  flour
2 teaspoons baking powder
1 tablespoon skim-milk solids
2 eggs

2 tablespoons honey
2 tablespoons brown sugar
3 tablespoons butter or margarine, melted
½ cup milk

Put blueberries in a paper bag, add about 1 tablespoon of the flour, and shake until coated—or toss them until coated in a small bowl. Sift remaining flour with baking powder and milk solids. Beat eggs with honey, sugar, melted butter or margarine, and milk. Combine dry and liquid ingredients and fold in the floured berries. Pour into small greased molds, filling ½ full; cover and steam according to directions on page 246 for 30 minutes. *Serves 6 to 8.*

STEAMED FRUIT BISCUIT ROLL

2 cups sliced naturally sweet
  fresh or frozen fruit or berries of any kind
2 tablespoons honey
2 tablespoons brown sugar
½ teaspoon cinnamon, nutmeg, or
  ginger

2 teaspoons grated lemon or orange rind
1 recipe for wheat-germ drop biscuit dough (page 195)
2 tablespoons butter or margarine, melted

Toss fruit gently with honey, sugar, spice, and ground rind until it is well coated. Make biscuit dough and roll it out on

248

floured board to ¼ inch thickness. Brush dough with melted butter or margarine. Spread fruit mixture over dough, leaving about 1½-inch margins all around, and roll or fold it over. Moisten edges of dough and press together firmly. Wrap the roll loosely in a clean cloth, allowing room for expansion, and place on rack or trivet above boiling water. Cover vessel and steam for 1½ hours. *Serves 6 to 8.*

GOOD-NUTRITION SAUCES

BLENDER FRUIT SAUCE

If you have an electric blender, you can make a deliciously nutritious sauce for almost any pudding (or ice cream) in a few minutes. Using whole sweet berries or cut-up naturally sweet unpeeled seasonal fruit of any variety except citrus, put a little at a time in the blender and run it at low speed until the fruit is puréed. If the fruit or berries are tart, you may add a little honey, dark molasses, brown sugar, or sugarless liquid sweetener —but not until the fruit is puréed. You will find that the purée is often sweeter than the whole fruit.

SUGARLESS WHIPPED TOPPING

½ cup skim-milk solids
½ cup ice-cold milk—or ice water

¾ teaspoon liquid sugarless sweetener

Put milk solids in a chilled mixing bowl. Add cold liquid and sweetener, stir until mixed, and beat vigorously until like sauce.

CITRUS SAUCE

2 eggs
¼ cup brown sugar—or 2 table-spoons sugar, 2 tablespoons honey—or 2 teaspoons sugarless liquid sweetener
½ teaspoon grated orange, lemon, or lime rind

pinch of salt
1 tablespoon skim-milk solids
½ cup warm milk
2 tablespoons orange, lemon, or lime juice

Beat eggs until frothy in top of double boiler. Beat in the

sweetener, grated rind, and salt. Put hot (not boiling) water in bottom of double boiler and place over very low heat. To mixture in top of double boiler add milk solids, warm milk, and fruit juice, continuing to beat until the sauce is smooth, warm, and slightly thickened—about 2 or 3 minutes.

PRUNE OR APRICOT SAUCE

1 cup pitted prunes or dried apricots
1 cup boiling water
½ cup orange juice

2 tablespoons dark molasses or honey
¼ teaspoon cinnamon

Pour boiling water over dried fruit and soak for 2 hours. Bring to the boiling point, lower heat, and simmer gently for 20 minutes, until fruit is soft. Remove fruit and purée it in blender or food mill. Thin pulp with orange juice, and, if necessary, add a little of the cooking water. Sweeten with molasses or honey and flavor with cinnamon. Mix well. (Save cooking water in refrigerator for other sauces, or a repeat of this one. Use instead of plain water.)

SPICY APPLE CIDER SAUCE

1 tablespoon butter, melted
1 tablespoon whole-wheat flour
1 cup warm apple cider
⅛ teaspoon ground cloves

⅛ teaspoon ground ginger
(honey, dark molasses, or brown sugar—if needed)

Blend melted butter with flour in saucepan. Set over low heat and slowly stir in the warm apple cider. Add spices and bring to boiling point, stirring; then remove from heat. Taste when cool enough, and add—if necessary—a little honey, dark molasses, or brown sugar.

HOT BUTTERY WINE SAUCE

If you use a good, sweet fruit or berry wine you won't have to add sugar.

2 egg yolks
6 tablespoons butter, melted
1 cup sweet fruit or berry wine

¼ teaspoon grated nutmeg, ginger, or cinnamon

Beat egg yolks thoroughly and stir into melted butter. Set over low heat and stir in wine, beating with wire whisk to blend thoroughly. Add spice and serve when hot, smooth, and thickened.

COCOA SAUCE

2 tablespoons cocoa
1 tablespoon cornstarch
pinch of salt
2 tablespoons butter or margarine, melted
⅛ cup skim-milk solids

¾ cup milk
2 tablespoons brown sugar—or 2 teaspoons liquid sugarless sweetener
½ teaspoon vanilla

Combine cocoa, cornstarch, and salt. Blend with melted butter or margarine to a smooth paste. Add milk solids, milk, and sweetener; stir and cook over low heat until slightly thickened. Remove from heat and stir in vanilla. Set pan in ice-cold water and stir until cool—about 5 minutes. Sauce will get thicker as it cools.

GOOD-NUTRITION FROZEN DESSERTS

FREEZER POPS

Many a child has been switched from sugary ice pops to Mom's clever substitutes: In individual plastic ice cube cups, or in plastic trays out of which you can press a single cube, pour any natural fruit juice your child likes—orange, pineapple, berry, mixed-fruit, etc. Place a pop stick or small drinking straw in a corner of each cup and let it rest on the outer rim. (Several doctors' wives I know use narrow tongue depressors for the sticks.) Freeze.

These are popular with children in warm weather, especially since you need not put maternal restrictions on the number they can have. (Why is it children always seem to ask, "Can I have two?") Each pop represents only a small portion of what would in its original form be a glass of fruit juice. Older children soon learn to make their own out of favorite fresh, reconstituted frozen, or canned fruit juices—a pleasant form of parental permissiveness. Puréed baby fruits can also be used, although the juices go further and contain less added sugar, or none at all.

251

"ICE CREAM" POPS

Children who balk at drinking milk will accept these. For an ice cube trayful, mix ½ cup skim-milk solids with 1 cup whole milk and flavor with vanilla, fruit juice, a little chocolate syrup, instant cocoa, or—treat of treats—instant decaffeinated coffee. You may be able to get away without adding sweetener. If not, sweeten the mixture before pouring into the trays with honey or dark molasses. Freeze as in preceding recipe for Freezer Pops.

SUGARLESS FRUIT SHERBET

two 6-ounce cans unsweetened frozen juice concentrate (orange, pineapple, grape, berry, etc., singly or in combination)

3½ cups cold water
2 tablespoons liquid sugarless sweetener
1 cup skim-milk solids

Put all ingredients in a large bowl (or electric mixer, if you have one) and beat vigorously until well blended. Pour into ice cube trays or flat dishes and freeze only until mushy—about 1 hour. Return to chilled mixing bowl and beat at low speed until soft, then at high speed until creamy—about 3 to 5 minutes. Pour into trays or dishes again and freeze. Serve in chilled sherbet glasses or dessert dishes topped with crushed fruit or berries. *Makes about 1½ quarts.*

SUGARLESS FROZEN CUSTARD

1¼ cups milk
½ cup evaporated milk
2 teaspoons unflavored whole gelatin
½ cup skim-milk solids

½ cup cold water
1 tablespoon liquid sugarless sweetener
2 teaspoons vanilla *
½ cup ice water

Combine milk and evaporated milk, and scald. Remove from heat. Soften gelatin in cold water and add to scalded milk. Add sweetener and vanilla, and stir well, until thoroughly mixed. Pour into ice cube trays and cool to room temperature. When cool, freeze until center is mushy (edges may be frozen). Pour into chilled bowl and beat at low speed until smooth and creamy.

---

* For other flavors, omit vanilla. Before second freezing, beat ½ to 1 cup any mashed or puréed fruit or ½ cup banana flakes. For coffee custard, add 1 tablespoon instant regular or decaffeinated coffee to scalded milk.

In separate chilled bowl dissolve milk solids in ice water and beat vigorously until it has the consistency of whipped cream. Fold whipped milk into former mixture, return to trays, and freeze until firm. *Makes about 1 quart.*

HONEY-BERRY ICE CREAM

2 cups hulled sweet full-ripe strawberries, raspberries, or blackberries	2 tablespoons honey
⅓ cup milk	½ cup whipping cream—or ½ cup skim-milk solids and ½ cup ice water

Mash or purée berries, stir in milk and honey, and blend thoroughly. Pour into ice cube trays and freeze until mushy. Pour into chilled bowl and beat at low speed until smooth and creamy. Whip cream—or dissolve skim-milk solids in ice water and beat until it has the consistency of whipped cream. Fold into fruit mixture, return to trays, and freeze—or freeze in sherbet glasses if these are heavy (thin ones may crack in the freezer). *Makes about 1½ pints.*

GOOD-NUTRITION CAKES

As with everything else you cook, the choice is yours when you bake a cake. You can concentrate on its gorgeous height, its perfect symmetry, its fine texture, and its melt-in-your-mouth sweetness—or you can consider its contribution to good diet.

You know by now that I am not happy about the amount of white flour and white sugar consumed by the American public—even that part of it which says, indignantly, "I never use sugar!" The individual who may not so much as put a sugar bowl on the table nevertheless manages to swallow more than a hundred pounds of it a year. You doubt this? Please refer to my earlier book, *Low Blood Sugar and You,* published by Grosset & Dunlap, in which you will find a great deal of information about the unsuspected ways in which high sugar intake is causing illness for us; and a table listing the sugar content of many popular foods. For example, there is ½ teaspoon of sugar in a stick of chewing gum—and there are 15 teaspoons of sugar in a single serving of frosted chocolate cake. There are 3 to 5 teaspoons of sugar in a 6-ounce glass of cola or carbonated soda pop—and up to 7 teaspoons per small-sized candy bar.

While you'd expect to find sugar in generous amounts in these and other foods classified as "sweets," which you say you never eat, there is a surprising quantity of it in many foods not classified as sweets—in canned vegetables, for example, and frozen heat-and-serve main courses or complete dinners, in commercial bread and rolls and breakfast cereals. In addition, restaurant patrons unwittingly eat enormous amounts of sugar. It seems that when a chef, like a food processor, is stumped for a condiment to add to a recipe to ensure its palatability, his reflexes move his arm automatically toward the sugar bin. There is sugar in restaurant and cafeteria gravies, stews, pot roasts, meat loaves, casseroles, spaghetti sauces, and some creamed vegetables.

My opinion of white flour can be found elsewhere in this book, preceding the bread section.

Except for the dedicated gourmet crowd and determined seekers after truly optimum nutrition (the two are not necessarily mutually exclusive), American housewives who bake the family's cakes from scratch are becoming as scarce as their sisters who bake the family's bread—which is to say, they're vanishing like the American whooping crane.

Yet, who can blame the millions of busy homemakers for turning to prepared cake mixes as naturally and gratefully as flowers turn their faces to the sun? Cleverly and delectably compounded, these mixes are attractively packaged and found on supermarket shelves in such mouth-watering variety as to make flour sifting and resifting, shortening blending, and endless beating as old hat as bending over a washboard. As further seduction, several of the cake-mix companies include in their packages disposable cake pans or mixing bags. Not even any bowls to wash! And to make absolutely certain the home cook is freed of further decision and responsibility, some companies offer ready-to-mix ingredients for frostings.

While I cannot quarrel with streamlined techniques which improve the lot of the busy housewife, I can and do quarrel with any food whose repeated use at the expense of good nutrition may impose hidden or deferred taxes on the body's well-being. The run-of-the-mill commercial cake mix is composed of refined white flour, refined white sugar, and not-so-refined artificial flavorings and colorings. There is, to be sure, some sort of enrichment program afoot, and "enriched" has become a magic word even on cake mix boxes. The word has about as much real meaning as the word "large" on a can of olives. To get really large olives, you have to look for the word "jumbo." To get really enriched cake, you do one simple thing: Make your own cakes from recipes with ingredients whose nutrient values are intact, which do not rely heavily on sugar for palatability, and on synthetic preservatives, dyes, and artificial flavors.

Except for gingerbread, spice, and other dark cakes, making a cake out of whole-wheat flour may seem a little on the odd side to the eyes—if not the taste—of people accustomed to airy-fairy angel-food and other pale cakes. And while not even this adamant antagonist of white sugar will try to make you bake all your cakes without any sugar at all, you will be asked to try brown sugar and, in some recipes, to replace some of the sugar with molasses or honey. (It is also possible to use sugarless sweeteners for cake baking, and the pharmaceutical houses which manufacture the sweeteners to be found on any dietetic shelf will be delighted to send you their recipe booklets. See also Where to Find Special-purpose Foods, page 28.)

SUNBURNED ANGEL CAKE

1½ cups brown sugar
½ cup strained orange juice
1 cup sifted whole-wheat pastry flour
¾ teaspoon cream of tartar

¼ teaspoon salt
8 eggs
1 tablespoon strained lemon juice
½ teaspoon vanilla or almond extract

Stir sugar into orange juice and cook over low heat, stirring, until sugar is dissolved. Continue to cook without stirring until mixture becomes syrupy, forming a thread when a small amount is dropped from a spoon. Remove from heat. Resift—at least 4 times—the flour with cream of tartar and salt. Separate the eggs and beat the yolks well. Add lemon juice and beat again. Beat the egg whites until stiff but not dry; then slowly beat in the sugar-orange syrup and extract. Add yolk mixture to dry ingredients; then fold in the beaten egg whites. Pour into an ungreased angel cake pan, "cut" the batter with a knife to eliminate air bubbles, and bake at 375° for 15 minutes. Reduce heat to 250° and bake 15 to 20 minutes longer. Remove pan from oven and invert on rack or trivet. Let it cool for at least 1 hour before removing the cake from the pan.

WHEAT-GERM BUTTER LAYER CAKE

1½ cups sifted whole-wheat pastry flour
3 teaspoons baking powder
¼ teaspoon salt
½ cup skim-milk solids
3 teaspoons wheat germ

½ cup butter
1 cup sugar
3 eggs
1 cup milk
½ teaspoon vanilla, almond, or maple extract

Resift flour with baking powder, salt, and milk solids. Stir wheat germ into mixture, distributing it evenly. Cream butter and sugar. Stir eggs into milk with a fork. Combine flour mixture with creamed sugar and liquid, and beat with 250 strokes by hand or 2½ minutes in electric mixer. Stir flavoring into batter. Pour into 2 lined or greased-and-floured layer cake pans and bake at 350° for 35 minutes. Remove from pans; cool on rack or trivet. Spread one layer with custard sauce (page 237) with added slices of naturally sweet fresh or frozen fruit or berries. Top with second layer.

WHEAT-GERM GINGERBREAD

2 cups sifted whole-wheat flour
½ teaspoon salt
2¼ teaspoons double-acting baking powder
1 teaspoon cinnamon
1 (or 2) teaspoon(s) ginger
3 teaspoons wheat germ
¼ cup skim-milk solids

1 cup dark molasses
⅓ cup butter, margarine, or vegetable shortening
½ cup buttermilk or light sour cream
1 egg, beaten
2 tablespoons brown sugar

Thoroughly mix together all dry ingredients except sugar. In small saucepan heat molasses and shortening together until melted. Stir and cool somewhat—not too much. Combine mixture with buttermilk (or light sour cream), beaten egg, and brown sugar, and add to the dry ingredients. Mix batter well without beating, and pour into lined or greased-and-floured cake pan and bake at 350° for 40 minutes. Serve hot or cold with custard sauce (page 237) or sugarless whipped topping (page 249).

FLOURLESS CARROT CAKE

5 eggs, separated
1 cup brown sugar
1 teaspoon vanilla
¼ teaspoon salt

½ pound carrots, grated fine
½ pound almonds, ground or pulverized
¼ cup wheat germ

Lightly beat egg yolks and mix with sugar, vanilla, and salt. Add and stir in the grated carrots, ground almonds, and wheat germ. Beat egg whites until stiff but not dry and fold into mixture. Bake in spring form at 350° for 1 hour.

OATMEAL SPICE CAKE

2 cups boiling water
1 cup seedless raisins
1 cup oatmeal
1 cup sifted whole-wheat flour
4 teaspoons wheat germ
1 cup brown sugar
2½ teaspoons baking powder

½ teaspoon each cinnamon, nutmeg, cloves
¼ cup skim-milk solids
½ cup solid shortening
1 egg
1 cup milk or buttermilk

Pour boiling water over raisins to plump them; then drain and reserve. Combine all dry ingredients and mix thoroughly. Cut in shortening with pastry blender or two knives. Stir egg into milk and add to flour mixture. Beat to blend thoroughly, stir in raisins, and pour into lined or greased-and-floured cake pan. Bake at 350° for 40 minutes.

GRAHAM CRACKER CAKE

1 cup brown sugar
½ cup solid shortening
2 eggs, beaten
1 cup sifted whole-wheat flour
¼ cup skim-milk solids
2 teaspoons baking powder

¼ teaspoon salt
¾ cup graham cracker crumbs
2 teaspoons wheat germ
1 cup milk
½ teaspoon vanilla, almond or maple extract

Cream sugar and shortening together. Stir in beaten eggs; then beat until very well blended. Resift flour with milk solids, baking powder, and salt; then stir into mixture the crumbs and wheat germ, distributing evenly. To creamed sugar add flour mixture alternately with liquid, stirring to blend. Stir in flavoring. Pour into lined shallow cake pans and bake at 350° for 30 minutes. Serve squares topped with custard sauce, fresh or frozen fruit or berries, or whipped topping.

NUT CAKE

⅓ cup softened butter or margarine
½ cup brown sugar
½ cup dark molasses
½ cup milk
½ teaspoon vanilla
2 eggs

1 cup whole-wheat flour
¼ cup skim-milk solids
2 teaspoons baking powder
½ teaspoon salt
¼ cup wheat germ
1 cup broken nut meats

Cream butter with sugar. Add molasses, milk, vanilla, and unbeaten eggs, and stir to blend well. Sift flour with milk solids, baking powder, and salt, and stir into this mixture the wheat germ, distributing evenly. Combine flour mixture with liquid, stirring to mix well. Fold in nuts. Pour into lined or greased-and-floured loaf pan and bake at 375° for 45 minutes.

HONEY-MOLASSES SPICE CAKE

¾ cup honey
½ cup dark molasses
¼ cup softened butter
¼ cup softened shortening
2 eggs, separated
1 cup milk
1½ cups sifted whole-wheat flour
   (½ cup may be soybean
   flour)

½ cup skim-milk solids
2½ teaspoons baking powder
½ teaspoon salt
1 teaspoon cinnamon
½ teaspoon each nutmeg and
   cloves
2 teaspoons wheat germ
1 tablespoon cold water

Combine honey, molasses, butter, and shortening. Add egg yolks and beat until blended. Add milk slowly, stirring to mix thoroughly. Resift flour with milk solids, baking powder, salt, and spices, and add to milk mixture, stirring only enough to moisten and blend ingredients. Beat egg whites with 1 table-spoon of cold water until stiff but not dry, and fold into batter. Pour into lined or greased-and-floured cake pan and bake at 350° for 40 minutes.

UPSIDE DOWN CAKE

2 cups sifted whole-wheat flour
3 teaspoons baking powder
¼ cup skim-milk solids
¾ cup brown sugar
¼ teaspoon salt
3 teaspoons wheat germ
4 tablespoons solid shortening

¾ cup milk
1 egg, beaten
4 tablespoons melted butter
1 teaspoon cinnamon
1 tablespoon cream
3 large apples, cored and sliced *

Resift flour with baking powder, milk solids, *2 tablespoons* of the sugar, and salt. Stir in wheat germ. Cut in shortening with

---

* Make this also with fresh peaches or apricots—or canned peaches, apricots, or pineapple.

pastry blender or two knives until mixture is mealy. Combine milk and beaten egg and stir into flour mixture, blending to a soft dough. Set this aside while you combine melted butter with remaining brown sugar, cinnamon, and cream. Spread the sugar mixture over the bottom of a well-greased cake pan. Press apple slices firmly into this in a single layer. Spread reserved dough evenly over the fruit. Bake at 350° for 50 to 60 minutes.

HONEY FRUIT CAKE

1 cup each seedless raisins, chopped dates, chopped figs	3 cups sifted whole-wheat flour
¼ cup butter	1 teaspoon cinnamon
1½ cups honey	½ teaspoon each, ginger and cloves
½ cup brown sugar	4 teaspoons wheat germ
½ cup water	1 cup chopped or broken nuts

Combine fruit, butter, honey, sugar, and water, and simmer over low heat for 10 minutes. Remove from heat and cool to room temperature. Sift flour with spices and stir in wheat germ, distributing evenly. Add sweetened fruit mixture and nuts, mixing well. Bake in very well-greased pans at 300° for 1½ hours. Serve with buttery wine sauce (page 250).

REFRIGERATOR CHEESE CAKE

2 tablespoons unflavored whole gelatin	1 teaspoon grated orange or lemon rind
½ cup cold water	1 teaspoon vanilla
2 egg yolks	½ cup skim-milk solids
½ cup sugar	½ cup ice water
½ cup milk	2 egg whites
1 teaspoon salt	½ cup graham cracker crumbs
2 cups cottage cheese	2 teaspoons wheat germ
½ cup sour cream or yogurt	
3 tablespoons orange or lemon juice	

Soak gelatin in cold water and set aside. In saucepan or double boiler combine egg yolks, sugar, milk, and salt. Stir over low heat or boiling water until thickened. Remove from heat and add gelatin solution, stirring until it is dissolved. Chill this mixture in refrigerator, or by putting pan in another pan of ice water.

Combine cottage cheese, sour cream, juice, rind, and vanilla, and beat until smooth. Add cheese mixture to the chilled custard mixture and stir until blended. In chilled bowl, mix milk solids with ice water and beat until it is the consistency of whipped cream. Beat egg whites until stiff but not dry. Fold into the cheese mixture first the whipped milk, then the egg whites. Pour into a glass pie or cake pan. Combine graham cracker crumbs and wheat germ and sprinkle over top. Refrigerate for several hours before serving.

CAKE MADE WITH YEAST

KAFFEEKLATSCH CAKE

This is a good one to have on hand when "the girls" drop in for a visit. The girls are usually trying to lose or control weight, and when confronted with homemade cake they suffer pangs of frustration or guilt—depending on whether they resist or succumb. This one, however, is almost permissible. It is economical of fat, minimal in sugar, and moistened with nonfat milk. Moreover, because it's made with yeast and whole-wheat flour with wheat germ added, it supplies important B vitamins reducers may lack in their diets. The sweet topping suggested, while not entirely innocent of calories, is certainly better than most of the all-sugar, buttery frostings which usually grace coffecakes.

½ cup skim-milk solids
enough hot water to make 1¼ cups skim milk
⅓ cup butter or margarine
¼ cup sugar
½ teaspoon salt

1 cake compressed yeast, or 1 package dry yeast
2 eggs, beaten
4 cups whole-wheat flour
4 teaspoons wheat germ
2 teaspoons lemon juice

Make 1¼ cups skim milk with hot water and remove ¼ cup of it. To 1 cup hot skim milk add butter, sugar, and salt. Stir and allow to cool to lukewarm. In remaining ¼ cup of skim milk, cooled to lukewarm, dissolve yeast. Add to previous milk mixture. Add well-beaten egg, stir, and add 2 cups of the flour and all of the wheat germ. Beat with a heavy spoon until well blended; then add enough of the remaining flour to make a fairly smooth dough, working with your hands. Cover with clean cloth and let rise in a warm place until double in bulk—about 1 to 1½ hours. Pat dough into a greased oblong or round pan, spread with topping (recipe below), and let rise again for 40 minutes. Bake at 350° for 20 minutes.

Topping for Kaffeeklatsch Cake

¼ cup water or skim milk
2 tablespoons butter or margarine
1 tablespoon brown sugar
2 tablespoons honey

2 tablespoons dark molasses
½ teaspoon vanilla
½ cup chopped nuts, cocoanut or wheat germ—your choice

Mix water, butter, sugar, honey, and molasses together in a small saucepan and simmer over low heat until well blended. Remove from heat; stir in vanilla. Spread over coffecake in pan before second rising; then sprinkle with chopped nuts, cocoanut, or wheat germ.

STOLLEN

Yeasty, rich with eggs and milk proteins, and low in sugar, this recipe makes 3 or 4 stollens for holiday serving or giving.

½ cup skim-milk solids
1½ cups milk
2 cakes compressed yeast, or 2 packages dry yeast
3 cups sifted unbleached or enriched flour
3 cups sifted whole-wheat flour
1½ cups softened butter or margarine
⅔ cup sugar (or ¾ cup brown sugar)
4 eggs

1 teaspoon salt
⅛ teaspoon nutmeg
1 teaspoon grated lemon rind
½ cup seedless raisins
1 cup finely chopped mixed citron, candied orange, and lemon peel
1 cup chopped nut meats (blanched almonds are traditional)
melted butter for brushing

Dissolve milk solids in milk and scald. Remove from heat. When lukewarm, crumble or sprinkle yeast over milk and add 1 cup of either flour. Stir and set aside in a warm place for 1 hour or more. Gradually add sugar to softened butter or margarine, blending until creamy. Beat in eggs one at a time until mixture is smooth, adding salt, nutmeg, and grated lemon rind as you beat. Combine this mixture with the yeast-milk sponge and mix well. Add most of the remaining flours and knead until dough is smooth and elastic. In reserved flour (about ½ cupful) toss raisins, chopped mixed fruits, and nut meats; then work into the dough. Cover dough with a clean cloth and let rise in a warm place until double in bulk—about 1 hour or more. Turn out onto floured board or waxed paper; divide into 3 or 4 equal parts. Roll or pat each part out slightly, brush with melted butter, and fold over once, shaping as you fold into long ovals. Set as far apart as possible on greased baking sheet, brush with melted butter, and let rise again until double—about 1 hour. Bake at 350° for 45 minutes.

CAKE FROSTINGS

Please don't ruin a carefully nutrition-guarded cake by smearing it with an icing made by using the usual 1, 2, or 3 cups of sugar! Best of all, of course, would be cake with no icing at all—a taste that can be acquired. For those who insist on gilding the lily, however, here are three frostings which do not lean too heavily on sugar for their appeal.

WHITE OR TINTED FROSTING

2 tablespoons cream or strong coffee

2 teaspoons vanilla—or 1 teaspoon almond or maple extract

3 tablespoons softened butter

½ cup powdered sugar

¾ cup skim-milk solids

Combine ingredients and beat vigorously until smooth and creamy.

263

CREAM CHEESE FROSTING

2 packages (6 ounces) cream
cheese
1½ tablespoons sweet or sour
cream
⅔ cup confectioners' sugar

1½ teaspoons grated orange or
lemon rind
½ teaspoon vanilla, almond, or
rum extract

Cream the cheese and cream together, working with a fork until mixture is soft and fluffy. Gradually beat in the sugar; then add and beat in the rind and flavoring.

HONEY FROSTING

1 cup honey   2 egg whites

Boil honey for 10 minutes, until a cooking thermometer reads 238°. Remove from heat and allow to cool for 10 minutes. Beat egg whites until stiff. Pour honey very slowly over beaten egg whites while continuing to beat, until mixture is thick. Let cool before spreading over cake.

GOOD-NUTRITION COOKIES

Cookies are eligible for the nutritionist's seal of approval—provided they are made with good nutrition in mind. They take kindly to brown sugar or molasses. They can be made with whole-wheat or unbleached flour. They can be fortified with additional skim-milk solids and with wheat germ. They are good made with yeast. Truly conscientious mothers can cut down on the sugar.

In other words, it is possible to satisfy children's demands for after-meal and between-meal snacks with something they'll welcome instead of scorn and still cram their apparently bottomless (when it comes to sweets, not vegetables) stomachs with good nutrients.

Chocolate recipes are omitted from a good nutrition cook book,

264

because it is a highly allergenic food, usually containing too much sugar, and has a stimulant in it similar to that in coffee or tea— which you usually deny to your small ones. If you want to introduce chocolate in cookies or other recipes, obtain carob at your health food store. This is the Biblical St. John's bread, and when ground and roasted tastes exactly like chocolate, but has better food values, is innocent of any stimulant, and doesn't bother those allergic to chocolate. It comes in carob candy bars, powder for icings, cocoa, etc.

SPICED OATMEAL COOKIES

½ cup softened shortening
⅔ cup brown sugar
1 egg, beaten
½ teaspoon vanilla
¾ cup sifted whole-wheat or unbleached flour
¼ cup skim-milk solids

½ teaspoon baking soda
½ teaspoon cinnamon
¼ teaspoon cloves
¼ teaspoon ginger
¾ cup oatmeal
2 teaspoons wheat germ
½ cup seedless raisins

Cream shortening and sugar. Add egg and vanilla, and beat until light and fluffy. Resift flour with milk solids, soda, and spices, and stir into the egg mixture. Add oatmeal, wheat germ, and raisins, and mix thoroughly. Drop by rounded teaspoonfuls onto greased baking sheet and bake at 350° for 15 minutes. *Makes 3 dozen.*

DAY-BEFORE OATMEAL MACAROONS

2 cups quick-cooking rolled oats
⅓ cup sugar
2 teaspoons grated orange rind
¼ teaspoon salt

⅓ cup cooking oil
1 egg, well beaten
¼ cup chopped nut meats

Combine oats, sugar, orange rind, and salt. Add cooking oil, stir well, and store overnight, covered, in the refrigerator. Add beaten egg and nuts to the chilled mixture, blending well. Drop by the teaspoonful onto ungreased cookie sheet and bake at 350° for 15 minutes. *Makes about 3 dozen.*

BANANA-OATMEAL COOKIES

1½ cups sifted whole-wheat or unbleached flour
¼ cup skim-milk solids
1 cup brown sugar
½ teaspoon baking soda
1 teaspoon salt
¼ teaspoon cinnamon
¼ teaspoon nutmeg
¾ cup softened butter, margarine, or shortening
1 egg
2 or 3 ripe bananas, mashed
1 cup quick-cooking rolled oats
3 teaspoons wheat germ

Resift flour with milk solids, sugar, soda, salt, and spices. Cut shortening into this mixture with pastry blender or two knives, working until it has the consistency of coarse meal. Add and stir in unbeaten egg and bananas, blending well. Add oats and wheat germ and blend thoroughly. Drop by the teaspoonful onto a greased baking sheet, spacing the cookies about 1 inch apart. Bake at 400° for 12 to 15 minutes. *Makes about 4 dozen.*

BETTY'S COOKIES

1 cup butter or margarine
3 tablespoons sugar
1 egg, or 2 yolks
2 level teaspoons baking powder
1 teaspoon vanilla
¼ cup soybean flour
2 cups unbleached flour
½ tablespoon wheat germ
3 tablespoons skim-milk solids

Cream butter and sugar. Add egg or yolks and blend well; then add remaining ingredients one by one, mixing thoroughly. Drop by the teaspoonful onto greased baking sheets, or put through a cookie press. Bake at 375° for 15 minutes. *Makes about 4 dozen.*

Note: This recipe is a starting point. The content of soy flour, wheat germ, and skim-milk solids can be raised to reach ultimately a level equivalent to the protein value of meat. Try the recipe in its present form. Next time, raise one of the special ingredients a little. You will discover the level of soybean flour, wheat germ, and skim-milk solids below which you must stay if the cookies are to be pleasing to your family. Even as given above, the recipe is commendably nutritious.

HONEY WHEAT-GERM COOKIES

½ cup softened shortening
½ cup sugar
½ cup honey
2 eggs, beaten
2½ cups sifted whole-wheat flour
¼ cup skim-milk solids

2 teaspoons baking powder
1 teaspoon cinnamon
1 teaspoon nutmeg
3 teaspoons wheat germ
¼ cup milk

Cream shortening and sugar, add beaten eggs, and beat until light and fluffy. Resift flour with milk solids, baking powder, and spices, and mix with wheat germ until evenly distributed. Alternately add to dry ingredients the egg mixture and the milk, blending thoroughly. Drop by the teaspoonful onto a greased baking sheet and bake at 350° for 18 minutes. *Makes about 3 dozen.*

APPLESAUCE BRAN COOKIES

½ cup softened margarine or
    shortening
1 cup brown sugar
1 egg
1½ cups sifted whole-wheat or
    unbleached flour
½ teaspoon salt

1 teaspoon baking soda
½ teaspoon each cinnamon, nut-
    meg and cloves
1 cup breakfast-cereal bran
3 teaspoons wheat germ
1 cup unsweetened applesauce
1 cup seedless raisins

Cream shortening and sugar. Beat in egg until mixture is very smooth. Resift flour with salt, soda, and spices, and add bran and wheat germ, mixing to distribute evenly. Alternately add applesauce and combined dry ingredients to the shortening mixture, blending thoroughly. Fold in raisins. Drop by the teaspoonful onto greased baking sheets, spacing the cookies about 1½ inches apart. Bake at 375° for 18 to 20 minutes. *Makes 3 dozen.*

MOLASSES COOKIES NO. 1

These are especially good, somewhat reminiscent of German lebkuchen and a favorite with men.

½ cup oil
6 level tablespoons brown sugar
½ cup dark molasses
2 egg yolks
¼ cup sweet or sour cream, buttermilk, or milk
1 cup sifted whole-wheat flour
½ cup skim-milk solids

2 tablespoons brewers' yeast
2 teaspoons baking powder
½ teaspoon salt
½ teaspoon each cinnamon, ginger, and nutmeg
2 teaspoons wheat germ
(½ cup chopped nuts or seedless raisins, optional)

Combine and beat thoroughly the oil, sugar, molasses, egg yolks, and cream (or milk)—best and most quickly done in an electric blender. Resift flour with all other dry ingredients except wheat germ, adding this to the sifted ingredients and stirring to distribute evenly. Combine with beaten mixture and blend thoroughly. (Fold in nuts or raisins.) Drop by the teaspoonful onto polished or greased baking sheet and bake at 350° for 12 to 15 minutes. *Makes about 2 dozen.*

MOLASSES COOKIES NO. 2

¾ cup butter, margarine, or solid shortening
¾ cup dark molasses
2 eggs
2¼ cups sifted whole-wheat or unbleached flour
½ cup skim-milk solids
½ teaspoon salt
¾ teaspoon baking soda

1 teaspoon cinnamon
½ teaspoon ground cloves
2 tablespoons brewers' yeast or yeast flakes
½ cup milk
1 cup seedless raisins
1 cup chopped walnuts, pecans, or cashews

Cream shortening and gradually beat in molasses. Add and beat in eggs. Resift flour with all other dry ingredients and add to the molasses mixture, alternating with the milk. Blend well. Fold in raisins and nuts. Drop by the teaspoonful onto greased baking sheets, spacing the cookies about 1½ inches apart. Bake at 400° for 8 to 10 minutes. Remove from sheets with spatula and cool on a rack. *Makes about 5 dozen.*

WHOLE-WHEAT BUTTER THINS

½ cup softened butter
⅓ cup sugar
2 egg yolks
½ teaspoon vanilla *
1 teaspoon lemon juice

¼ teaspoon grated lemon rind
1 cup sifted whole-wheat flour
¼ cup skim-milk solids
2 teaspoons brewers' yeast
⅛ teaspoon salt

Cream butter and sugar. Add egg yolks, vanilla, lemon juice, and rind, and beat until smooth and well blended. Resift flour with milk solids, brewers' yeast, and salt, and stir into beaten mixture, blending thoroughly. Chill in refrigerator. Put through cookie press onto lightly greased and floured baking sheet; or —pinch off walnut-sized pieces of dough, roll into balls, and flatten between sheets of waxed paper, removing to baking sheet with a spatula. Bake at 375° for 10 minutes. *Makes about 2½ dozen.*

PEANUT BUTTER COOKIES

½ cup butter or margarine
¾ cup brown sugar
1 egg
1 cup peanut butter
½ teaspoon vanilla
1¼ cups sifted whole-wheat or
    unbleached flour

½ teaspoon baking soda
½ teaspoon salt
1 tablespoon brewers' yeast
2 teaspoons wheat germ

Cream butter with sugar until very smooth. Beat in egg, peanut butter, and vanilla. Resift flour with soda, salt, and brewers' yeast. Add and stir in wheat germ, distributing well. Combine flour mixture with peanut butter mixture and mix thoroughly. Pinch off small pieces of the dough, roll them into balls, and place on greased baking sheets. Flatten them with the tines of a fork or stamp with a fancy cookie mold and bake at 375° for 15 minutes. *Makes 5 dozen.*

---

* These cookies, so sparing of sugar, generous with nutrients, and easy to make, can be your cookie-jar staple. Vary the flavorings from time to time. Instead of vanilla, use ½ teaspoon almond extract, or 1 teaspoon maple extract, or 1 to 2 teaspoons ground anise seeds.

RED-SKIN PEANUT OATMEAL COOKIES

½ cup softened butter or margarine
¾ cup brown sugar
1 egg, well beaten
½ teaspoon vanilla
1¼ cups sifted whole-wheat flour
¼ cup skim-milk solids

1 teaspoon baking soda
1 teaspoon cinnamon
¼ teaspoon salt
1 cup quick-cooking rolled oats
2 teaspoons wheat germ
(about) 1 cup red-skin peanuts

Cream butter, adding sugar gradually and continuing to cream until fluffy. Beat in egg and vanilla. Resift flour with milk solids, soda, cinnamon, and salt, and add to first mixture, blending well. Combine oats and wheat germ, and work into dough until well distributed. Dough will be rather stiff. Roll out on lightly floured board to about ⅛ inch thickness. Cut into rounds or fancy shapes. Place on greased baking sheets and press several peanuts into the top of each cookie. Bake at 350° for 10 to 12 minutes. *Makes 4 dozen.*

Note: Peanuts are often acceptable to children in lieu of candy—and red-skins are much more nutritious than the larger, skinless kind.

COOKIE-JAR SPICE COOKIES

1 cup butter or margarine
1 cup brown sugar
1 cup dark molasses
2 egg yolks
1 tablespoon lemon juice
4 cups sifted whole-wheat flour
½ cup skim-milk solids

2 tablespoons brewers' yeast
1 teaspoon baking soda
1 teaspoon salt
3 teaspoons ginger
½ teaspoon cloves
½ teaspoon cinnamon
½ teaspoon nutmeg

Cream butter or margarine and sugar, beating until smooth and well blended. Beat in molasses, egg yolks, and lemon juice. Resift flour with remaining dry ingredients and work into first mixture, blending well. Divide dough into easily handled lumps and roll each out between sheets of waxed paper until about ⅛ inch thick. Cut into rounds or fancy shapes, remove with spatula to greased baking sheets, and bake at 350° for 10 minutes. *Makes about 6 dozen.*

270

COTTAGE CHEESE COOKIES

¼ cup butter or margarine
¼ cup creamed cottage cheese—
    or one 3-ounce package cream
    cheese
½ cup sugar
¼ cup honey
2 egg yolks
1 tablespoon lemon or orange
    juice

2 tablespoons milk
1 cup sifted whole-wheat or un-
    bleached flour
2 teaspoons baking powder
¼ cup skim-milk solids
½ teaspoon salt
2 teaspoons wheat germ

Soften butter or margarine and combine with cheese, working with a fork until well blended and smooth. Cream this mixture with sugar and honey. Add egg yolks, juice, and milk, and mix thoroughly. Resift flour with baking powder, milk solids, and salt, and add wheat germ to this mixture, distributing evenly. Combine with first mixture and stir to blend. Drop by the teaspoonful onto greased baking sheet and bake at 350° for 8 to 10 minutes. *Makes about 2 dozen.*

SPICY REFRIGERATOR COOKIES

½ cup softened butter or marga-
    rine
½ cup brown sugar
4 tablespoons dark molasses
2 eggs
2 cups sifted whole-wheat or un-
    bleached flour
2 tablespoons brewers' yeast

2 teaspoons baking powder
¼ cup skim-milk solids
¼ teaspoon salt
¼ teaspoon ginger
½ teaspoon nutmeg
½ teaspoon cinnamon or cloves
4 teaspoons wheat germ

Cream butter and sugar until very smooth. Add and beat in molasses and eggs. Resift flour with all remaining dry ingredients except wheat germ, adding this to flour mixture, stirring to distribute evenly. Combine both mixtures by stirring or beating until well blended, and chill in refrigerator. When stiff enough to handle, roll dough on waxed paper without using any more flour. Form into several long rolls. Wrap rolls in foil or waxed paper and store in refrigerator until thoroughly cold—overnight, or longer. Slice as thin as possible and bake on greased baking sheet at 375° for 8 to 10 minutes. *Makes about 5 dozen.*

SESAME SEED COOKIES

¼ cup softened butter or marga-
    rine
½ cup brown sugar
1 egg, beaten
1 cup sifted whole-wheat flour

¼ cup skim-milk solids
½ teaspoon baking powder
⅛ teaspoon salt
½ cup toasted sesame seeds *

Cream butter or margarine and sugar until light and fluffy. Add beaten egg. Sift flour with milk solids, baking powder, and salt, and add to egg mixture. Add and blend in sesame seeds until well distributed. Drop by the scant teaspoonful onto greased and lightly floured baking sheet, spacing well apart. Bake at 375° for 8 to 10 minutes. *Makes about 2 dozen.*

CARROT COOKIES

½ cup butter or margarine
½ cup solid shortening
¾ cup brown sugar
1 egg, well beaten
1 teaspoon vanilla
½ teaspoon grated lemon rind
1 cup cooked, mashed carrots

2 cups sifted whole-wheat or un-
    bleached flour
½ teaspoon salt
2 teaspoons baking powder
¼ cup skim-milk solids
1 tablespoon brewers' yeast

Cream butter or margarine wth shortening and gradually blend in sugar until very smooth. Add egg, flavorings, and mashed carrots, and mix thoroughly. Resift flour with remaining dry ingredients and combine with carrot mixture, blending thoroughly. Drop by the spoonful onto greased baking sheet and bake at 400° for 12 to 15 minutes. *Makes about 3 dozen.*

---

* To toast sesame seeds: Spread a thin layer in a large, shallow baking pan. Place pan in a 350° oven and bake until lightly browned—about 20 minutes.

YEAST COOKIES

1 cake compressed yeast, or 1 package dry yeast
¼ cup warm vegetable water
3 cups whole-wheat flour
¼ cup butter or margarine

½ cup brown sugar
1 egg
¼ teaspoon salt
½ cup milk—or orange juice

Crumble or sprinkle yeast over warm vegetable water, stir in ½ cup of the flour, and let stand while you proceed. Cream butter and sugar. Add egg and salt, and mix well. Stir in milk or orange juice. Add yeast mixture; then add and mix remaining 2½ cups of flour. Blend well. Drop by the spoonful onto a greased baking sheet and bake at 350° for 10 to 15 minutes, until browned. *Makes about 2 dozen.*

CANDY-SUBSTITUTE COOKIES

DATE AND NUT SQUARES

5 tablespoons sifted whole-wheat flour
2 teaspoons baking powder
⅛ teaspoon salt
½ cup brown sugar

1 pound pitted dates, chopped
½ cup nut meats
½ cup wheat germ
3 eggs, well beaten
1 teaspoon vanilla

Resift flour with baking powder and salt. Combine with sugar, dates, nut meats, and wheat germ. Stir in beaten eggs and vanilla. Spread over bottom of greased shallow baking pan and bake at 325° for 45 minutes. While still hot, cut into small squares. *Makes 2 dozen.*

ALMOND DELIGHTS

1 cup softened butter or margarine
¼ cup sugar
1 cup unblanched almonds (skins
and all)

2 cups sifted whole-wheat, unbleached, or enriched flour
2 teaspoons vanilla

Cream butter and sugar until very smooth. Grind almonds in a meat grinder, putting them through the finest blade 2 or 3 times. They should be oily rather than powdery. Combine creamed butter, almonds, flour, and vanilla, beating until thoroughly blended. Cover and refrigerate for several hours, until stiff. Cut or break into 3 or 4 pieces; with palms of hands roll each piece on waxed paper into long ropes about the diameter of an ordinary pencil. Cut each strip into 2-inch pieces and bend into circles, horseshoes, or crescents. Arrange on greased baking sheet and bake at 300° for 12 to 15 minutes. *Makes about 3 dozen.*

NUT MERINGUES

2 egg whites
⅛ teaspoon cream of tartar
pinch of salt

½ cup brown sugar
½ teaspoon vanilla
½ cup chopped nut meats

Beat egg whites with cream of tartar and salt until stiff but not dry. Add sugar very slowly, beating stiff after each addition. Fold in vanilla and nut meats. Cover baking sheet with heavy (ungreased) paper. Drop from a spoon in peaks and bake at 275° for 40 to 50 minutes. Remove at once to plate or tray to cool. *Makes 3 dozen.*

RAISIN-NUT DROPS

½ cup butter or margarine
¾ cup brown sugar
2 eggs
½ cup whole-wheat, unbleached,
or enriched flour

2 tablespoons skim-milk solids
1 teaspoon cinnamon
½ teaspoon baking soda
1 cup chopped nut meats
½ cup seedless raisins

Cream butter and sugar until smooth. Add and blend eggs. Sift flour with skim-milk solids, cinnamon, and soda, and combine with egg mixture. Fold in nuts and raisins. Drop by the half-teaspoonful or in smaller amounts onto warmed baking sheets and bake at 350° 10 to 12 minutes. *Makes 4 dozen.*

VITAMIN-PROTEIN COOKIES

These may sound strange, but actually they're pretty good. At least they're something for a reducer, a therapeutic dieter, or a dietary-problem child to nibble on when fats and carbohydrates must be kept to a minimum. Children have been known to enjoy them for the chewing exercise they provide, and they offer a solution in households where children refuse to eat meat or where the dental bills are in ratio to high sugar consumption.

½ cup skim-milk solids
¼ cup wheat germ
½–1 teaspoon liquid sugarless
   sweetener

one 3½-ounce jar of strained baby
   food *

Add milk solids, wheat germ, and sweetener slowly to baby food. Stir to mix thoroughly. Drop by the teaspoonful onto lightly oiled (or shiny, ungreased) baking sheet and bake at 325° for 20 to 25 minutes. Remove cookies with a spatula and allow to cool. Store in the refrigerator in a covered jar or in freezer bags. *Makes 12 to 15.*

GOOD-NUTRITION PIES

The luscious, memory-laden, mouth-watering, homemade pie does not deserve the unsavory reputation it has acquired at the insistence of diet alarmists. It can be nutritionally acceptable as it is popular for a family dessert just so long as you don't cancel out its perfectly good ingredients by making it unnecessarily sweet, bulging with superfluous calories.

---

* Experiment with baby foods. Start with the fruits or custards and alternate with vegetables and even with some of the strained meats. These can be made even more nutritious by adding up to 1 tablespoon of brewers' yeast or yeast flakes.

Remember, please, that one important part of this book's intent is to guide you toward optimum, or at least improved, nutrition. The path to this goal inevitably bypasses some old traditions about food and emerges in clearings where new or modified concepts await you.

It may have been all very well even as recently as the turn of the century to top off a six- or seven-course meal with an enormous two-crust pie filled with Heaven only knows what caloric richness and garnished with great dollops of thick yellow cream. In those days the people gathered around the table were burning up calories in reasonable proportion to intake. Papa worked longer and harder hours at his job, and his leisure time was usually spent in physical activities more strenuous than sitting behind the wheel of an automobile or in front of a television set. Mama could expend plenty of calories bent over the washtub or wielding a broom. The children hiked to school; and more of their play time was spent in active doing, instead of in being entertained.

But it is not only an excess of calories which dictates that modern desserts, including pies, be considerably less lush than those of yesteryear. The meal preceding the moment when a pie is carried proudly to the table may have left something to be desired in protein-vitamin-mineral supply. No matter how conscientiously the homemaker plans, shops, and cooks, there are bound to be some gaps in nutrient availability for the simple reason that she must use the foodstuffs available to her. Don't misunderstand me. Despite the nutrient-robbing aspects of some current agricultural, processing, and preservative methods, these foodstuffs are not "bad." They are merely devitalized. They are not the same foodstuff equivalents on which standards of minimum daily requirements were based when the first books on nutrition were written.

With a day's average diet supplying an overabundance of refined carbohydrates, ample fats, and far too few proteins, it makes no nutritional sense to make the lopsided balance even

more precarious with a dessert which throws it further out of
kilter. And let's face it—a pie can be the repository of more
carbohydrate and fat than the average man, woman, adolescent,
or child needs to round out the day.

From a food value standard, the ideal pie is tall in the pan
and presents an open face. A tall pie means narrower servings,
with the bulk of substance in a filling which can provide excellent
nutrition. An open-face pie means only half of the crust's carbohydrates and fats. However, for those to whom a pie is a pie
only if it has two crusts, there are ways to imbue those crusts
with nutritional meaning.

PIE CRUSTS AND TART SHELLS

General Instructions

Work rapidly and lightly.

Add liquid a little at a time, unless otherwise specified—just
enough to moisten the dry ingredients.

Take care not to stretch the dough while handling or rolling;
otherwise it will shrink when baked.

For prebaked shells: After lining pie pan with dough, trim-
ming, and crimping, fit slightly smaller pie pan in the shell for
the first 5 minutes of baking.

For covered pies: After lining pie pan with bottom crust and
filling it, roll out second crust between sheets of waxed paper.
Fold in half, paper and all, and with scissors or very sharp knife
cut slits or a design through the "sandwich," starting at the
fold. Remove outer waxed paper. Put folded edge of crust down
at the center of the filled pie, unfold, and remove remaining
waxed paper. Roll edge of top crust under edge of bottom crust,
press together, and crimp with fork or fingers.

CRISP PIE CRUST

All ingredients and utensils should be at room temperature before starting.

1¾ cups sifted whole-wheat or unbleached flour
1 teaspoon salt
¼ cup skim-milk solids

2 teaspoons wheat germ
½ cup cooking oil
3 tablespoons milk or water

Resift flour with salt and milk solids into a mixing bowl. Stir in wheat germ. Combine oil and milk, and pour into a well in the center of the flour mixture. Stir with a fork until flour is just damp and dough begins to hold together. Divide dough in half and form each half into a ball, using a knife or spoon—or your fingers. If possible, refrigerate dough balls for 30 minutes or more. Put each ball between two sheets of waxed paper and roll out into circles about ⅛ inch thick. *Yield:* two 9-inch pie crusts, or 8 tart shells.

Prebaked shells (see page 277): Preheat oven to 450°. Prick bottom of crust in several places with a fork. Bake at 450° for total of 15 minutes.

For pies to be baked with filling: See individual baking times for each recipe.

FLAKY PIE CRUST

All ingredients and utensils should be thoroughly chilled before starting.

1½ cups sifted whole-wheat or unbleached flour
1 teaspoon salt
2 teaspoons wheat germ

⅓ cup lard
⅓ cup butter
(about) ¼ cup ice water

Resift flour with salt. Stir in wheat germ. Cut lard and butter into flour mixture with pastry blender or two knives—only until lumps of shortening are approximately the size of peas. Sprinkle ice water—a little at a time—over these ingredients, pushing aside pieces of dough as they begin to hold together. Don't over-mix. The dough should be barely moist, and the lumps of shortening should not be allowed to start melting. Refrigerate dough

278

for at least 30 minutes before proceeding. Turn dough out onto a cold board covered with waxed paper. Working with a knife, separate dough into two parts and flatten each into an irregular ball or square. With cold rolling pin, roll each to a thickness of ½ inch. Fold in half and roll again. Repeat. Cover with waxed paper and roll to ⅛ inch thickness. Remove top sheet of waxed paper and invert pastry into a pie pan, removing remaining waxed paper. Shape to pan quickly; prick in several places with a fork. Repeat if you are preparing for prebaked shells. Trim edges and crimp with fork. *Yield:* two 9-inch pie crusts or 8 tart shells.

Prebaked shells (see page 277): Preheat oven to 425°. Bake for a total of 10 minutes.

For two-crust pies (see page 277): Individual baking times given for each recipe.

To make tart shells out of crisp or flaky pie crust: Cut circles from dough after it has been rolled out to ⅛ inch thickness. Either place inside muffin cups, pressing against the sides, or shape over backs of muffin cups. Trim edges, flute or crimp them, and prick sides and bottom of dough with a fork.

CHEESE CRUST

For precooked or uncooked fillings.

1 cup sifted whole-wheat or un-bleached flour
¼ cup skim-milk solids
2 teaspoons wheat germ

½ cup butter or margarine
½ cup cottage cheese or cream cheese (½ of large package—4 ounces)

Resift flour with milk solids. Stir in wheat germ. With pastry blender or two knives, cut butter into flour mixture. Add cheese and mix to a smooth dough. Form into ball and chill in refrigerator for 30 minutes or more. Roll out between sheets of waxed paper and line pie pan as in either of preceding pie crust recipes. Bake at 450° for 8 to 10 minutes. *Yield:* one 9-inch pie crust, or 4 tarts.

CRUMB CRUST

For precooked or uncooked fillings, or for unbaked pies.

1¼ cups toasted fine whole-wheat
    bread crumbs
2 teaspoons wheat germ
6 tablespoons butter or margarine,
    melted

1 teaspoon honey
2 teaspoons dark molasses

Combine bread crumbs and wheat germ. Stir in melted shortening and sweeteners, blending thoroughly. Reserve about ½ cupful of the mixture and press remainder firmly into a well-greased deep pie pan, shaping it against the bottom and sides. Chill in the refrigerator for at least 1 hour. Bake at 350° for 10 to 15 minutes. Or—fill, sprinkle remainder of crumb mixture over top, and bake as directed for individual pies. *Yield:* one 9-inch pie crust.

BERRY OR FRUIT PIES BAKED IN PASTRY SHELLS

OPEN-FACE DEEP PIES

1 recipe crisp or flaky pie crust
    (page 278)
5–6 cups berries (whole or sliced)
    or apples, peaches, or apricots
    (thinly sliced)
½ cup or less brown sugar, depending on sweetness of fruit

2 tablespoons sifted whole-wheat
    flour
⅛ teaspoon salt
½ teaspoon cinnamon
⅛ teaspoon nutmeg
2 teaspoons lemon juice
1 tablespoon butter or margarine

Make pie crust, line a deep pie pan, and refrigerate while you prepare the filling:

Put berries or fruit in a rather large, flat bowl or dish. Combine all dry ingredients and sprinkle over fruit, turning it gently with a slotted spoon until well coated. Fill cold pastry shell with fruit and sprinkle with lemon juice. Dot with butter. Cover pie with inverted pie pan or lightweight ovenproof lid, and bake at 425° for 10 minutes. Reduce heat to 350° and bake 30 minutes. Remove lid and bake 10 minutes more.

DEEP BERRY OR FRUIT PIES WITH WHEAT-GERM TOPPING

1 recipe crisp or flaky pie crust
  (page 278)
4–5 cups berries (whole or sliced)
  or apples, peaches, or apricots
  (thinly sliced)
2 teaspoons lemon juice

½ cup sifted whole-wheat flour
½ cup wheat germ
½ cup brown sugar
½ teaspoon cinnamon
⅛ teaspoon salt
⅓ cup butter or margarine

Make pie crust and line a deep pie pan. Place unsweetened berries or fruit directly in pastry-filled pie pan and sprinkle with lemon juice. Combine all dry ingredients, blending well, and cut in butter or margarine with pastry blender or two knives until mixture resembles coarse crumbs. Spoon this mixture over fruit and bake the pie at 350° for 30 to 40 minutes, until fruit is tender.

TWO-CRUST BERRY OR FRUIT PIES

1 recipe crisp or flaky pie crust
  (page 278)
3–4 cups berries (whole or sliced)
  or sliced fresh or unsweetened canned fruit *
½ cup brown sugar
3 tablespoons sifted whole-wheat

flour—or 1½ tablespoons cornstarch plus 1½ table-spoons wheat germ
1½ tablespoons orange or lemon juice
½ teaspoon cinnamon or nutmeg
1 tablespoon butter

Make pie crust and line a shallow pie pan with half of the dough, keeping this and remaining half of dough in refrigerator while you prepare the filling:

Place berries or fruit in bowl. Combine all remaining ingredients except butter and sprinkle over bowl. Stir gently until well distributed and blended, and let stand in refrigerator for 10 minutes. Pour into pastry-lined pan and cover with top crust (page 277). Bake at 425° for 8 to 10 minutes. Reduce heat to 325° and bake for 35 to 40 minutes, or until crust is golden brown.

---

* If you are using canned fruit, reduce total baking time to 30 minutes.

FILLINGS FOR BAKED PIE CRUSTS

UNCOOKED BERRIES

Uncooked berries are preferred for good nutrition. Berries are high in vitamin C content, and cooking is not kind to vitamin C.

2 cups any berries in season　　　　**1 baked pie shell of any kind**
honey or brown sugar to taste

Hull and wash berries and sweeten to taste. Fill baked pie shell and top with whipped topping (page 249). Serve with or without refrigerating. Or top with *molasses meringue:*

2 egg whites　　　　　　　　　**⅓ cup dark molasses**

Beat egg whites until foamy. Add molasses slowly, continuing to beat until mixture peaks. Pile on berry pie, level with spatula, and place directly under broiler until lightly browned—just a minute or two.

COOKED BERRIES

4 cups berries in season　　　　　**⅛ teaspon salt**
½ cup brown sugar　　　　　　　**2 tablespoons whole-wheat flour**
1 tablespoon orange or lemon　　**2 tablespoons butter or margarine**
**　juice**　　　　　　　　　　　**1 baked pie shell of any kind**

Hull and wash berries. In saucepan, mash 1 cup of the berries to permit flow of juices. Combine remaining berries with sugar and add to saucepan. Cook, covered, over low heat until berries are soft, stirring occasionally to prevent scorching. When enough liquid forms, pour off about ½ cup of it and let it cool a little. To the liquid add orange or lemon juice, salt, and flour, and stir to a smooth paste. Stir this into the cooking berries and stir until mixture thickens. Remove from heat, stir in butter or margarine, and cool. Pour into baked pie shell before serving. Decorate, if you like, with whipped topping (page 249) or serve with custard sauce (page 237).

UNCOOKED FRUIT

2½ cups any peeled, sliced, soft, naturally sweet fruit (apricots, peaches, nectarines, plums)

1-2 tablespoons brown sugar or honey, depending on sweetness of fruit

1 baked pie shell of any kind

Toss fruit in sweetener and fill any baked pie shell. Decorate with whipped topping (page 249).

CITRUS FRUIT JUICE CHIFFON PIE

1 tablespoon unflavored whole gelatin

¼ cup cold water

4 eggs, separated

½ cup sugar

½ cup unsweetened orange, lemon, grapefruit, or lime juice

½ teaspoon salt

1 tablespoon grated orange rind

1 prebaked cheese, crumb, or nut crust (pages 279-280)

Soften gelatin in cold water. Beat egg yolks until light and add sugar, juice, and salt. In top of double boiler, stir and cook these ingredients until they are custardy. Add softened gelatin and grated orange rind, and stir to mix well. Remove from heat and, without stirring again, let mixture cool at room temperature until it begins to thicken (on a warm day, refrigerate). Beat egg whites until stiff, but not dry and fold into mixture. Pour into baked pastry shell and refrigerate until serving. (Decorate with whipped topping, if you like—page 249.)

BANANA-CITRUS-PINEAPPLE CHIFFON PIE

1 ripe banana

⅓ cup orange juice

2 tablespoons lemon juice

2 tablespoons drained crushed (canned) pineapple

1 envelope unflavored whole gelatin

¼ cup cold water

⅓ cup boiling water

½ cup sugar

⅛ teaspoon salt

½ cup heavy cream

1 baked pastry shell (pages 277-280)

Cut peeled banana into very thin slices and combine with mixture of orange juice, lemon juice, and crushed pineapple.

283

Sprinkle gelatin over cold water and stir into boiling water, adding sugar and salt. Stir until dissolved and combine with fruit mixture. Refrigerate for 1 hour. When thoroughly chilled, beat until fluffy. Whip cream until stiff and fold into gelatin mixture. Pour into baked pie crust just before serving.

STEWED FRUIT–BANANA PIE

2 cups cooked pitted prunes, apricots, or peaches—or mixture of all three
2 cups sliced ripe bananas
½ cup honey
¼ cup butter or margarine
1 teaspoon lemon juice
½ teaspoon grated lemon rind
⅛ teaspoon salt
1 baked pastry shell of any kind

Cut cooked fruit into small pieces. Cream honey and butter together until thick and smooth. Add cooked fruit, sliced bananas, lemon juice, rind, and salt. Combine by stirring or beating and pour into baked pastry shell. Decorate with whipped topping (page 249).

GOOD-AS-GOLD VEGETABLE CHIFFON PIE

1½ cups cooked (by baking or boiling) mashed pumpkin, squash, carrots, or sweet potatoes
2 eggs, separated
¼ cup skim-milk solids
¼ cup brown sugar
½ cup dark molasses
1 teaspoon cinnamon
1 teaspoon ginger
½ teaspoon nutmeg
(⅛ teaspoon cloves, optional)
1 teaspoon salt
1 tablespoon unflavored gelatin
¼ cup cold water
1 baked pastry shell of any kind

Combine mashed vegetable, egg yolks, milk solids, sugar, molasses, and spices (including salt) in top of double boiler over gently boiling water and cook for 10 minutes, stirring frequently. Soften gelatin in cold water and stir into the hot vegetable mixture until thoroughly blended. Refrigerate until chilled and mixture begins to thicken and set. Beat egg whites until stiff but not dry, and fold into chilled vegetable mixture. Pour into baked pastry shell and return to refrigerator until served. Decorate with whipped topping (page 249).

CREAM OR CUSTARD PIES

There are dozens of nutritionally acceptable rules for custard or cream pies, with or without fruit or berries, in most recipe books. They call for eggs, milk, cornstarch or flour, and a reasonably moderate amount of sugar. Rather than take the space to repeat them all here, I suggest that if you avoid chocolate and add up to ½ cup of skim-milk solids to any of the recipes you may feel that you have done your nutritional duty.

However—to make a cream pie that's just a little different and quite a bit more nutritious, try one of the following:

BEIGE CREAM PIE

2½ tablespoons sifted whole-wheat flour
6 tablespoons skim-milk solids
⅛ cup brown sugar
¼ teaspoon salt
3 egg yolks, beaten
1 tablespoon butter or margarine

2 cups scalded milk
1½ teaspoons vanilla, or ¾ teaspoon almond or maple extract
1 baked pie crust of any kind (pages 277–280)

Combine dry ingredients and add to beaten egg yolks. Blend well. When smooth, transfer to top of double boiler and stir in butter and scalded milk, continuing to stir over boiling water until mixture is smooth and thickened. Cool, add flavoring, and pour into baked pie shell. If you like, top with molasses meringue (page 282) and brown under broiler for 1 or 2 minutes.

SOUR CREAM PIE

2 whole eggs
2 egg yolks
½ cup brown sugar
½ teaspoon cinnamon
¼ teaspoon nutmeg

1 teaspoon lemon juice
2 tablespoons skim-milk solids
1 cup heavy sour cream
1 cheese pie crust (page 279)
½ cup wheat germ

Beat eggs and egg yolks slightly and put in top of double boiler. Add sugar, spices, and lemon juice, and stir. Combine milk solids and sour cream, and add to pan. Stir well and cook over boiling water until mixture is smooth and thick. Allow to cool before pouring into baked pie crust. Sprinkle generously with wheat germ and heat in 275 to 300° oven for 15 or 20 minutes.

BANANA FLAKE NESSELRODE PIE

1½ tablespoons unflavored whole
    gelatin
¼ cup cold milk
1¾ cups light cream
¼ cup skim-milk solids
3 eggs, separated
pinch of salt
2 tablespoons granulated sugar
2 teaspoons rum flavoring

¼ teaspoon nutmeg
½ cup maraschino cherries, rinsed, drained, and coarsely chopped
¼ cup chopped citron
¼ cup sliced blanched almonds
4 tablespoons banana flakes
1 baked flaky pie crust (page 278)

Sprinkle gelatin on cold milk and let soften. Combine cream and skim-milk solids, and scald in top of double boiler. Remove from heat. In a bowl, beat egg yolks with a fork, and stir in salt and sugar; then slowly stir in scalded cream. Return mixture to double boiler and cook over hot (not boiling) water, stirring constantly, until as smooth and thick as custard sauce (it should coat the spoon)—about 5 minutes. Remove from heat and let stand 10 minutes; then stir and add softened gelatin. Add rum flavoring and nutmeg, blend thoroughly, and refrigerate for at least 30 minutes. When mixture begins to set, remove from refrigerator and fold into it the cherries, citron, and almonds. Beat egg whites until stiff, slowly adding banana flakes as you beat. When quite stiff, fold into custard mixture, pour into baked pastry shell, and refrigerate again until thoroughly set.

Sane Food Shopping

12

Sane Food Shopping

If I attempted to explore for you the expertise a nutritionist would apply in choosing or rejecting products in the supermarket, this chapter would expand into a textbook. By way of compromise, so you may realize that behind the philosophy of a good-nutrition cook book, there is a formidable (and steadily growing) science, let me cite three supermarket products, and tell you why a nutritionist would not serve them to your family.

The first is a convenience food, and as I list the ingredients for you, try to guess what the product is:

Water
corn syrup
shortening with freshness
  preserver
sugar
whey solids
food starch modified
dextrose
sodium caseinate
gelatin
whole milk solids
monosodium and diglycerides
salt

vinegar
polysorbate 60
vanilla
monsodium phosphate
sugar gum
lecithin
sodium bicarbonate
ammonium bicarbonate
white flour
sorghum grain flour
artificial flavoring and
  artificial coloring

You mean you didn't guess it is labeled: "Lemon Cream Pie"?

Aside from the anomaly of a lemon cream pie that may legally be innocent of containing either lemon or cream, please note: The major ingredients in this pie are cheap sweeteners. The starch has been modified, meaning that it deliberately is made to be less digestible than ordinary starch—and no more nutritious. The diglycerides are, in a manner of speaking, artificial soaps. The sorbates have been found to alter the shape of human cells, and in high concentrations, to kill them. This is merely an aspect of their function of inhibiting the growth of bacteria and fungus organisms in pie. Interestingly, that information came from one government agency, but the use of sorbate is licensed by another government agency! Artificial colors and flavors, an American Medical Association symposium was recently told, can be squarely indicted as causes of hyperactivity in children. The freshness preserver is either BHT or BHA, or both. I have commented earlier on the action of BHT in changing (undesirably) the behavior of animals, and the effect of BHT in causing skin cancer in animals.

Unnecessary question: isn't baking your own pies, not only free of these additives but filled with *good* nutrition, worth the investment of time, effort, and a few extra cents? What price are you willing to pay for the illusion of convenience? I say "illusion" because the illnesses, minor and major, of a family with third-grade health because of fourth-grade foods and inexcusable additives will be costly of time and money and heartache.

A second convenience food is French toast. The bread is the usual absorbent cotton, with its roughage removed, and perhaps some twenty vitamins, minerals, and other nutrients depleted. Three vitamins are restored; this is—with a sense of humor—called enrichment. Twenty years later, you'll be taking injections of those vitamins for diabetes, or whatever; or eating medically prescribed high-roughage crackers in an effort to recover from the constipation and the diverticulosis you developed from eating bread without roughage. This is—with no sense of humor—called modern medicine.

290

The label of the French toast tells us that it contains artificial color, which means that it doesn't have enough eggs to be an honest yellow. It is also spiked with the ubiquitous BHA and BHT. Question: having baked your own good, honest, nutritious bread, how long does it take to dip it in egg-and-milk, and prepare French toast, minus dangerous additives, that contributes to your family's well-being?

The third product is found in a thousand foods. It is ordinary white sugar. Consider it from the point of view of the wife who has just been told by the family doctor that her husband is pre-diabetic. Predictably, her first question is: "What shall I feed him?" I submit that you should ask that question *now,* before the trouble starts. What nutrition cures, it may prevent, or at least mitigate. Wouldn't it be intelligent if we all ate as if we were pre-diabetic? And would not sugar be the first target for taboo?

That, of course, explains why this *Cook Book for Good Nutrition* makes sugar a condiment, modestly used as condiments should be, rather than a major source of calories, which it is in many American diets. Let us, by way of demonstrating how little the average person knows of the effects of common poor foods, take a look at sugar, the worst of all common foods, supplying empty calories, devoid of the life-sustaining nutrients that every natural food (free of man's touch) supplies.

In 70 percent of the men who eat the national average of more than one hundred pounds of white sugar per person, per year, physicians find the following changes in the body:

The adhesiveness of blood platelets is abnormally increased, making clots—and heart attacks—more likely. The blood triglycerides rise, as well as the uric acid, cholesterol, fasting insulin, and cortisol levels. These comprise the chemical "profile" of men who are in more than usual risk of heart attacks. The adrenal gland and the liver enlarge; the pancreas shrinks. None of these changes is normal, none desirable. Sugar contributes to the risk of low blood sugar, paradoxically, because it overstimulates the pancreas, which may result in overproduction of insulin, driving blood sugar down. The overstimulation may eventually exhaust the pancreas, resulting in diabetes. Low blood sugar causes symptoms ranging from unprovoked anxiety to suicidal depression, from impotence in men to frigidity in women. Diabetes can lead to hardening of the arteries, heart disease, and cancer. The obvious moral: a cook book with recipes which begin with two or three cupfuls of sugar is surely most useful as a starter for fires in these days of energy shortages.

Now that I have justified the emphasis on buying foods and preparing recipes low in sugar, I can anticipate your reflex move: toward brown sugar, raw sugar, turbinado sugar, and honey. Despite the eulogies of these substitutes in health food literature, they offer no advantage over white sugar. In fact, honey is somewhat more undesirable, because it contains fructose, in addition to sucrose (white sugar) although one tends to use less because it is sweeter. Fructose, also known as levulose, is the "natural" sugar of fruits, too—but anything sucrose does, fructose does more intensely and more undesirably. None of this means discarding brown or raw sugar or honey, or eliminating fruits from the diet. It means moderation. Reduce the sugar in your recipes, exactly as I have in those of the *Cook Book for Good Nutrition.* There are lower levels of sugar content that still turn out baked products of satisfactory texture (which sugar affects) and sufficient sweetness. If you decrease the sweetness of your foods gradually, your family will take the change in stride.

Useful hints: Buy waterpacked canned fruit, or self-juice packed. Honey being sweeter than sugar, a saving on sucrose intake is achieved if you must add a touch of honey to satisfy the family's sweet tooth. Buy frozen fruits packed au naturel—without the heavy overcoat of sugar crystals common to such. There are brands of canned fruits in which sugar syrup use has been reduced so much that the total sugar content—syrup and fruit—is no greater than that of the fresh. Freeze your own fruit: blueberries and strawberries, for example, can be frozen as is, without added sugar. Be aware of the tremendous concentration of hidden sugar in foods: twelve teaspoonfuls per portion of ordinary apple pie; large amounts in ketchup; five teaspoon-

292

fuls in a plain doughnut, seven in a glazed doughnut; and one teaspoonful of sugar in every six of average ice cream. Salad dressing, frankfurters, canned meats, practically all breads, vitamin and medicine tablets, cough syrup, indigestion remedies, presweetened cereals (a particularly bad buy, because the sugar content raises the price by an amount equivalent to buying sugar at $2.00 per pound) are some of the hidden sources of a large part of our sugar intake. Persuade your family to taste beverages *before* they sweeten them, which will almost surely reduce their sugar intake. (If you discount that source, you're due for the surprise Merv Griffin encountered. He discovered he had low blood sugar when he was tested, after I had discussed the subject on his television program. He further discovered, he told us on the air, that he was drinking thirty cups of coffee a day, each with two teaspoonfuls of sugar; and he remarked on how much better he was feeling since he had reduced his intake of the sweetener.)

Readers who know that starch is converted into sugar (glucose) in the body will want to know if this type of carbohydrate must necessarily be as undesirable. Not so: starch has none of the undesirable effects of sugar. While both starch and sugar ultimately yield glucose, sugar also yields fructose. It is this type of sugar that is the mischief-maker, and this, of course, is dominantly supplied—as fructose—from honey, all forms of sucrose, and fruits.

If you have a young baby, you will keep away from baby foods that are oversweetened and oversalted—as so many of them are. These ingredients are added because mothers taste baby foods; the baby couldn't care less. Another ingredient in baby foods that should be avoided is modified starch. I have already pointed out that the modification is specially aimed at making the starch less digestible; and it is an overprocessed carbohydrate besides. As for salt: depending on the genetic history, high-salt intake can be a pathway to hypertension. Without any resort to the salt cellar, the sodium content of human blood will stay within normal range. Only under conditions inducing intense perspiration or abnormal intake of fluid is there the need to pay attention to the salt intake. With either sugar or salt, you start an undesirable habit for an infant.

There is a long list of *don'ts* based on food additives which are known to be dangerous—and don't let us waste time discussing the failure of the Food & Drug Administration to protect the public. The best, quickest answer to that question is the remark made by an FDA commissioner upon his retirement from office. Asked by a reporter to outline the problem that bothered him most as chief of the agency, his reply was: "The belief of the public that this agency protects the public." So let us take our lead from the advice given by the FDA itself, which reads: "The best protection for the consumer is the alertness of a well-informed consumer."

Among the food additives which should have been banned here long ago, as some of them already have been in countries where regulatory agencies aren't susceptible to commercial pressures:

Butylhydroxytoluene (also known as BHT, freshness preserver, oxygen interceptor, anti-staleness ingredient).

Butylhydroxyanisole (also known as BHA; same uses as described above for BHT).

Sodium butyrate; sodium nitrite; sodium nitrate; sorbate; propyl paraben; methy paraben; sodium hexanoate; sodium decanoate; Red #2.

The last is a food coloring agent found in lipstick, medicine and vitamin pills, soda pop, and in about 10 percent of all the other foods and beverages sold in this country. It deforms the unborn young.

Saccharin and cyclamates are difficult to evaluate. Certainly, the evidence on both sides is so strong that one should not stop the abuse of sugar only to turn to abuse of the synthetic sweeteners. The tests indicting saccharin and cyclamates as causing cancer are undoubtedly of dubious validity, since the test conditions were in no way related to the ways in which the artificial sweeteners are actually used. Cancer derived from suspending a tablet of saccharin in the bladder of an animal simply means that you should not allow anyone to suspend a tablet of saccharin in your bladder. Astronomical doses of cyclamates, causing cancer, simply mean that astronomical doses are unwise; and in any case, the cyclamate research has been demonstrated to be invalid, and is now being repeated. With saccharin, there is one observation that seems valid and susceptible to practical application: a few days of abstinence from it allows the body to clear virtually all of the chemical from the tissues. In any case, our objective is not that of finding safe substitutes for sugar. We should try to re-educate our palates so that our tastebuds are no longer anaesthetized by a tide of sugar, and we can again enjoy the fine natural flavors of good foods.

In the bread department: ideally, you will be baking most of your bread. When you *must* fill in, avoid commercial white bread and rye (which is virtually identical with the white). Genuine pumpernickel doesn't exist, for all practical purposes. What you are buying is a fermented, overprocessed rye-wheat combination, colored with burned sugar—and the term "caramel coloring" is usually the warning flag. Real whole grain does not require darkeners. "Reducing" bread doesn't exist. French and Italian breads are worse than commercial white bread—pale only because they are made with water instead of milk. The supermarkets now carry some natural loaves of genuine whole-wheat, without additives, and a very few white loaves which have been raised in nutritional value by the addition of wheat germ, soy, and non-fat milk. If wheat germ has not been restored, avoid the bread. If the wheat germ used is defatted, the restoration becomes largely pointless, for the unsaturated fats, hormones, neuromuscular factor, and Vitamin E are removed when the germ loses its fat content.

The presence of nitrites and nitrates strikes any number of common meat products from the shopping list. These include canned corned beef, bologna, salami, Kosher beef fry, frankfurters, and some brands of ham and bacon.

Few cereals are worth buying, since the large majority are preserved with BHA and BHT, messed up with added sugar, processed to the point where the vitamin loss is significant, even in the few breakfast cereals that *are* whole grain. Quite a few are tinted with Red #2 and other coal tar dyes, some of which (based on past experience with the coal tar "approved food color list") may prove to be cancer-producing, teratogenic (fetus harming), or just plain toxic. Oatmeal—packed without sugar—is a good cereal; wheat germ itself is a fine one and can be added to other cereals for augmented nutritional value; and the various brands of granola (if unsweetened) are good nutrition. If you want a quick appraisal of most of these breakfast cereals, ask your veterinarian about feeding them to valuable dogs.

In the supermarket meat department, you are faced with any number of unknowns. While the use of diethylstilbestrol, which has caused hundreds of cases of vaginal cancer in girls whose mothers took the hormone in pregnancy, is no longer permitted as a method of increasing weight gain in cattle, there are at least six hormones or hormone-like substances unknown to the public, still legally in use by the feeder lots. Time alone—a phrase that might cover a great deal of harm and many tears—will tell us whether any of these is a threat to the well-being of the consumer, as diethylstilbestrol tragically was. So long as ten cents worth of such a chemical will yield weight gain equal to thirty-five days of additional feeding, the economic motive will be strong enough to preserve the doctrine of "innocent until proved guilty."

The extenders for hamburgers and meat loaves need scrutiny. If they do not contain sufficient soy, they are diluters of protein—substituting starches for protein, a nutritional disaster for the growing body of a child. The price of soy has leaped astronomically, and is approaching the point where it is as costly as meat. The labels of these products will bear increasing attention, as this trend persuades manufacturers to cheapen the product by the addition of extenders which do not really extend. As for the products sold as substitutes for broiling chicken, read the labels. Much of the time, you are paying about twenty-seven cents an ounce for bread crumbs—better derived from your own good home-baked bread.

If a nutritionist accompanied you through the supermarket,

these are some of the alternatives he would choose, in lieu of average items freely bought by the average housewife:

Cream instead of "non-dairy whitener." The whitener has virtually no nutrition and contains casein which makes it off-limits for anyone allergic to milk. It is usually made with coconut oil, the only vegetable oil that raises blood cholesterol more effectively than animal fats.

Fresh meats, instead of canned luncheon meats and frankfurters.

High-protein macaroni and spaghetti, made with wheat germ instead of the higher carbohydrate, overprocessed products. When you "extend" cheese or meat with ordinary macaroni, you are falling far short of what you could accomplish. The high-protein products contain 85 percent more protein than ordinary macaroni and spaghetti, and are made with wheat germ, supplying the entire Vitamin B Complex natural to wheat, yet removed in the ordinary product.

Blocks of natural cheese, in place of the sliced, paper-separated varieties. You pay an unbelievable premium for slicing and separating. Also, natural cheese in place of "cheese spread" and "cheese food"—names which mean that full cheese values are not present.

Fresh potatoes, in place of instant mashed potatoes. The term "instant" apparently means that all nutritional values are instantly removed by processing, which doesn't explain what the numerous additives in such products are preserving. The philosophy of taking the path of least resistance is exemplified in these American convenience potato products—those imported from Europe are frequently devoid of additives. The European variety are usually available in forms for making potato pancakes or dumplings. For other purposes, buy fresh potatoes. If you boil them for fifteen minutes before baking, you save time (and energy) in baking them.

Cottonseed oil, instead of other cooking oils. Cottonseed oil, when you can find it, usually has no BHT and BHA, as virtually all other supermarket oils do because it contains enough natural Vitamin E to act as a preservative.

Unbleached flour in place of bleached, brominated flour. The bromine is added because commercial bakers like it, to produce more loaf volume—a euphemism for balloon bread with more air than bread. The bleaching destroys what little Vitamin E is left when the wheat germ is removed from the flour.

Vacuum-packed wheat germ which has not been defatted, in place of any other type of packaging which does not exclude air. Wheat germ, like all good foods, doesn't keep. Remember the nutritionist's rule of thumb: if it keeps, throw it out. If it will spoil, eat it before it does. Defatted wheat germ has lost its wheat germ oil, and numerous important nutrients with it.

Fresh fish, in place of breaded fish sticks. Bread is often the major part of the food, thereby diluting the protein values.

Brown rice, in place of white rice. "Long grain" has no nutritional significance. White rice was one of the earliest recognized causes of beri-beri. Converted rice is a compromise—better than white, inferior to brown. Wild rice, which is a good food, is a misnomer; it's actually a kind of barley. In any case, the name is appropriate: the price drives you wild.

Sugar-freed canned vegetables, in place of products like canned peas, carrots, and others which frequently contain added sugar.

Juice-packed pineapple and other canned fruits free of sugar syrup, when available.

Applesauce minus added sugar. The ordinary kind is 50 percent higher in calorie value—all from sugar.

Special note: I never *buy veal.* The veal which carries a premium price is white. It would be red if the calf were fed any iron, so that the whiteness is a testimony to the deliberately induced anemia in the poor little animal. That anemia may be so profound that the calf must be constantly and heavily dosed with antibiotics, lest an infection overcome its weakened defenses.

Maple syrup in place of pancake syrup. The natural product at least has slight mineral values. The other has synthetic flavor in some brands, and synthetic butter flavor is included, with sugar and coloring.

Plain yogurt, in place of the fruited types. The latter most frequently represent added jam or preserves in so high a concen-

298

tration that in some brands, sugar contributes more calories than yogurt. The plain vanilla type reeks with sugar. Add your own natural vanilla flavoring or unsweetened fruit.

Fruit juice in place of fruit "drink," "punch," "ade," or whatever. Most of these products offer you water at a high price, garnished sometimes with added Vitamin C at five times the cost of a Vitamin C tablet of equal potency, plus added sugar. The actual juice content may be as low as 10 percent legally. The irony: in some states which do not tax food, these drinks are taxed as soft drinks—which is what they really should be labeled.

One type of juice product deserves special attention: the powdered imitation orange or other fruit juices, the frozen imitations, or those which combine the imitation with the real. You may recall that the astronauts on one space shot developed heart irregularities which were ultimately traced to a lack of potassium. They were drinking a reconstituted powdered substitute for orange juice, on which the manufacturer has capitalized to the point where some children must be convinced that the entire moon program was arranged as a backdrop for imitation orange juice advertising. Had the space men been provided with the real juice, they would have had their potassium. This, it seems to me, dramatically emphasizes the deficits you incur by indiscriminate food shopping: little debits add up and cause large troubles.

A thousand topics remain undiscussed, but common sense—and reading of labels—will ultimately make you expert enough so that you buy properly by reflex. That is what arises from an overall philosophy such as that of my good friend, Adelle Davis. She coined a quick phrase to steer you away from additives of dubious (and unproved) safety: "If you can't pronounce it, don't buy it." That may be oversimplified, but your family will never be harmed by chemicals they don't swallow. A second, less oversimplified axiom, was suggested by another friend, Dr. John Yudkin: "Keep away from foods with which man has overmeddled." As Dr. Yudkin pointed out, man can't get inside an egg. (But he *can* create "egg improvers" which seem to rival eggs in nutritional values, so long as the comparison doesn't mention the nutrients real eggs contain.)

A concluding admonition: there are those made anxious by the realization that *you* are protecting your family in ways *they* don't. Their reaction to their own inner guilt feelings, which are usually subconscious, is hostility, which takes shape in deriding you, labeling you as a food faddist, or announcing that you have to die of something, so . . . At those moments, remember what a Swiss historian said: "The essence of tyranny is making the complex simple." Then you won't surrender to tyranny—not when it is aimed, consciously or not, at keeping you in ranks of the conformists whose definition of good health is any state of well-being that allows them to walk on the street, if the wind is blowing in the right direction.

Index

Index

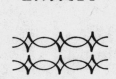

304

The Carlton Fredericks Cook Book